I0885987

"I love this book. A while back I undertook the assignment of writing a chapter about Artemisia Gentileschi. As a mostly self-taught art scholar, and more importantly, as a man writing about the art and experience of a woman, I felt a deep need to seek help to make sure I got her right. I turned to Elissa Weichbrodt, whose generosity of time, spiritual wisdom, and scholarly insight didn't just bring Gentileschi's art to life for me but her story as well. Here, Weichbrodt weaves together a measured, compelling, and honest view of the tropes under discussion, which, in turn, has helped me learn to be a better man. Put yourself in the hands of this faithful narrator to better understand the dignity of womanhood."

—**Russ Ramsey**, pastor and author of *Van Gogh Has a Broken Heart*

"If you were as grateful as I was for *Redeeming Vision*, you will love *Look like a Lady* and the way it zooms in on the hidden women of our past and the visuals that have formed—or malformed—our image of women. Thankfully, Elissa Yukiko Weichbrodt does not leave readers with a mere unveiling of the deforming stories but highlights counter-stories that transform our imagination of women: from objects to subjects, from biological mothers to spiritual cultivators, from monsters to sisters."

—**Jessica Hooten Wilson**, Pepperdine University; author of *The Scandal of Holiness*

"Based on the title of this book, a reader may be tempted to believe it's primarily for women. It's not. It's a book for men as well, a book that men should read with humility and heed with generous spirits. Elissa Yukiko Weichbrodt's book is so very good in the way that it retells the power of images throughout history, particularly as they have led to the diminishment or denigration of women. I pray that Weichbrodt's book finds a wide readership and results in the generation and appreciation of life-giving images that tell the true story of our belovedness."

—**W. David O. Taylor**, Fuller Theological Seminary; author of *A Body of Praise* and *To Set the World Aflame*

"*Look like a Lady* is a warm, intelligent journey through art history, women's history, and culture. It's an astonishingly rich book—visually, imaginatively, and intellectually. More than simply looking at the past, however, Elissa Weichbrodt points the way forward by envisioning what womanhood can look like when we embrace women in their full humanity, complexity, and potential."

—**Karen Swallow Prior**, author of *The Evangelical Imagination: How Stories, Images, and Metaphors Created a Culture in Crisis*

LOOK *LIKE A* LADY

LOOK *LIKE A* LADY

five visual tropes of womanhood
and how to see ourselves differently

elissa yukiko weichbrodt

BrazosPress
a division of Baker Publishing Group
Grand Rapids, Michigan

Published by Brazos Press
a division of Baker Publishing Group
Grand Rapids, Michigan
BrazosPress.com

Printed in the United States of America

Library of Congress Cataloging-in-Publication Data
Names: Weichbrodt, Elissa Yukiko, 1982– author
Title: Look like a lady : five visual tropes of womanhood and how to see ourselves differently / Elissa Yukiko Weichbrodt.
Description: Grand Rapids, Michigan : Brazos Press, a division of Baker Publishing Group, [2026] | Includes bibliographical references.
Identifiers: LCCN 2025053286 | ISBN 9781587436925 paperback | ISBN 9781493455126 ebook
Subjects: LCSH: Christian women—Religious life | Christian women—Conduct of life | Women—Religious aspects—Christianity | Self-perception—Religious aspects—Christianity | Christianity and art
Classification: LCC BV4527 .W4345 2026
LC record available at https://lccn.loc.gov/2025053286

All line drawings are the author's renderings.

Cover art by Nicole Kaufman Illustration

Baker Publishing Group publications use paper produced from sustainable forestry practices and postconsumer waste whenever possible.

26 27 28 29 30 31 32   7 6 5 4 3 2 1

For my mom,
who remains faithful

And for all my Women, Art, and Culture students
who held on to hope

Contents

Introduction

Paper Doll Dresses and Stories That Shape Us

Why won't it fit?

I shift the paper doll's dress a little more to the right, hoping that the cardstock arm will somehow align with the elegant, ruffled sleeve. It doesn't, and I'm deeply disappointed.

Maybe I should just cut her arm off. Then she could wear the dress.

When I was an eight-year-old girl, my copy of *Tom Tierney's American Family of the Colonial Era* paper doll book was both a prized possession and a source of deep vexation. Fresh from a family trip to colonial Williamsburg, I adored the detailed, colorful illustrations of late eighteenth-century fashion, especially the women's ornately trimmed, floor-sweeping gowns. I happily spent hours with a tiny pair of scissors, snipping around delicate locks of hair and ruffled hems.

My frustration came from realizing that the dolls' clothes were not interchangeable. Prudence could not wear Hannah's quilted dress because she was facing the wrong direction. Sarah and Prudence were the same height and both looking to the right, but they couldn't share clothes either. I hoped that the voluminous garments might conceal and transform the paper doll's chemise-clad form. But when I laid Prudence's elegant fuchsia gown over Sarah's body, the folding tabs refused to align and part of her arm remained stubbornly visible outside the lace-edged sleeve (see fig. I.1).

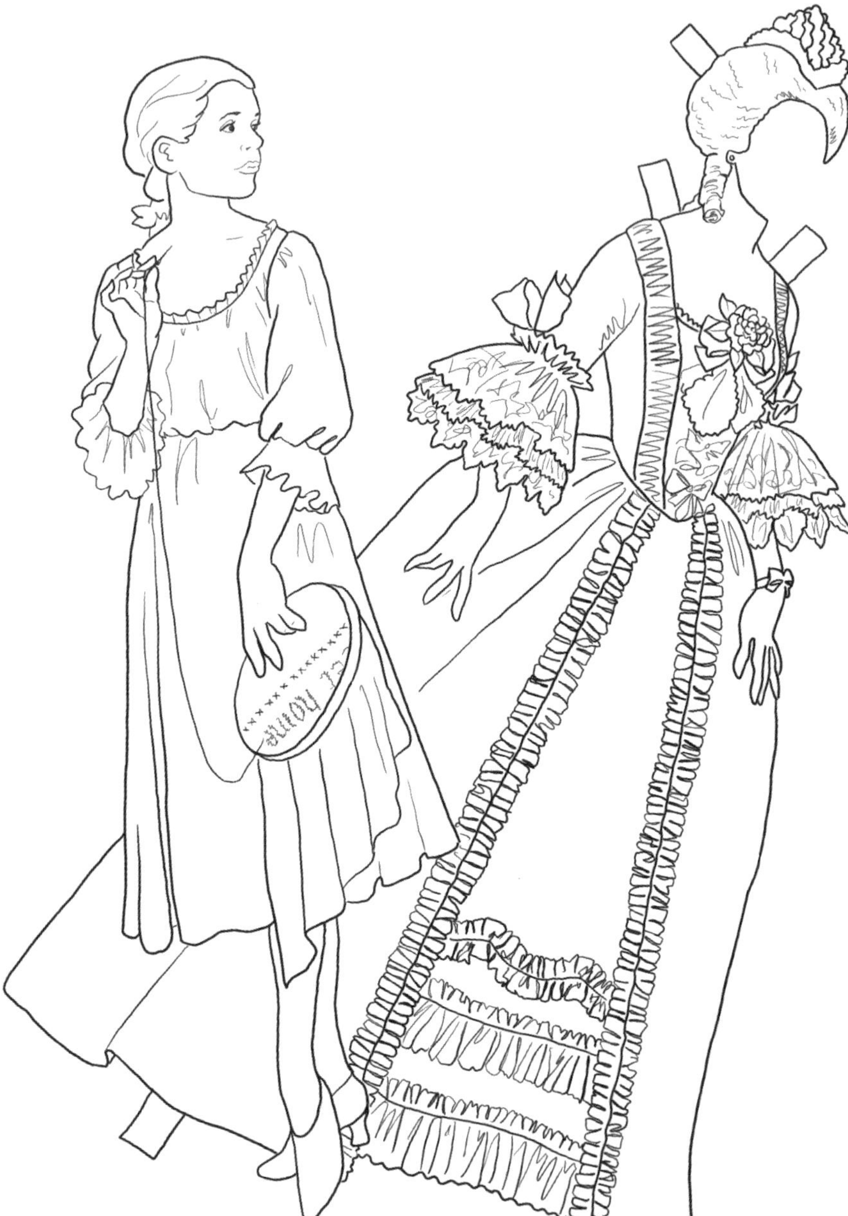

Figure I.1. Paper dolls

Decades later, I regard my initial solution with mild horror. *Maybe I should just cut her arm off?!* I was willing to amputate the doll's limbs, to alter her body, so she could fit the inflexible contours of the garment.

Eventually, I realized that it made far more sense to create new paper gowns for each doll than to mutilate the dolls to fit the gowns. It took me far longer to understand that the same could be said for my own body and the various stories of womanhood that—like paper doll dresses—I contorted myself to fit.

Stories That Shape Us

Stories are the sticky threads of our imagination, pulling together seemingly unrelated experiences into something we can grab hold of. We tell stories to make sense of our world, to describe why things are the way they are. Some stories—we might use the fancy word "metanarratives"—set out to explain *everything*. Are we just collections of atoms that exist only to collect and protect resources for our own survival? Are we part of a story of slow but inevitable progress? Or, as my faith teaches, are we participants in the greatest rescue story ever told—loved, pursued, and delivered by the God of the universe?

Other stories are more narrowly focused. They are identity stories, narrating who we believe ourselves to be in the world. These stories shape us as people, molding us to respond in certain ways, to move our bodies according to a particular choreography, to say yes to some things and no to others. When my husband and I moved our young family from St. Louis to Chattanooga, we told each other, "I guess we're outdoors people now." In St. Louis, we relished our more urban lifestyle; we could walk from our house to a train station and take public transportation to a Major League Baseball game. In Chattanooga, that option simply didn't exist. Yet we *could* walk from our house to a national park. Telling each other the story "we're outdoors people" prompted us to buy a trail guide and devote every Saturday to exploring the Cumberland Plateau. And because we hiked up creek beds and through gulches and along escarpments each weekend, we fell more and more in love with our new surroundings and more eager to spend time in them. Changing our story also changed us.

Where do these identity-shaping stories come from? Parents, teachers, doctors, pastors, news media, and actual storybooks—novels—might teach us using words. But we also learn these stories through the images and objects that make up our visual culture. Visual culture is more than just the paintings and sculptures deemed worthy of museum collections. It includes movies and TV shows; album covers; news photographs; images of a newly opened coffee shop posted to social media; illustrations in children's books and Bibles; and advertisements for skin care, clothing, furniture, protein powder, streaming services, and anything else you can think of.

Most of us see hundreds if not thousands of images every day, and we file those impressions away in our personal internal archives.[1] These images often reference other, older images, coalescing over time and shaping our ideas about the world. Our visual archive is what makes us confident enough to judge, often without conscious thought, what a "good" vacation, sunset, and cup of coffee look like. We do the same to identify a "worthy" politician, hero, mother, and so forth.

Sometimes—and for good reason—we assume that the biggest negative effect of visual culture is the set of impossible body standards it offers.[2] "If only," we tell ourselves, "we had more plus-sized models—or models with belly rolls, disabled models, dark-skinned models, models with natural hair, models with wrinkles, and models with stretch marks—we could create a gentler, healthier, more welcoming culture." There's some research that bears this out.[3]

But the stories that visual culture tells us about gender extend far beyond ideal body types. What do we expect men's and women's appearances, behaviors, and desires to be? From a young age, we've been told—over and over again—not *who* women and men are but *how* they should act in order to be women and men.

When it comes to gender, Western visual culture repeats a limited set of identity stories. Some of these stories offer desirable identities, like the maverick hero. Others, like that of the bumbling dad, serve as cautionary tales. *Don't act like this, or no one will respect you.* For men, a Western emphasis on individuality has resulted in a kind of long visual culture buffet with regularly changing options. There's a sturdy George Washington, feet firmly planted on the bow of a boat as he crosses the Delaware River. But there are also the brooding genius of a Romantic author, the lone figure looking out over a vast landscape, the impossibly muscular bodies of ancient Greek gods, the valiant soldier dying in the arms of his comrades, and—though we sometimes forget it—the opulent ermine cape and scarlet high heels of King Louis XIV. Certainly, this buffet comes with a distinct brand of anxiety; you can never be sure if your preferred dish—your flavor of masculinity—will remain on offer. But that's another book.

Women, meanwhile, have inherited a narrower and eerily consistent set of shaping stories. These scripts have been repeated so often and for so long that we often fail to recognize them as stories at all. We find them in art museums, billboard ads, school textbooks, and influencer feeds across the political spectrum. Sometimes we're told that the stories are divinely ordained, biblical models. Yet as we'll see throughout this book, there's a suspicious overlap between the teachings offered by some Christians and the guidance found in mainstream fashion magazines, celebrity profiles, TikTok videos, and so on.

As the stories repeat themselves, they snatch up authority that does not belong to them. The outsized familiarity makes these limiting stories seem like massive, natural rock formations, so unyielding that a road must change its trajectory. In reality, though, they're much more like paper doll dresses that simply weren't made for the wearer.

The distinction is crucial. We easily recognize the futility of trying to stick paper doll outfits onto flesh-and-bone humans who bend and turn and move. But if we confuse a limiting story with an essential truth about the world, we risk contorting ourselves—or dismembering others—to fit a shape that does not belong to us. We might even doubt that we're meant to be a woman at all.

The Story we've been given is so much better. I believe that the triune God made humanity—male and female—as the *imago Dei* (Gen. 1:26). God gifted them a story—*the* Story—to live into: "Be fruitful, multiply, fill the earth, and subdue it" (1:28). Both man and woman were the image of God, and they needed each other to steward the world they were given.[4] But Adam and Eve rejected God's gracious abundance in favor of a twisted story. They doubted the fullness of God's love for them and believed the lie that they needed to be like God themselves (3:1–6). Their disobedience resulted in broken relationships with God, with creation, with each other, and even with their own selves (3:7–19).[5] Now, as humans, we long for restoration (Rom. 8:22). We desperately grasp at rules or even hierarchies that promise us a sure and stable place in the world.

But Jesus—fully God and fully man, born of a woman—offers us a path back to that good, true Story.[6] Through his life, death, and resurrection, Jesus became the "firstfruit" of the reconciliation to come (1 Cor. 15:20). He lives fully into the Story and promises that we, his family, will someday do the same. Jesus's resurrection, his conquering of death by death, is what theologian N. T. Wright describes as "the hope for God's renewal of all things, for his overcoming of corruption, decay, and death, for his filling of the whole cosmos with his love and grace, his power and glory."[7] Jesus invites me to discard the parts of my identity I've constructed on my own and to enter into the fullness of myself in him (Col. 2:9–10).[8]

This capacious, beautiful Story of stories anchors me. I know that I, Elissa Yukiko Weichbrodt, am a particular child of God (1 John 3:1). I am the image of God (Gen. 1:27). I am remarkably and wondrously made (Ps. 139:14). God knows my name, and he numbers the hairs on my head (Isa. 45:3; Luke 12:7). My body matters, and I will be resurrected (Job 19:25–27). He gives me a hope and a future (Jer. 29:11). He is for me (Rom. 8:31). I am beloved.

Why would we settle for anything less than this? When false, constricting stories conceal our belovedness, when they hide us from ourselves, we become like eight-year-old me, trying to fit Prudence's dress onto Sarah's body, wondering if we should just cut off an arm to make the gown fit.

Stories . . . and Counterstories

So, what *are* the limiting stories—the ill-fitting paper doll dresses—we've given women in the West? This book explores five powerful visual tropes and the histories behind them: Venus, Vessel, Maiden, Mother, and Monster. Each chapter begins by recounting a moment not when someone else told an untrue story about me but when *I* told it about myself. One reason these scripts were so convincing to me is because I saw and heard them in both my conservative evangelical world and mainstream popular culture. The stories were also always connected to an image, and that image was part of a web of similar objects and pictures.

Studying art history helped me recognize the constricting stories for what they were. As I learned more about the artworks that incessantly repeated the various scripts, I also realized that these stories concealed or flattened much more complex realities. Rather than being accurate reflections of stable norms, the bodies, postures, and narratives came *from* somewhere. They could also be reinterpreted to serve shifting cultural needs or soothe new anxieties. And importantly, *women* actively participated in perpetuating and policing these tropes.

Telling this history in an honest way comes with real challenges. One approach has been to simply add brilliant, high-achieving women back into our existing historical narratives. Artists like Artemisia Gentileschi and Élisabeth Vigée Le Brun may have been forgotten, but if we just pop them into our canon of artistic geniuses, then we'll prove that women can do anything. However, this strategy often ignores the social structures and cultural assumptions that led to these women being ignored or discarded from our shared histories in the first place. We need histories that account for how ideas of womanhood have changed over time as well as why those shifts happened and who benefited. Another temptation is to flatten historical women into either helpless victims of misogyny or unquestionable heroines who overcame it. What we need instead are histories that acknowledge women's agency, that show us how they chose to negotiate systems that typically weren't built for them. We need histories that consider how race and class shaped women's lived experience and how women themselves have often thrown limiting stories, like straightjackets, onto other women. It's in the thick complexity of the past that we find the courage to acknowledge our own humanity and to imagine how we, too, might choose to negotiate our present.

We also need more than just a critique of existing stories; we need new, different ones. Shorter "counterstory" essays follow each dominant script, focusing on an artwork made *for* or *by women* in the West. The counterstories are Witnessing, Being, Moving, Cultivating, and Partnering. Thus, while each dominant story is a noun, set and unyielding, the counterstories are continuous verbs that suggest the beautiful spaciousness of being beloved by God.

Story	Counterstory
Venus	Witnessing
Vessel	Being
Maiden	Moving
Mother	Cultivating
Monster	Partnering

These are not simply inversions or reversals.[9] They do not turn the victim into the hero or give the bad guy his comeuppance. Such approaches can be useful in shaking an old story loose, and I offer examples of more modern and contemporary artists who do that work effectively. But these counterstories challenge an accepted narrative by rejecting its assumptions altogether. If the Venus script tells women that we must be desirable or be worthless, a counterstory dismisses such artificially limited options and approaches from another angle—directing us to a space that may seem new but was really there all along.

If you had told me about this book idea twenty years ago, I would have guessed that all the counterstories would come from artworks made after the 1970s. Perhaps there might be one artwork from the 1920s, at the earliest. I mistakenly believed that there were no earlier examples of women grappling with and reimagining the stories of Venus, Vessel, Maiden, Mother, and Monster. In the end, in a surprising reversal of my earlier view, the counterstories I've chosen to share actually come from older artworks.

My Protestant upbringing meant that I had limited knowledge of medieval theology and monastic practices. I also had a truncated understanding of how women have historically served or seen themselves in the Western church. But as I studied, taught, and traveled to see other, older artworks, I realized that some lesser-known works from the medieval and Renaissance periods can help us correct and expand our own vision of womanhood today, *especially* within the Christian church.

The counterstories I offer are also not the only ones available to us! They are simply some of the images and objects I've found so far that have prompted a more faithful, expansive imagination of how I might live as a daughter of God, awaiting the day when all the sad things, including the denigration and suppression of women, are made untrue.

This book is an accounting of the limiting stories of womanhood that I've told myself. Because of that, it is not a history of gender in evangelicalism or a history of misogyny in Western culture more broadly. This is not a book about the biblical womanhood movement or a critique of it. It's not an argument about women's roles in the church or home. It's also not a consideration of womanhood around the globe. Western visual culture has been a powerful shaping force for me, so I focus on that here.

Even more specifically, I've been formed by a constellation of communities and cultural resources that made me softly receptive to some limiting stories and unexpectedly resistant to others. I grew up in a Christian home as the oldest child and only daughter. We were homeschooled, but in Hawaii, culturally a world apart from the families in matching plaid featured on the covers of national homeschooling magazines. I was shaped by the purity culture of the nineties and early aughts but escaped the regular shaming that often occurred at my peers' Christian schools or church youth groups. I was raised in a church that narrowly prescribed men's and women's roles but also encouraged and included women in serious theological study. I attended a conservative Christian college where some students felt stifled, but I felt empowered to ask more questions about my faith than ever before and to explore both the richness and the historic harms of my theological tradition. Add to all this the particularities of my ethnicity: half Japanese, half European, and raised in a predominantly Asian American, collectivist culture. My longing has always been to find a place where my body, my interests, and my abilities could make sense together.

I have also always been a lover of art. As a child and then a teenager, I drew almost constantly. When I was younger, most of my drawings were pulled from my own imagination. As I grew older, however, I increasingly filled my sketchbooks with copies of old European masterworks alongside figures and faces lifted from fashion magazines and beauty ads. These drawings were another way that I absorbed limiting stories of womanhood.

That experience prompted my decision not to include photographs of the many artworks I reference in the stories of Venus, Vessel, Maiden, Mother, and Monster. You'll be familiar with many of them already; they are sitting in your own visual archive. So instead of reproducing images of the originals, I chose to draw them myself. The line drawings allowed me to both emphasize certain sections of the artworks and deliberately resist the further objectification of the represented women. I wanted to make these familiar objects strange to us again, to make us blink our eyes and wonder, "How did I not see it that way before?" Redrawing the artworks—in a sense reimagining my teenage sketchbooks—helped me pay attention in new ways. Sharing those drawings with you can, I hope, do something similar.

How to Read This Book

Every spring semester, I teach a class called Women, Art, and Culture. The course considers women as the makers and subjects of art in the West, from the classical period through the 1970s. Female students make up the majority of the roster, but a few male students always join us as well.

On the first day of class, I ask my students to do three things. Regardless of your gender, I offer the same encouragement to you here too:

1. Read with generous humility. We can be humble about what we don't know or how we have been shaped by forces we didn't recognize at the time. Believing that we are purposefully made by God to be finite, living within the limits of bodies and culture, frees us to express gratitude and repentance. It's okay to learn new histories and to change our minds. It's also okay to carefully interrogate unfamiliar ideas. Reflect on what you've read and make connections to your own experiences.
2. Read with hope. We live in a culture that rewards outrage. But snappy takedowns and public shaming are often motivated by despair, not a desire for change. I caution my students to resist the temptation to let anger fester and calcify into bitterness. God does, however, welcome our lament. We can bring him our grief over

the ways that limiting stories of womanhood have harmed both women and men. We do so because we believe that he hears and that he *cares*. Read with resurrection hope, unafraid to confront the brokenness because you know that Jesus is coming back to make all these sad things untrue.

3. Welcome interdependence. We were never meant to be alone, and we were never meant to do it all. Because we are the image of God, we are made to be in relationship. Read with friends, with your spouse, or with your child. Ask each other questions and listen to each other's experiences. Embrace the reality of a shared calling to cultivate and steward creation and culture, side by side, together.

Beyond the Niche

When I tried to fit that fuchsia dress onto the wrong paper doll, I hated the way that the woman's arm exceeded the limits of the ruffled sleeve. I wanted everything to line up neatly, to fit within the precise parameters. I had no imagination for anything beyond the rigid edges.

It took looking at a different kind of art altogether to adjust this way of thinking.

Early seventeenth-century Dutch flower paintings are meticulous affairs. They are also a bit stiff. In a 1618 painting by Ambrosius Bosschaert the Elder, tulips, roses, irises, and columbine fan out from a delicate vase in unnatural symmetry. The bouquet sits on a stone ledge, perfectly framed by an arched window niche. While beautiful and rendered with great attention to detail, the flowers test the limits of believability. The crisply rendered, perfect blooms contradict their reality as organic things. After all, even after being cut, flowers respond to light and water, petals unfurling, stems drooping, and buds curving toward sunlight.

By the end of the seventeenth century, most Dutch painters favored lush compositions with flowers that elegantly arced and tumbled from vases. In a still life completed around 1726, now in the collection of the Toledo Museum of Art, the renowned floral painter Rachel Ruysch presents us with a boldly asymmetrical bouquet. Like Bosschaert, Ruysch places her vase of flowers in a stone niche. Her blooms, however, seem to both recede backward into the dark niche and burst forward into our shared space. A bright-white rose near the center of the composition, surrounded by delicate pink blossoms, immediately attracts our attention. Meanwhile, Ruysch creates both dramatic movement and precarious balance with a scarlet poppy that seems to curve away from us in the top right corner and a ruffled, deep-orange marigold that flops toward us in the bottom left. Its pompom-like form hangs over the stone ledge, petals fluttering out like a dancer's skirt. Instead of remaining contained by the architecture, Ruysch's blooms spill over each other, tumbling out of their vase and breaching the edges of the niche.

The marigold is not an errant flower in need of correction. It—and the other animated blooms—is evidence of delightful, overflowing plenty. The painting seems almost to vibrate with pent-up energy. A tiny caterpillar inches along one sweeping stem, while a white butterfly perches on golden petals. A fat, striped bee nestles into an open poppy. Browning leaves, riddled with insect bites, slowly curl inward, even as vine tendrils spiral upward and a plush bud seems ready to burst. The arrangement is firmly anchored in the niche, but its expansive exuberance is a welcome expression of the flowers' liveliness.

What if we could tell each other stories that embrace this kind of abundance?

1

Venus

The Venus of Coca-Cola

I wonder if I look like the girl in the Coke ad.

I'm eleven, sweeping up grass clippings in my family's tiny backyard in Honolulu, Hawaii. A welcome breeze sweeps past the apartment, rustling through trees and bushes and swirling my long, straight, dark hair off my shoulders and around my face. Almost unthinkingly, I lift and turn my chin toward the wind, locking one knee and pushing the opposite hip out, adopting what I hope is a pose of casual elegance. But instead of paying attention to the way that the moving air cools my slightly damp skin—instead of experiencing the wind in and through my own body—I try to imagine how my body appears to others.

Do I look like a lady?

Decades later, I'm struck by the clarity of this memory. It's the first time I remember imagining myself from the outside, as the object of another's gaze. I was a preteen in a pre–social media world, wearing a baggy T-shirt and shorts and still fidgeting with the unfamiliar straps of a training bra. But I held my body up to a visual template—a desirable woman on display, dancing on a balcony in a yellow, off-the-shoulder dress—and found the edges where I did not align. I told myself a story about who I could and should be as a *woman*. That story has haunted me ever since.

I've since realized that it wasn't just the Coke ad girl who was telling me how to be a woman. She lived in a mental folder of "beautiful women" already packed full of pictures that spanned centuries of Western history and ranged from high art to popular culture. There were Sandro Botticelli's *Birth of Venus* from a "masterpieces everyone should know" book, the women with high cheekbones and airbrushed skin in drugstore makeup ads, the tanned girls with perky breasts and butts in surf apparel posters, and the ladies with voluminous hair and pearly smiles in Miss America pageants. And since I was in my Jane Austen stage, there were also Regency-era portraits and the BBC's *Pride and Prejudice* costumes.

While the hair color, ethnicity, and even bodily proportions of the depicted women varied, all the images told me the same story: To be a woman is to be an object of desire. Truly, it was more than that. The pictures taught me that to be a woman is to desire to be desired.

This is the story of Venus.

Once you have met Venus, you will find her everywhere. Of course, she fills entire galleries of art museums. She's also lounging on rumpled beds or draped over sports cars, selling everything from luxury handbags and perfume to vacations and Viagra. Her classic standing pose, the one I tried to mimic as an eleven-year-old, still fits perfectly within the 9:16 dimensions of social media videos. Even now I find myself reciting her script when I scrutinize my reflection in the mirror before heading out for the day, surveying my body from the outside, as an object to be seen.

Pointing out the existence of this story and critiquing its effects are hardly new. Well-known works by twentieth-century scholars decry what they call "the male gaze," or the accepted practice in art and literature of presenting women as sexual objects for the pleasure of a presumably straight male viewer or reader.[1] British cultural commentator John Berger neatly summarizes this state of affairs in his 1972 book *Ways of Seeing*: "Men act and women appear."[2] According to Berger, thanks to a long line of cultural artifacts, a woman "must continually watch herself" from the imagined perspective of a man.[3] She turns herself and other women into an object of desire and regulates herself accordingly. Indeed, Berger says, she cannot even weep at her own father's funeral without worrying how she looks while weeping.

How did we get here? It is easy to blame "the patriarchy," implying that a clandestine group of powerful men chose to imprison helpless women in their lustful gaze for most of Western history. But as I study art history, I have to admit that the creation, function, and circulation of Venus images are far more tangled and textured than merely an appeal to a straight man's libido. Such complex histories also help me understand my own frustratingly paradoxical relationship to this narrative. Art history isn't to blame for this limiting story; it actually exposes the story's deep flaws and contradictions.

Venus Arrives

There's a sculpture in the Capitoline Museum in Rome, Italy, that stands alone in a small, octagonal-shaped room paneled with decorative granite and capped with a honeycombed dome. Light streams in through an oculus, bathing the sculpture and its pedestal in light. After hall after hall packed with antique marbles, the spare nature of this installation is striking. "This is important art," the curators seem to announce. "This is hallowed ground."

It's a beautiful sculpture. A young woman, slightly larger than life-sized and carved from creamy marble, stands atop a cylindrical base. Beside her, also carved from marble, is a tall, elegant vase, partially draped with a tassel-edged cloth. Her smoothly polished body curves in a slight S shape, one leg bending slightly as her weight shifts over the opposite, jutting hip. Art historians call this pose, introduced and refined by the ancient Greeks, *contrapposto*. Her right arm reaches up to cradle—or perhaps cover—her round, firm breasts. Her left arm curves down as her hand modestly shields her pubis.

I'm caught in a figure eight of lithe limbs, my eyes trailing across one arm, down another, then down one leg and back up to the swell of her buttocks and nipped waist. When I finally manage to look at her face—smooth and symmetrical and crowned with a pile of wavy tresses—her averted gaze and dropped chin point me back to the endless loop below: breasts, groin, legs, hips, breasts, groin, legs, hips.

My museum map tells me that I'm standing in the Cabinet of Venus, looking at the *Capitoline Venus*. The sculpture is actually a copy of the famous *Aphrodite of Knidos*, carved by the Hellenistic sculptor Praxiteles in the fourth century BCE and credited as the first monumental female nude sculpture in Western art history. Though the original was destroyed long ago, Praxiteles's work was an important beginning—not just a blip—in Western art history. The sculpture cemented Praxiteles's fame in his own time and became the new prototype for representations of the goddess of love and beauty. When, a few centuries later, the ancient Romans adopted and adapted Greek religion and art, Aphrodite became Venus, and even more variations of the unclothed goddess developed.

We can group the dozens of surviving sculptures into various types. Praxiteles's pose—with the body curved like an S and a hand shielding the pubis—is the Venus Pudica, or "modest Venus." The Venus Anadyomene languidly raises her arms to wring out her hair as she emerges from the sea. The Venus Callipyge arches her back and glances over her shoulder at her own buttocks (see fig. 1.1). The Crouching Venus, depicted on the cover of this book, drops to one knee while pulling an arm across her chest.

All these ancient poses are eerily recognizable. We see them in advertisements for swimsuits and underwear, in social media feeds, and even perhaps in our own photos from trips to the beach. Sometimes we call them "flattering" or perhaps "empowering." They're so familiar that they crowd out most other possibilities of how we might inhabit our bodies.

In the Cabinet of Venus, I walk around the sculpture, following the inlaid stone trapezoids and circles on the floor like a game piece moving along a checkered route. By the time I'm halfway around the room, I can see what is unnoticeable from the doorway. Venus is not actually standing calmly. Instead, she's bent slightly at the waist, and her shoulders are curled inward. She seems to be withdrawing into herself, her buttocks squeezed together as her hips pull to the left and her torso twists to follow (see fig. 1.2).

Two sets of competing visual cues collide. The architecture of the room, the artwork's placement, and the sculptor's purposeful rendering of curving limbs all seem to invite a desiring gaze. Yet the woman's hollowed, retreating posture—more visible from the side and rear of the sculpture—suggests not just a reluctance to be on display but an active attempt to *conceal* herself from view.[4]

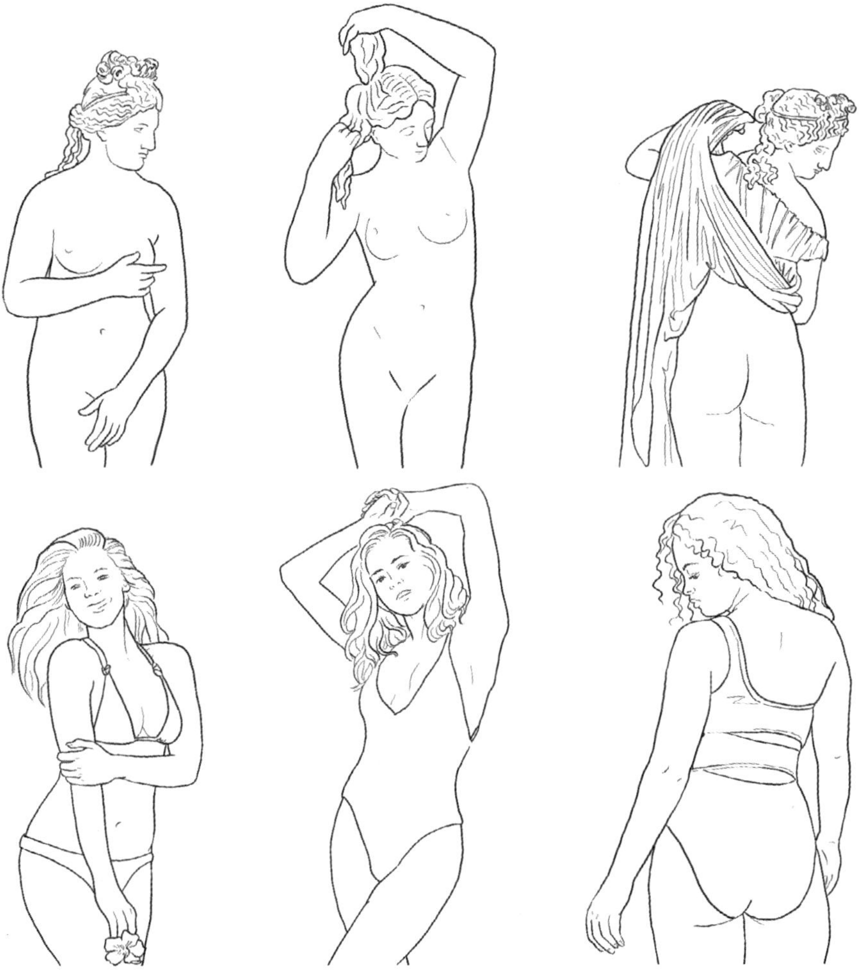

Figure 1.1. Drawings of a Venus Pudica, a Venus Anadyomene, a Venus Callipyge, and their swimsuit model counterparts

The friction feels familiar. Though eleven-year-old me eagerly hoped to be like the Coke girl, joining the ranks of beautiful women like this Venus sculpture, my high school self was more conflicted. I rode the bus to work, standing stiffly, shoulders tense, resolutely avoiding eye contact. Every commute felt like a gauntlet of gazes. Increasingly, I deemed the ride a success if I could make it off the bus without a teen guy or older man commenting in some way on my appearance. Occasionally, I was humiliated and afraid. One day a boy swore at me as he exited the bus with a group of leering, whistling friends. I learned that even when I wasn't striking a pose, my body remained on display.

And from the looks of it, the *Capitoline Venus* is in the same bind.

But *why*? How is it that the goddess of love and beauty—supposedly the most beautiful woman of the ancient world—is simultaneously cowering from view *and* providing a template of desirability that will persist for thousands of years? The sculpture's history reveals that this tension isn't an accident.

In the fourth century BCE, the renowned Greek sculptor Praxiteles carved two versions of a slightly larger-than-life Aphrodite. According to the Roman historian Pliny the Elder, one of the figures adhered to tradition, depicting the goddess of love and beauty wearing a draped chiton.[5] But Praxiteles also made a daring variation. In this one, Aphrodite's body was laid bare. A nearby, long-necked ceramic vessel used for carrying water suggested that the goddess was at her bath and thus unclothed. Praxiteles offered both sculptures for sale at the same price. The people of Kos chose the first statue, believing it to be the more appropriate depiction of the goddess. But their rivals, the people of Knidos, purchased the rejected sculpture and built a new temple where Aphrodite could be viewed from all angles.[6]

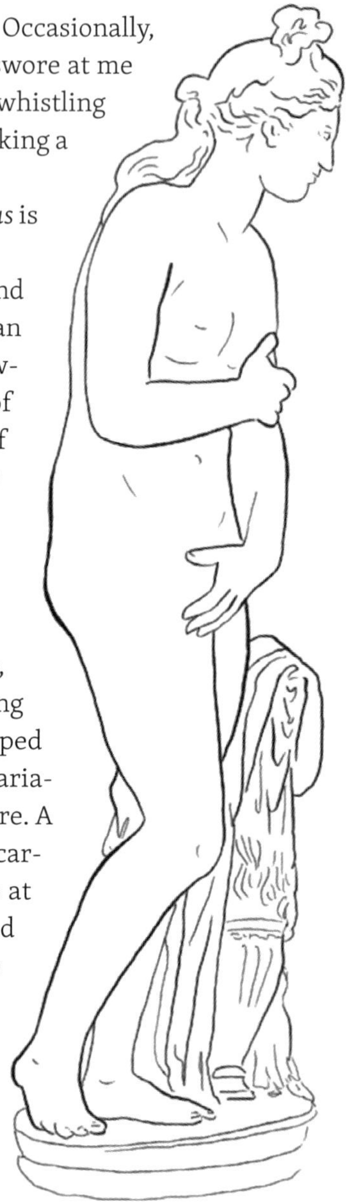

Figure 1.2. Drawn from the *Capitoline Venus*, a Roman copy of Praxiteles's fourth-century *Aphrodite of Knidos*

Why was the town of Kos appalled by Praxiteles's naked Aphrodite? If you've spent any amount of time in an art museum with works from Western Europe, you've probably seen a lot of paintings and sculptures of nude women. Such artworks, however, were not always as popular and pervasive as they now seem to be.

In earlier periods of Greek history, the only figures—divine or human—depicted without clothes were men. Ancient Greeks celebrated the male body as the most excellent form of humanity, the embodiment of moral and aesthetic excellence. Male athletes competed naked, and those muscular bodies were further idealized and used to represent the Greeks' superhuman gods.[7]

In sculptures and paintings, women—both divine and human—were almost always clothed. The only exceptions were scenes meant to express humiliation, such as sexual violence within a war narrative, or sexual availability, such as prostitutes depicted on the bottom of drinking vessels.[8] In sculptures from the classical period, Aphrodite, the goddess of love and marriage, is always clothed, her pleated chiton veiling her body. This modesty reflected the lived experience of free Greek women, who were largely hidden from public view and valued for their chastity.

So, what happens when Praxiteles carves an *unclothed* Aphrodite? Should we see it as an artistic innovation, a saucy break from tradition by a genius rebel? Is this part of a natural evolution, a move toward increasing illusionism in art? Does it reflect a universal appreciation of the beauty of the human body? Scholars have told the story in numerous ways.[9]

According to art historians Nanette Salomon and Nigel Spivey, Aphrodite's original male viewers understood the sculpture in explicitly sexual terms.[10] Praxiteles's obvious narrative—that Aphrodite is bathing—doesn't just explain the goddess's nakedness. It *eroticizes* the view. Visitors to the temple become voyeurs. The fact that we're not supposed to see the goddess naked heightens the appeal. She is desirable because she does not want to be seen. Her attempt to cover herself ends up drawing *more* attention to her genitals, encouraging the viewer to fill in the blank. She is somehow more arousing in her vulnerability.

We might scoff at this—who would be turned on by cold, white marble? But the work was originally painted. Tinted hair, lips, eyes, and skin created an even more believable appearance of a real woman. Indeed, the illusion was so compelling that a Greek poet imagined Venus encountering the sculpture and exclaiming, "When did Praxiteles see me naked?!"[11] Other early accounts suggest that the sculpture could be mistaken for or was interchangeable with an actual woman. In one story, an enthusiastic visitor rushes up and kisses the marble Aphrodite.[12] In another, a young man is so consumed with lust that he spends the night in the temple and attempts to copulate with the statue! The following morning, ashamed by the stain he left behind, he throws himself off a cliff into the sea.[13] Of course, such tales should not be understood as reliable documentation of actual viewers' reactions. The popularity and persistence of these accounts, however, suggest that men's arousal was not an unexpected result.

Why, after centuries of only clothed depictions of women, does Praxiteles's Aphrodite establish itself so firmly as a new visual type? Does this shift reflect the influence of Phoenician religion on Hellenistic Greeks?[14] Is it a response to the painting of a nude Helen of Troy by the famed artist Zeuxis?[15] Does it serve as a means of asserting ongoing masculine control even as women enjoyed greater legal rights?[16] Does the beautiful, vulnerable Aphrodite offer an opportunity for ancient "locker room talk," a communal affirmation of a woman's desirability as a means of male bonding?[17] Grappling well with the past means we need to make room for multiple, overlapping causes rather than insisting on a singular, simple answer.

It's precisely the textured and frequently re-narrated history of the sculpture's origin that actually disrupts the seemingly pure facade of the Venus story. The constant repetition of the sexualized Venus from ancient Greece onward suggests that all women naturally desire to be desired. But the sculpture's history helps us see that this is a visual script that had a start date.

I wish I could give this history to my teenaged self. She knew none of it, but she sensed an impossible bind. Even when she did not want to be the object of sexual attention, others expected her body to be available. She should want to be wanted. My younger self *did* know that the constant surveillance felt wrong, and she wondered why things were this way. Even more importantly, what could she do about it?

A Virtuous Venus?

When I was fifteen, I worked my way through a then-standard set of purity culture books, including Elisabeth Elliot's *Passion and Purity* and Josh Harris's *I Kissed Dating Goodbye*. My other reading material was less expected for an adolescent girl. My dad introduced me to the world of systematic and applied theology, and soon I was charging my way through Augustine, John Calvin, Louis Berkhof, Hans Rookmaaker, William Dyrness, and others. My mind prickled with ideas and questions.

Somewhere between being harassed on the bus for my body and being frustrated in my quest to find someone—besides my father—who would talk to a fifteen-year-old girl about theology, I hatched a new plan. I wanted to be desired, but I wanted to be desired for what I believed were the "right" reasons: my virtue and my intelligence. And I found what I thought might be a good model in a Renaissance painting.

After a lull in the medieval era, the story of Venus regained prominence in fifteenth- and sixteenth-century Italy. Responding to renewed interest in classicism and humanism, Florentine and Venetian artists revived the tradition of the female nude in visual culture. Among the most famous of these was Sandro Botticelli's *Birth of Venus* (ca. 1485–86)—a five-and-a-half-foot-tall, nine-foot-wide painting—which depicted an unclothed Venus, posed like Praxiteles's Aphrodite, riding to shore on a clam shell.

I filled sketchbooks with the perfect oval face and Disney princess hair of this Venus, but I didn't want to be *her*. No, I found my model at the center of Botticelli's other large-scale mythological painting from the same period, *Primavera* (see fig. 1.3).

Completed sometime between 1477 and 1482, *Primavera*, or Springtime, is an over-ten-foot-wide painting of nine mythological figures—six women, two men, and a soaring toddler cupid—in an orange grove. Botticelli carefully arranges his figures in a horizontal band that moves us across the composition. Beginning on the far right, we see the blue-winged Zephyrus, the god of the west wind, diving into the frame. His arms reach toward the nymph Chloris, here depicted as a blond woman in a diaphanous robe. Chloris is running, her body tipping forward slightly as she looks over her shoulder at the pursuing god. Immediately to the

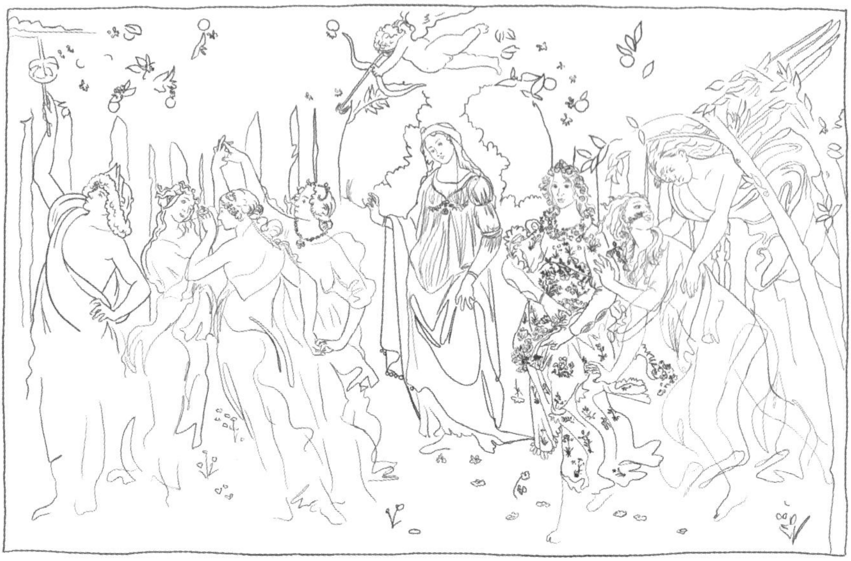

Figure 1.3. Drawn from Sandro Botticelli, *Primavera*, ca. 1477–82

left, we find a buoyant Flora, the goddess of spring, clad in a flower-covered gown and scattering roses as she steps toward the center of the composition. Next, we find my preferred Venus. She stands a little way back from the rest of the figures, framed by an arch of orange tree branches. Though she wears a long, gathered gown, her pose is still that of the Venus Pudica: Her hips and waist form a sinuous, exaggerated curve, while one hand holds a red and blue drape at the apex of her thighs. She raises her other hand in greeting as she steadily meets our gaze. Above her, a blindfolded cupid pulls back his bowstring, and we follow the implied line of his arrow to the left and the trio of dancing women—the Three Graces. The central sister looks over her shoulder to the left, directing our attention to the final figure: the dark-haired god Mercury, swathed in red and reaching up to touch his staff to a swirling cloud.

Even if we can't identify the figures in the painting by name, it's clear that Venus is the composition's visual linchpin. Framed by a central arch and elevated above the other figures, she steadily returns our gaze. Her gauzy dress, auburn hair, and slightly protruding belly unify her with the other women in the painting, but her red drape also connects her to Mercury on the left. She's not—as they say—like other girls. She's modest and elegant, confident and controlled.

As a teenager, I read that the painting was a kind of intellectual puzzle and a reflection of a Renaissance worldview. Botticelli's subject matter demonstrated the renewed fifteenth-century interest in classical humanism. According to Neoplatonic thinkers of the period seeking to blend Greek philosophy and Christian theology, Venus served as the allegorical embodiment of divine love and beauty. Instead of inciting lust, her physical beauty would direct the viewer to contemplate *spiritual* beauty.

Given my conservative evangelical context and ambivalence toward my own body, this idea made sense to me. The painting offered an appealing model of a *virtuous* Venus. The women in sheer dresses were trying too hard, and the lady in the floral dress had the kind of supermodel status I knew I would never attain. But the Venus in the middle? She was the one with our attention and respect. Her restraint seemed powerful.

It wasn't hard to translate this painting into the language of purity culture. Both the Christian books I read and my experiences commuting on the bus taught me to believe that boys were just lust-crazed animals. Both sources also seemed to suggest that my body was primarily a sexual object. But purity culture also offered me a strange kind of agency. I didn't have to accept being ogled as the norm. I believed *I* could do something different.

In her book *Passion and Purity*, widowed missionary and conservative womanhood guru Elisabeth Elliot tells a story about a man in her Bible school class who she catches staring at her. She attributes his attention to the fact that she is different from other, flirtatious women. "Something signaled a mystery," she explains, "and it fascinated him."[18] She ends the anecdote by connecting mystery to modesty and "true" beauty: "A woman's beauty should reside, according to the Apostle Peter, in the inmost center of her being."[19]

I took Elliot's words to heart. Dressing modestly—defined by hemlines and strap widths—would allow my inner beauty to shine. I could, in effect, transcend my body and be valued for my mind and my goodness. Other girls might put their bodies on display, cheapening themselves while causing men to stumble with impure thoughts. I, however, hoped that by covering my body I could deflect a desiring, sexual gaze and my "true" self could be appreciated. Like the Venus in Botticelli's *Primavera*, I could redirect—even elevate—men's thoughts.

And then, maybe, someone would want to talk to me about Augustine's *Confessions*.

It never quite worked out that way. Still, I persisted. Rules offered certainty in the midst of adolescent upheaval, and I could cling to a flimsy sense of moral superiority.

Years later, when I returned to *Primavera* with a new set of interpretive tools, I was stunned. The more I learned about the work's history, the more I recognized the surprisingly extensive overlap between Botticelli's fifteenth-century painting and twentieth-century purity culture. The painting didn't exist just as an illustration of an abstract idea. It actively shaped at least one man and woman's lived experience of love, sex, and marriage.

Primavera is not an easy artwork to make sense of. Scholars continue to argue over when it was painted, why it was painted, what classical texts might be referenced, and whether Botticelli was even aware of the Neoplatonist philosophy I had read about in high school.[20] But what happens if we consider the work's real-world location, audience, and impact?

Scholars believe the painting was commissioned to celebrate the marriage of Lorenzo di Pierfrancesco de' Medici, a member of the most powerful banking family in fifteenth-century Florence. The painting was one of several hung in a room adjacent to the bedchamber he shared with his bride, Semiramide Appiano.[21] Florentine husbands put great effort—and funds—into decorating the bedrooms for their young brides. These choices were not merely aesthetic.[22] Renaissance viewers understood the formative power of art. Pictures were beautiful, yes, but they also shaped character and action.

What lesson was being taught? According to art historian Lilian Zirpolo, Botticelli's painting hews closely to common marriage advice at the time, offering guidance to the bride on chastity, submission, and procreation.[23]

Chastity was *the* primary virtue for women in fifteenth-century Italy. At the time, women—not men—were believed to have a greater, more animalistic sexual appetite, and this needed to be controlled both before and after marriage. (We'll return to this notion when we examine the stories of the Vessel and the Monster.) For noblewomen like the bride Semiramide, virginity was considered part of their dowry. It was their most valuable possession. Once they were married, their modest behavior was supposed to signal their sexual faithfulness and thus their value as women. Popular books like *On Wifely Duties* by Francesco Barbaro advised wives to achieve this chastity by "preserv[ing] an evenness and restraint in the movements of the eyes, in their walking, and in the movement of their bodies." He continued, "The wandering of the eyes, a hasty gait, and excessive movement of the hands and other parts of the body cannot be done without loss of dignity."[24] The message was clear: Women's bodies were dangerous in their natural state and needed to be controlled in order to be desirable.

In *Primavera*, we see this emphasis on chastity in a few ways. The Three Graces wear pearls in their braided hair, a common symbol of virginity. Instead of dancing wildly, the mythological sisters strike refined, restrained poses. Every flick of the wrist and tilt of the head is calculated to convey their chastity according to Barbaro's dictates. Importantly, their poise also contrasts with the slightly bent, awkward figure of Chloris, the nymph on the far right of the composition.

The three figures on the right side of the painting offer another lesson to the bride: submission. Botticelli seems to illustrate a story told by the classical poet Ovid. In Ovid's poem *Fasti*, Chloris, a wood nymph, catches the attention of Zephyrus, the god of the west wind. Zephyrus pursues Chloris. She runs away, but he overpowers her and rapes her. To make "amends for his violence," the god marries Chloris and makes her the goddess of spring: the beautiful Flora.[25]

In Botticelli's painting, a powerful, blue-skinned Zephyrus swoops between trees and reaches toward a stumbling Chloris. She turns back to look at him, her hair in disarray, her limbs flailing like those of a skittish animal trying to escape a hunter. Her lips part as if crying out in fear. But Botticelli completes the tale by also representing Chloris's transformation into Flora. He paints a chain of flowers that emerges from the nymph's open mouth, then seamlessly becomes part of the floral pattern on the beautiful woman's gown. But why include *this* story of pursuit and sexual violence in a wedding gift?

Botticelli's choice was not unusual. Florentine brides brought their belongings to their husband's home in large, elaborately decorated marriage chests known as *cassoni*. Many of these chests depicted other mythological scenes of sexual abductions, such as the rapes of Proserpina, Europa, and the Sabine women.[26] To modern viewers, it may seem cruel—even unconscionable—to give such illustrations to a young bride. But for fifteenth-century Italian women, these stories reiterated the need to submit to their husband's sexual demands and serve the greater social good.

In his legendary history of Rome, first-century historian Livy recounts that Romulus, the first king of Rome, is worried by the lack of women in his city. He leads his male followers to abduct wives from the nearby Sabine people. Though initially indignant, the Sabine women accept their kidnappers as husbands and subsequently broker a peace between the two peoples, leading to the growth and glory of the new Roman kingdom.[27] In the Renaissance, the story was told to women to emphasize the social importance of marriage for stability and prosperity.[28] Their role, like that of the Sabine women, was that of submission and obedience.

Botticelli's Chloris offers another reason to act in this way. Once she submits to Zephyrus, the clumsy, bestial nymph transforms. She becomes the elegant, poised, and fertile goddess Flora, scattering blossoms—gathered in her gown, near her womb—across a fruitful garden.

This is *Primavera*'s third lesson. Semiramide's chastity and submission both serve the ultimate goal of a Renaissance marriage: procreation. Most Renaissance marriages were arranged affairs, chosen for economic or social reasons. Thus, a marriage's main purpose was not romantic fulfillment but the strengthening and extending of a family line. Botticelli visually draws attention to Venus's belly, suggesting her body's capacity to sustain and bear new life.

By the time I saw *Primavera* in person for the first time, I was married and in my thirties. As I stood under the bright lights of the bustling Uffizi Gallery in Florence, a stone lodged in my throat as I blinked back tears. Perhaps the hundreds of tourists around me, snapping photos with their phones and listening to their guides explain Neoplatonism, thought I was moved by the sheer beauty of the painting. But my emotion stemmed less from the aesthetic experience and more from acknowledging that Botticelli's crisp pastels served as a candy coating to a damaging, limiting story for women *and* men.

I cried because I imagined eighteen-year-old Semiramide seeing *Primavera* every day, not in a crowded museum but in her private room. I imagined what it would be like to have an ever-present reminder that to be a real woman—a desirable bride, a *Venus*—she must follow the painting's instructions. She must control her body—quieting her hands and averting her eyes—lest she appear unchaste; she must control her emotions and intuitions, remaining available to all her husband's sexual demands; and, somehow, she must control her own womb, lest she fail to produce more Medici children. I wept because I knew those standards from my *own* time and place.

Voices in evangelical purity culture, fueled by shame and absent of grace, echoed those same dictates. I could hear it all in my head:

> Dress this way, not that way, otherwise men will think you're a slut. Don't express sexual desire, and certainly don't act on it at all. If you have sex before marriage, you are permanently damaged and will be unable to properly bond with your spouse. Don't have ambitions or questions or dreams of your own, because your husband will be the one to cast a vision for the family. He's also going to want to have mind-blowing sex all the time, and your duty is to always say yes. All that sex should lead to an endless parade of babies, but you must stay attractive to your husband in between pregnancies in order to fulfill his needs.[29]

I imagined Lorenzo di Pierfrancesco, an uncommonly young husband, also seeing this painting day after day. He was ambitious and well-connected, groomed to take over the Medici legacy. I wondered if he was ever anxious about living up to the expectations he carried, if he was nervous that his powerful older cousin would change his mind and choose someone else to be his heir. Did he ever feel overwhelmed by the expectation that he must be perpetually decisive and active? Did he long for simple human connection but worry that such a desire made him weak? Did he ever wish that Semiramide would be playful or exuberant or pursue *him*?

After spending the last decade grappling with the ways purity culture had malformed me, my husband, and so many of our friends, I saw *Primavera* in a new light. I wanted to scold my high school self. I felt naive. How could I have believed the false promise of the virtuous Venus, that following rules would make me worthy of love? Why couldn't I see that the virtuous Venus was not so different from the nude Venus on display? The story behind their beautiful, placid faces was somehow still the same: A woman's body is fundamentally an object of desire.

But I wasn't the only one erroneously convinced that images of Venus were merely aesthetic artifacts or intellectual propositions. While Renaissance viewers readily acknowledged the social role of images, we've since become accustomed to seeing Venus in museums, divorcing her from her real-world impact, past and present. It's easy to forget that she is still shaping our stories. How did this supposed separation happen? The shifting interpretations of another well-known painting provide a helpful example.

But-It's-Art Venus

After leaving the Botticelli paintings on the main floor of the Uffizi, I find another famous Venus downstairs. Fifty years after Botticelli's *Primavera*, the Venetian artist Titian rotated the Venus Pudica eighty degrees and shifted her relationship to the presumed viewer. Now known as the *Venus of Urbino* (1538), the four-foot-wide painting depicts a young, nude woman with flushed cheeks and long, dark-blond tresses lounging on a bed with rumpled sheets. She holds a bouquet of red roses in her right hand, near her breasts, while her left hand reaches down to conceal—or perhaps stroke—her genitals. Unlike Praxiteles's sculpture, however, Titian's woman returns our gaze, and unlike Botticelli's Venus, this woman seems to be at home in sixteenth-century Italy. There is no Cyprian Sea in the background or mythological beings serving as escort. Instead, we find ourselves in a well-appointed Venetian bedroom, with a view of a

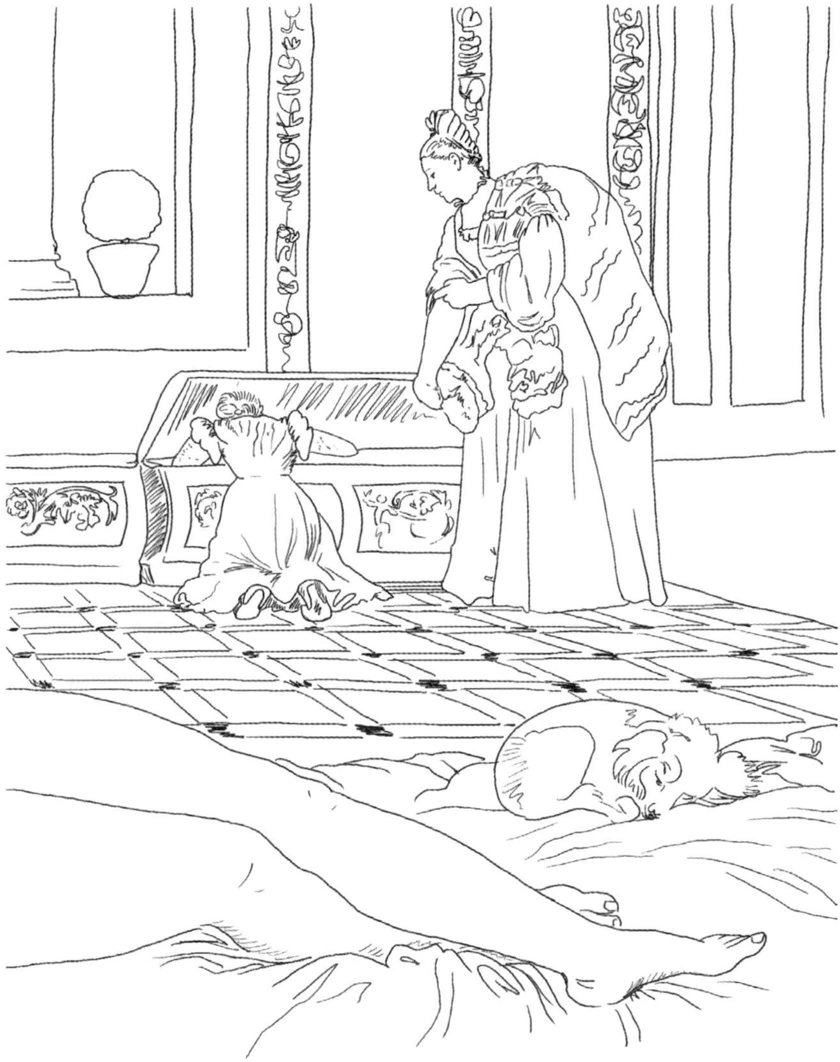

Figure 1.4. Detail drawn from Titian, *Venus of Urbino*, 1538

garden and two maids rummaging through a large, decorated chest on the far wall (see fig. 1.4).

Despite the activity and detail in the background, Titian calls our attention to the reclining woman. She fills the space closest to us, set off from the rest of the room by a dark paneled wall and heavy green velvet drapes. Her pale skin glows. Layers of translucent oil paint evoke a warm, sensuous tactility, so different from the cool rigor of Botticelli's *Primavera*.

Titian also makes other deliberate choices that direct us to a particular point in the composition. The vertical edge of the partition, the shadowed crease of the woman's right hip, the undulating contour of her shoulder, breast, and arm, and the inverted teardrop of her left thumb and forefinger all converge precisely at her pubis. Try as we might to look at her face, the roses, the maids, or even the tiny dog curled up at the foot of the bed, the very structure of the painting insistently leads us back to the apex of the woman's thighs. But instead of shying away, as Praxiteles's Venus seems to, Titian's woman looks back at us. What is she doing? What should *we* do?

As with *Primavera*, critics and scholars have long argued over this painting. Are we looking at a Roman goddess or a portrait of a brazen courtesan? Is this an allegory of divine Beauty or pornography for the elite?[30] Responding to what he understood as the artwork's frank sexuality, American author Mark Twain famously called it "the foulest, the vilest, the obscenest picture the world possesses."[31] But what was this painting actually *for*?

Today, we might assume, like Twain, that the painting was meant as erotica for a male viewer. Certainly, pornographic images for men did exist in sixteenth-century Italy. But this Venus was not that. Like Botticelli's *Primavera*, Titian's *Venus of Urbino* bears the hallmarks of typical Italian bridal gifts.[32] There are a myrtle tree in the background and red roses in the woman's hand, both symbols of love, marriage, and fertility. The tiny dog curled up at the foot of the bed represents marital fidelity. The women in the background are preparing to pack away the woman's bridal gown in her marriage chest. Finally, the subject matter of the "sleeping Venus" often shows up in both wedding poems and, believe it or not, the inside lid of marriage chests.

Yes, while mythological scenes of women's submission decorated the exterior of some brides' *cassoni*, the interior lid could contain a painting of a reclining, sensuous Venus![33] The image was private and certainly not meant for intellectual contemplation. When seen in flickering candlelight, in the privacy of the couple's chamber, the glimpsed nude could be both titillating and instructive.[34] According to Renaissance commentators, gazing upon physical beauty could stimulate fertility and result in more handsome offspring![35]

Titian's *Venus of Urbino*, though hung in the bedroom rather than set in a chest, follows the same template of instructions for a bride. Like *Primavera*, it still teaches the values of chastity, submission, and fertility. The reclining woman remains chaste, because she is ostensibly meeting the gaze of her husband, offering him access to her body.[36] The painting is, at least initially, a private image. But of course, none of this is immediately apparent to us as contemporary viewers, reverently approaching the *Venus of Urbino* in the solemn space of the Uffizi Gallery.

I certainly didn't know any of this history when I read my first art history textbook. I do remember being a little shocked by the image. The woman, with her frank appraisal and seductive pose, seemed to be the great-great-grandmother of *Sports Illustrated* swimsuit centerfolds and contemporary ads. Was she inviting objectification? Or, despite being painted by a man, was she the first girl-power or sex-positive feminist? My textbook dodged those questions altogether. Instead, it celebrated the painting as the "height" of Titian's artistic powers and lovingly described the formal elements of color and value that would "inspir[e] generations of painters in Italy and north."[37] Any social function of the work was deemed secondary to its value as an expression of artistic skill and influence.

Perhaps you'd expect Christian scholars to decry Titian's *Venus* as immodest and sinful. But in his book *Modern Art and the Death of a Culture*, which laid the foundation for most contemporary Christian engagement with visual art, art historian Hans Rookmaaker actually praises another one of Titian's reclining nudes as evidence of a Christian worldview. These Renaissance female nudes are not "real" naked women, he writes. Instead, they should be understood as metaphors, "figures through which invisible yet real concepts could be symbolized and visualized by means of painting."[38] For Rookmaaker, metaphors are an extension of a Christian conception of the world. Christians know that absolute virtues are real and exist independent of humanity. Thus, when Titian represents Venus as a symbol of love and beauty, he reflects a belief that "love and beauty [are] not just man's feelings and man's subjective taste; they [are] really there."[39] Rookmaaker—and other conservative modernist commentators—justify the Venus story by telling us that we're not really seeing a desirable woman, intended for titillation. We're seeing the manifestation of an abstract idea, one that they claim serves as an essential element of Western civilization.

When is a body not a body?

When it's a picture of an idea.

So how did this shift occur? How did Venus move from the privacy of the bedroom to the public halls of high art and culture? Once there, did she truly inhabit only the philosophical realm of ideas?

We get some sense of this relocation from a painting made by Johan Zoffany. The painting depicts the Uffizi Tribuna, an octagonal room in the Medici palace in Florence that was, by the eighteenth century, one of the first modern European museums. Zoffany crams his five-and-a-half-foot-wide canvas full of detail, including classical portrait busts, Madonna paintings by Raphael, and the *Venus de Medici*, the family's prized, ancient copy of Praxiteles's Aphrodite, purposefully evoking the sensuous cacophony he experienced in the Tribuna. Young men in powdered wigs rapturously gaze up at the marble figure; one holds a magnifying loop up to his eye to get an even better look. But Zoffany also adds additional works from the Medici collection that were not typically in the room, including the *Venus of Urbino* (see fig. 1.5).

Somehow, even amid this visual feast, Titian's painting becomes a focal point. The lounging, nude woman, now a painting of a painting, still catches and holds our gaze. Instead of hanging on the wall, the painting is held up for inspection in the composition's foreground by the gallery's curator.

The abundance of visiting British men, the reverence given to the contents of the Uffizi Tribuna, and the gallery's very existence as a public museum are all the results of major intellectual and cultural shifts in Western Europe. The Age of Enlightenment, usually dated from the late seventeenth through the eighteenth century, was marked by a belief in humanity's capacity to study and comprehend the world through empirical observation. Reason, rather than ancient or spiritual texts, should provide the basis for knowledge. Indeed, perhaps *only* that which could be apprehended rationally was real and worthy of consideration.

Museums developed as a means of organizing collections of knowledge and providing the public with the opportunity to make observations

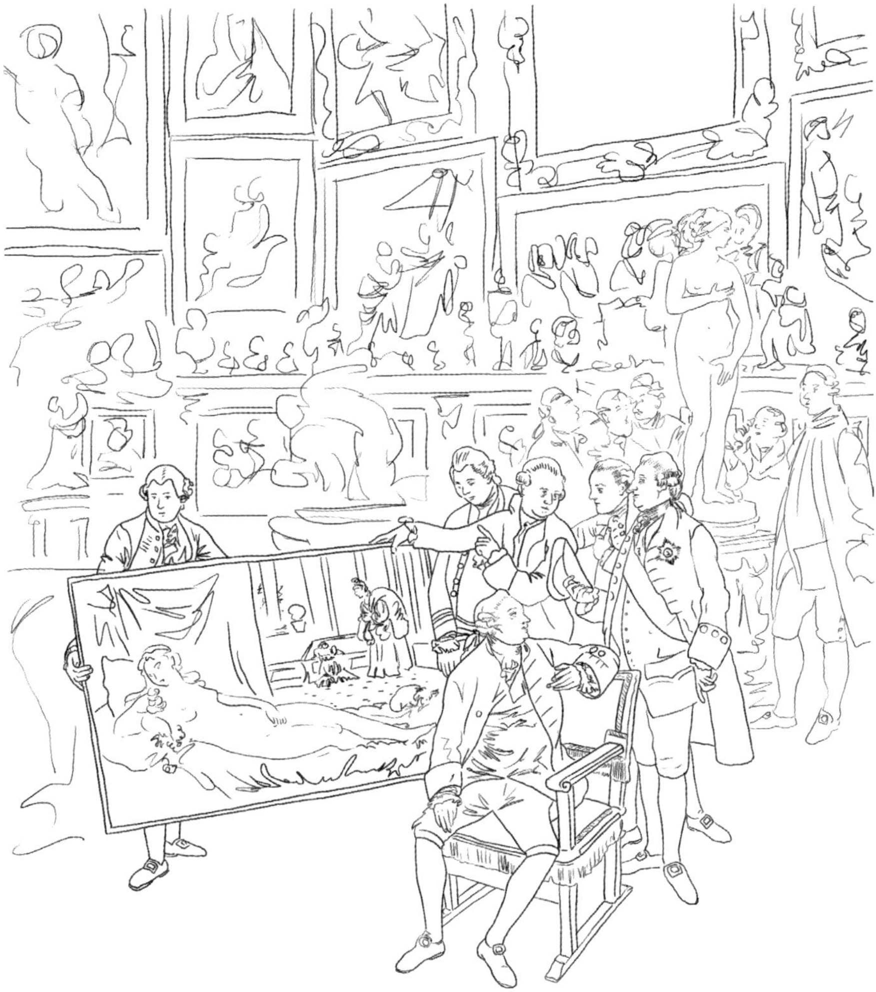

Figure 1.5. Detail drawn from Johan Zoffany, *Tribuna of the Uffizi*, 1772–77

themselves. What should fill these spaces? Much of the artwork made during the medieval era—quirky, cartoonish bodies and animals made to communicate theological, not empirical, truths—was deemed sadly lacking. Greek and Roman sculpture—with believably posed, beautifully proportioned bodies—and the Renaissance artworks that echoed those ideals were celebrated. The social functions of Praxiteles's *Aphrodite of*

Knidos or Botticelli's *Primavera* or Titian's *Venus of Urbino* were largely and purposefully forgotten. In their place, a distorted understanding of classical antiquity, one that reflected seventeenth- and eighteenth-century priorities, slowly emerged.

In this new story, the *Aphrodite of Knidos* never invited lustful leering! Ancient Greek men perceived her as a visualization of a mathematical algorithm. Her beauty was rational and therefore virtuous and transcendent! Eighteenth-century philosophers declared that contemplating the perfectly proportioned bodies of Greek art would feed the viewer's soul and influence the character of a nation.[40]

Unsurprisingly, the taste for classicism extended to the creation of new art and architecture as well. Rejecting the obvious drama and sensuality of much seventeenth- and early eighteenth-century art, artists in Italy, France, Britain, and the new republic of the United States favored crisp, linear paintings and pure white marble sculptures. Philosophers asserted that these formal choices stimulated the mind. Color, on the other hand, appealed to the weaker flesh.[41] Never mind that Greek and Roman sculptures had originally been painted. To Neoclassical artists and viewers, color applied to sculpture was deceitful artifice that hindered the purity and nobility of ideal form. White marble sculptures offered a kind of abstraction, distancing the unclothed bodies from the viewer and allowing for a completely cerebral engagement. Or, at least, that's what critics claimed.[42]

The reality, as we might expect by now, was more complicated.

While male connoisseurs tried to relegate Venus to the world of high art and the realm of ideas, wealthy women in France and England had other ideas. Historian Amelia Rauser has recently demonstrated that aristocratic women in the late eighteenth and early nineteenth centuries deliberately used fashion to turn themselves into classical "living statues."[43] Like sculptors and painters, they too rejected the artifice of the previous decades. Instead of wearing heavy, rigid gowns and powdered wigs, women adopted simple, low-cut dresses in gossamer-thin, white muslin that bared their arms and clung to their bodies. We see such classicized dress in Angelica Kauffmann's *Portrait of a Woman at Her Toilet*, where a young woman with tumbling curls elegantly pulls a draped shawl around her simple,

Grecian-inspired gown (see fig. 1.6). In the 1790s, some women even wore "belly pads" beneath their dresses, reshaping their bodies to mimic the curving, fertile stomachs of ancient statues and Botticelli's Venuses![44] Their visual quotations were deliberate. The goal was to be "a living spectacle of masterpieces of the most celebrated artists of antiquity."[45] In doing so, they could insert themselves into conversations otherwise reserved for men. But the potency—and potential threat—of this participation is evident in vicious cartoons from the period that mocked these women as silly, amateur, vacuous, and even ugly.[46]

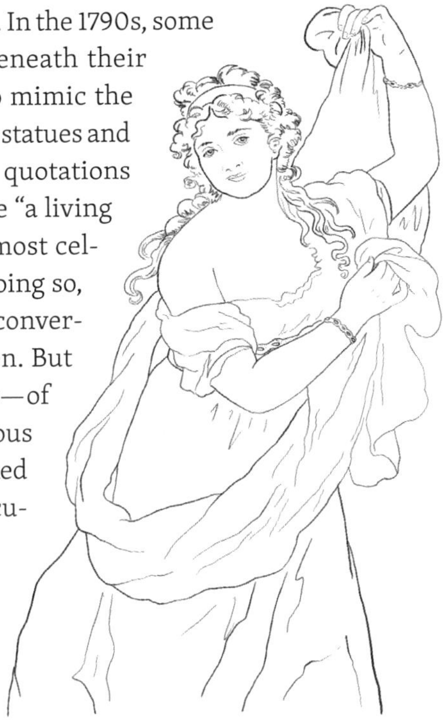

Figure 1.6. Detail drawn from Angelica Kauffmann, *Portrait of a Woman at Her Toilet*, 1795

Rauser's research reminds us of an important truth: Visual scripts are never simply laid down on helpless, utterly passive women. Women always maintain some degree of agency, engaging with, negotiating, and troubling these stories.

By the 1820s, the eclectic subjectivity and sentimentality of Romanticism had successfully challenged the dominance of Neoclassical aesthetics. But Venus's place was secured. Sanctioned as high art, the reclining, female nude became an expected part of the portfolio of any ambitious male painter or sculptor. The real social and cultural effects of displaying women's bodies in this way were ignored in favor of emphasizing a world of ideas.

The Other Venus

As I walk across the campus of my small Christian liberal arts college, I hear a long whistle coming from the chapel steps. An upperclassman is waving. "You know I have a thing for Asian women!" he yells. Maybe he's joking. Maybe he's being honest. I don't really want to find out, so I lift my chin and keep heading back to my room. I'm nineteen, and I've only just learned that there is an entire subgenre of the sex industry that specifically fetishizes Asian women as both exotically dangerous and willingly compliant. In the southeastern United States, my biracial body can be hard for people to categorize. But men who have "a thing for Asian women" tend to identify me as one. Then they tell me what that means to them.

My heart is still beating quickly when I enter my dorm. There's a storm in my chest. On the one hand, my skin crawls at being catcalled. On the other hand, I have to grudgingly admit that in a community overwhelmingly populated by women who fit white, Southern standards of beauty, there's a strange relief that *someone* claims to find me attractive. The Venus story sinks so deeply in my bones that I wonder if my desirability is proof of my womanhood. Maybe I can make myself powerful if I embrace whatever strange sway my body seems to hold over these men. Yet this supposed attractiveness also hinges on the belief that I am a deviant Venus, outside the norm.

I am the exotic other.

The problem is not that there's only a single Venus body type. After all, Botticelli's Venus is a tall, svelte ginger. Seventeenth-century Flemish painter Peter Paul Rubens renders blond nudes with round bellies, dimpled thighs, and double-D breasts. A century later, the French artist François Boucher paints Venus at her toilette with soft folds and powdered, gray hair. The desirable body morphs to accommodate shifting tastes. But there is one attribute that does seem consistent in the first two-thirds of my art history textbooks: Venus is of European descent.

And so, the first time I see a reproduction of Paul Gauguin's 1899 painting *Two Tahitian Women*, I gasp in delight (see fig. 1.7). Two golden-skinned, dark-haired, young women, standing close together and cropped at mid-thigh, fill the three-foot-high canvas. Both women adopt the familiar Venus pose, one hip slightly pushed out and tipped up. Is this the non-European Venus I've been looking for? Are Polynesian women being represented as beautiful and worthy of representation? It seems like a cause for celebration!

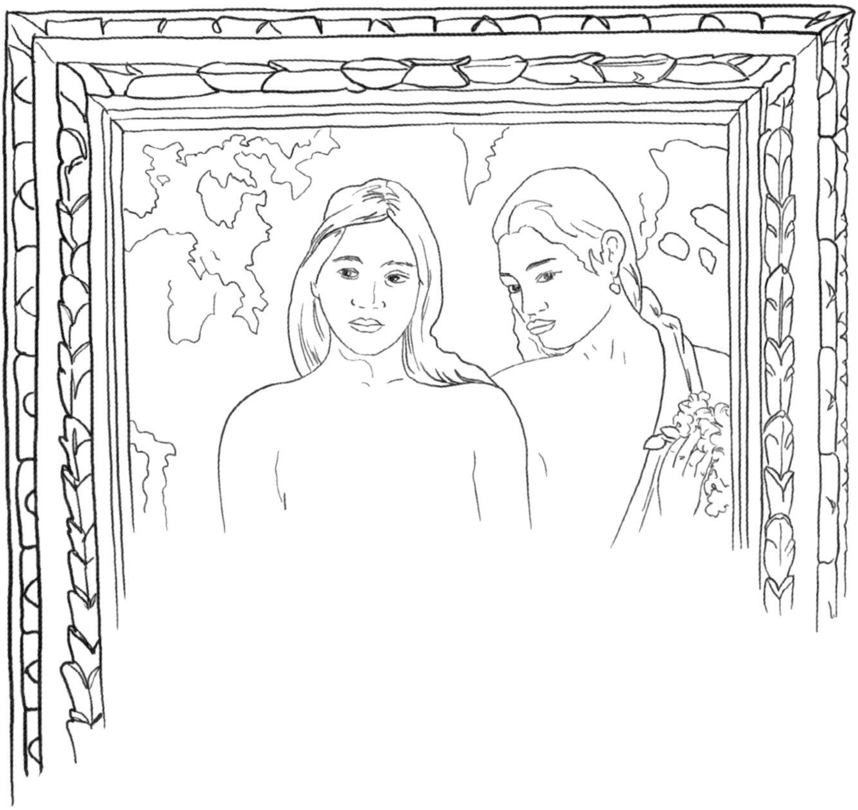

Figure 1.7. Detail drawn from Paul Gauguin, *Two Tahitian Women*, 1899

Now, though, I see the painting as a cause for lament. When the story of Venus is the sole—or the loudest—story we have, we can start to believe that the *only* way to honor a woman's body is to objectify it and declare it desirable. But again, the painting's particular history makes it clear: This work does not dignify these women. It flattens them into objects and pushes them into a cruel racial hierarchy.

Like all artists, Gauguin makes deliberate choices. In *Two Tahitian Women*, he unifies the women with the nature behind them while emphasizing their bare breasts. Gauguin uses the same colors in both the women's bodies and the dreamy, abstracted landscape behind them. The dark green of the background also shows up as shadows below their chins and breasts. The exact yellow-brown of their skin glimmers as a patch of light in the lower left background. The women seem to emerge from, while remaining connected to, the natural world.

Gauguin also directs our attention to the women's bare breasts using line and color. The woman on the right turns her face toward her companion but makes eye contact with the viewer. She wears a pale-blue drape that ties on one shoulder but scoops beneath one breast and holds a cluster of pink flowers in her hands, which are raised as if in prayer. The gesture also pushes one arm up under her visible breast. The second woman wears only a purple skirt. She cradles an oblong tray full of bright-vermilion fruit or flowers in her arms, and her pert, round breasts almost seem to rest on the dish, as if they, too, are on offer. Like Praxiteles's bathing *Aphrodite of Knidos* and Titian's *Venus of Urbino*, the very structure of the work encourages viewers to focus on the women's sexuality.

Gauguin was not the first European artist to depict a non-European woman as a Venus. From the late fifteenth through the sixteenth century, seafaring European nations explored the globe, discovering the existence of vastly different worlds far from their own shores. With the recent invention of the printing press, explorers' accounts could be widely shared, and artists' engraved illustrations helped the public imagine these distant lands and people. Of course, these illustrators were not actually recording what explorers encountered in their journeys. They inevitably interpreted accounts of these new cultures through their own, existing visual archives. Images and objects they had seen before shaped their current experiences. And so, women with unfamiliar skin tones, hairstyles, and adornments were represented in new travel accounts in a very familiar pose: the Venus in *contrapposto*. In depictions of Algonquian women in the new Virginia colonies and engravings of West African women encountered by Dutch traders, we find the same proportions and gestures of classical sculpture.[47] Are these early, multicultural Venuses celebrating a diversity of hair types and skin color?

Not quite.

In Europeans' minds, the lack of clothing in these unfamiliar cultures signaled, at best, a lesser degree of civilization and, at worst, moral degeneracy. Yet confusingly, the main European visual script for a naked or scantily clothed body came from revered classical and Renaissance models. Venus provided an easily understandable formula for representing women from these seemingly alien places.

As the seventeenth century continued, European exploration became colonization and domination. Representations of people in the Americas and Africa hardened into demeaning stereotypes, supported by the seemingly scientific, rational language of the Enlightenment. Naturalists claimed to use empirical observation and comparison to create new classifications for humanity based on certain physical differences such as skin color and hair texture. Historians have demonstrated how the notion of "race" as a biological fact also established and justified a hierarchy in which, unsurprisingly, Europeans sat at the top.[48] As the reasoning went, the land, resources, and women of these so-called inferior cultures were all available for European conquest and plunder.

Black women, however, received the heaviest blow. (We will look at this history more closely in the Monster chapter.) As the transatlantic slave trade began, demeaning images of African women as ugly and ape-like reinforced the claim that they were also animalistic in their mental capacity, sexual appetites, and morals.[49] Eventually, this trope became known as the "Jezebel" stereotype.

Later, in the nineteenth century, French artists like Jean-Auguste-Dominique Ingres and Eugène Delacroix painted lounging "odalisques," bedecked with peacock feathers and silk turbans. While the setting suggested that these women were ladies in the Ottoman court, their bodies were still recognizably European. In effect, the artists played on their audience's belief in the sexual availability of non-Western women while still offering bodies that aligned with conventional European beauty standards. Today, the trope of the spicy Latina—usually a light-skinned, curvy woman with a hot temper and abundant sexual energy—continues the same idea.

Paul Gauguin's *Two Tahitian Women* is part of this long history. Gauguin, also a French artist, accepted the idea that non-Western cultures were "primitive" when compared to the developed West. However, he—along with a number of other European poets, writers, and artists—also believed that this primitivism was a good thing. In their minds, it meant that these cultures had not been corrupted by Western modernism and could still get in touch with nature and the spiritual in an authentic way.[50] Gauguin left Paris for Tahiti in 1891, looking for an untouched paradise where people were governed by their senses and intuition rather than logic.

Gauguin didn't paint these Tahitian women because he saw them as dignified, worthy, and complex subjects. He painted them because they represented his desire to escape from what he saw as the stifling confines and expectations of industrialized European society.[51]

When Gauguin actually arrived at the main port of Papeete in Tahiti, however, he was disappointed. The island had been forcibly annexed by the French almost fifty years earlier, and European technology, culture, and religion had reshaped the island's culture. Still, the artist stayed for two years, making paintings and sending them back to Paris to be sold. Despite having a wife and five children whom he left behind in Denmark, Gauguin also took a thirteen-year-old native, Teha'amana, as his so-called native wife, or *vahine*. He claimed that she taught him about Tahitian folk religion and practices and that he accessed a kind of primordial knowledge through their sexual encounters. For Gauguin, Tahitian women were desirable because of their apparent *deviance* from European norms. They were exotic—outside of what he considered familiar. And so, he painted them as such, inviting others to gaze on their bodies in the same way.

I wonder how Teha'amana understood her relationship to Gauguin. Some scholars suggest that she and her family received financial security and increased social standing by having a relationship with a Frenchman.[52] When Gauguin left for an extended visit to France, Teha'amana remained behind. She refused to resume a relationship with Gauguin two years later, perhaps because she could see evidence of syphilis. She went on to marry a native man.[53]

It is very tempting to simply kick Gauguin out of the art historical canon as a creepy old Frenchman who had "a thing" for foreign girls. But history is most helpful when it helps me maintain complexity rather than justify my judgments. I do not have access to Teha'amana's inner life, but I suspect that, given her humanity, a storm of contradictory emotions raged at times inside her chest too.

The Veil of Venus

The Venus story is absurdly simple, diminishing women to objects of desire. Yet the script's complicated history also demonstrates its frustrating resilience through multiple variations. Praxiteles's Aphrodite is not a confident goddess willingly putting herself on display. Instead, her privacy is breached, and her vulnerability is precisely what makes her desirable. Hellenistic Greek masculinity is defined not by protecting defenseless bodies but by consuming them for pleasure. Botticelli's virtuous Venus rewrites the script as a rulebook for a Renaissance bride: Regulate your body, submit it to your husband, and you will be rewarded with children and stability. Titian's Venus even revels in her sexuality and promised fertility in the context of marriage. Enlightenment critics insist that real bodies have little to do with Venus. She is instead a beautiful, abstract idea—a cultural watermark. Yet women's bodies remain available in titillating, erotic prints and literature. Meanwhile, actual women assert their own warm, breathing bodies within the philosophical conversation, dressing as Venus sculptures come to life. Western colonialism applies the same script to non-European women, spreading the lie that the worst fate is to be deemed too ugly to be considered desirable. Surely you can find present-day iterations in whatever cultural spaces you inhabit. Over and over and over again, we see the same story—to be a woman is to be an object of desire.

History also shows us that the visual script is a flimsy concoction. Once we see it, we can see through it. It is almost as if its thinness allows it to be draped, folded, stretched, and twisted into innumerable contortions. Sometimes I still lay it on myself, wondering if there's an age limit to Venus, wondering if I'm trying too hard—or not enough—as a middle-aged woman, wondering if I would feel more empowered if I wielded my sexuality like a weapon.

Yet Venus *can't* be my story because it slices and flattens me into something less than a human, an image bearer of the living God. My tradition's catechism declares that I am made "to glorify God, and to enjoy him forever."[54] If this calling is not an abstract philosophical concept but an embodied reality, then the Venus story has to be untrue. *I* get to enjoy

God; I am not just a source of others' enjoyment. My primary purpose cannot be sexual objectification, whether that be done by men, women, or even myself.

Perhaps the best thing the Venuses in Botticelli's *Primavera* and Gauguin's colorful paintings can do is serve as a prompt to honest lament. I want to name the ways this Venus story has malformed me. I grieve how persistently I tried to shoehorn myself into a small story, excusing my own humiliation along the way. I mourn the times I tried to escape my body, unable to recognize its goodness as a particular, finite creation that bears the image of the living God. And I confess that in demeaning myself I also dehumanized others, stridently judging women for their bodies and actions and infantilizing men as incapable of anything other than lust.

But I don't want to stop there.

I want to tell a different story about looking altogether.

COUNTERSTORY:
Witnessing

Venus Takes Charge?

It's not terribly hard to find artworks by modern and contemporary artists that challenge the Venus story. Some seem to poke fun at the trope. Suzanna Valadon, once a model for famous French artists, later became a painter in her own right. One of her best-known works, *The Blue Room* (1923), depicts a woman lounging on a bed in a Venus-like pose. However, this thick-fingered, sunburned Venus with heavy breasts is wearing striped pajamas and smoking a cigarette. The Guerrilla Girls, a feminist art collective, parodied Ingres's *Grande Odalisque* in 1989 with their satirical poster *Do Women Have to Be Naked to Get into the Met. Museum?* Ingres's exotic woman now wears a gorilla mask, and bold text states, "Less than 5% of the artists in the Modern Art Sections are women, but 85% of the nudes are female." The poster humorously yet pointedly highlights a disparity of representation.

Artists also highlight bodies that the Venus story historically ignored or distorted. Months before she died from lymphoma, artist Hannah Wilke made a series of photographs titled *Intra-Venus* (1994). She struck familiar poses for the camera, implicitly asking if her bloated, bandaged body was still worthy of celebration and care. In a monumental 2017 painting, Harmonia Rosales reimagines Botticelli's *Birth of Venus* as the *Birth of Oshun*, substituting Yòrúba religion and West African bodies for classical mythology. Still other artists swap out the implied male viewer. Romaine Brooks explores lesbian desire in her stark painting of a dark-haired, nude woman titled *White Azaleas* (1910), and decades later so does Mickalene Thomas in her glossy, rhinestone-encrusted paintings of Black women.

Finally, some women choose to become Venus themselves. Well-known actresses, pop stars, and online influencers have directed photoshoots in which they adopt Venus's poses, harnessing their sexual powers for their own purposes and self-promotion.

But when we pull apart the flimsy threads of the Venus script, what remains? Does an awareness of a history of objectification necessarily change people's attitudes or actions? Is the goal simply to expand a desiring gaze, lengthening both the list of potential bodies and the list of potential viewers? Is *self*-objectification our best alternative? Is a consenting Venus a powerful Venus? All these options assume one thing: the presence of a consuming, objectifying gaze. I wonder, though. Is that the only look available to us?

A Visitation

There's a small wooden sculpture in the Metropolitan Museum of Art in New York that I always try to visit on my way out of the building. Made between 1310 and 1320, two female figures—just under twenty-four inches tall—turn toward each other, gazes locked and hands clasped (see fig. 1.8). The women's heads are slightly too large for their gently curving bodies, and their outstretched arms frame the most important part of the sculpture: lozenge-shaped crystals set into their torsos as glittering, pregnant bellies. The title, *The Visitation*, lets us know that these are two specific pregnant women: Mary and her cousin Elizabeth from the Gospel of Luke.

If we're familiar with the biblical narrative of Luke 1, we know that Gabriel has just told Mary that she will be the mother of God. Mary hurries to visit her older cousin Elizabeth, who is also miraculously pregnant. When Elizabeth hears Mary's greeting, her child—John the Baptist—leaps in her womb "for joy," recognizing the incarnate presence of the Messiah in Mary's womb (Luke 1:41–45). Given all this, we might expect Mary to be the obvious main character in this sculptural group. I'm struck, however, by how the artist—known to us now only as Master Heinrich of Constance—creates a unified whole.

Mary and Elizabeth echo and balance each other. They are carved from the same materials, wear the same garments, and share the same scale and mass. Even their faces mimic each other with their high, arched eyebrows, rosy cheeks, and enigmatic smiles. It is almost as if each woman is looking at a mirror image of herself. Still, each figure also asks for individual attention. When we look at Mary head on, Elizabeth is turned toward her in profile. Likewise, when we look at Elizabeth directly, Mary stands in profile.

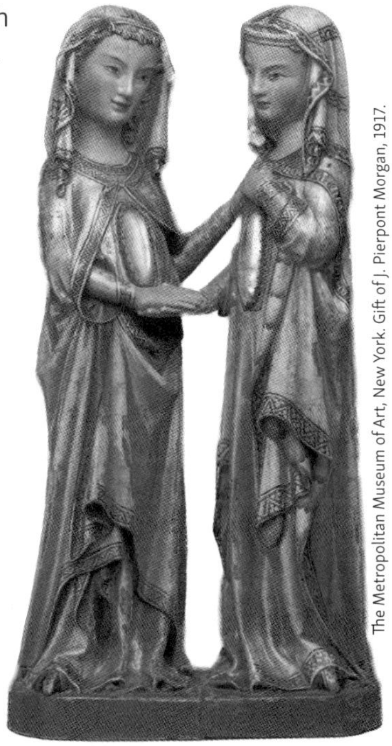

The Metropolitan Museum of Art, New York. Gift of J. Pierpont Morgan, 1917.

Figure 1.8. Attributed to Master Heinrich of Constance, *The Visitation*, ca. 1310–20, painted wood, gilding, and cabochon crystals. A full-color image of this sculpture is included in the color insert section.

The artist also unifies the figures using the lines of the women's arms. Mary stretches her right hand across her body to grasp Elizabeth's right hand. With her left hand, she reaches across to tenderly touch her cousin's shoulder. Elizabeth, in turn, brings her left hand up to her chest, her fingers just barely brushing Mary's. She holds a long, narrow scroll that curls around her shoulder, inscribed with her greeting to her cousin. The women's connected arms perpetually guide our looking. We follow the circuit around and around as it loops continuously around the most important elements of the sculpture: the inset crystals.

The use of transparent quartz also creates an important contrast. The sculpture is carved from walnut, a medium-density wood that holds detail well. Master Heinrich of Constance takes advantage of this property, using a variety of tools to transform a tree's limb into softly folded fabric with intricate, embossed borders, smooth faces with petite features, and long, limber fingers. The wood is painted, first with a chalky paint that smooths over the woodgrain, and then layered with translucent pigments. Shimmering gold glints on the decorations of their garments, and both figures are polished to a glossy shine. The women's garments, hands, and faces almost have the appearance of a hard candy shell. This contrasts with the lozenge-shaped stones set into the women's torsos. A misty, milky white, the crystals seem to glow. While the wood absorbs the light, the cabochons refract it. They are so different from the rest of the sculpture that we have to give them attention.

These formal choices also activate my body as a viewer. I find it impossible to stand still and look at the work from a single spot. I want—I need—to move, to tip my head and step slowly in a circle, watching the crystals sparkle and shift from milky white to pale rose.

After reading about a string of very famous Venuses, you might find this small, admittedly quirky sculpture an odd and insufficient source for a counterstory. In fact, you may think, like I initially did, that *The Visitation* is no more than a medieval Precious Moments trinket. Painted sculptures, especially at this scale, often seem more like kitsch than high art, and the crystal bellies certainly don't contradict that perception!

Still, this sculpture was made for a particular group of women, and it was made to help them tell a particular story about themselves and their relationship to each other. And as it turns out, it's a story I want to tell about myself too.

Living Transparently

This *Visitation* originally belonged to the fourteenth-century nuns of the convent of St. Katharinenthal near Lake Constance on the border of Germany and Switzerland. The women lived cloistered lives; they never left the convent, choosing to devote their whole lives to prayer and contemplation. Life within the abbey was rigidly structured and primarily communal. Sisters followed the same liturgy of regular prayer times, shared sleeping quarters, ate together, and had no personal possessions.

Still, individual sisters had deeply personal encounters with artworks in the convent church. This approach to liturgical artworks developed as part of the turn toward mysticism in the fourteenth-century Western church: the belief that Christians could experience intimate union with God in their life now, not just in the life to come. While upheaval and conflict raged among and between political and church leaders in Europe, mysticism emphasized personal devotion and transformation. In the context of the St. Katharinenthal convent, artworks like *The Visitation* could serve as teaching tools that also invited contemplation.[55] Sisters did not pray *to* the artworks but instead used the objects like a lens, gathering and focusing their attention so that they might experience the presence of God in a profound and embodied way.[56]

Some of the intense visionary experiences of nuns at this particular convent are recorded in a manuscript known as the *Katharinenthal Sister Book*.[57] The *Sister Book* contains the vitae, or brief biographical accounts, of sisters at the convent who lived between approximately 1245 and 1345. Some of them are very short—just a few sentences—while others are more extensive. Each begins, "There was a sister named . . ." and goes on to describe a key event or events in her life at the convent.

Some of the entries describe special grace or visions that sisters received following devoted prayer or acts of mercy. For example, one sister has a vision of Christ as a child who accompanies her through her day, resulting in an "inexpressible" feeling of "joy, sweetness, and companionship."[58] Another sister chooses to break her usual practice of silent prayer in order to comfort a struggling novice. Later, she is rewarded with a vision of the Christ child.[59] Other entries, however, record sisters' lack of faith or incorrect behavior. The Virgin Mary appears to one sister to chastise her pride over her acts of mercy. Another has a vision disappear because she refused to help a fellow sister; the loss prompts her to repent of her selfishness. Together, the short biographies offer instruction by means of both positive and negative examples.

As a twenty-first-century reader and viewer, I admit that both *The Visitation* sculpture and the *Sister Book* offer glimpses into a deeply unfamiliar culture. I am, quite frankly, shaped by Enlightenment beliefs about the natural world. I am not always sure what to make of crystal wombs or visions of the infant Christ. The nuns are not abiding by the scientific method or standards of contemporary journalism! At the same time, their longing to know that they are loved by God in the midst of personal doubt and social upheaval *does* seem familiar. So, is there something we can learn from how they shepherd this yearning?

An overlap between the wooden *Visitation* sculpture and the language of the *Sister Book* offers a valuable insight. Just as Mary and Elizabeth have translucent wombs, the nuns' visions frequently involve transparency.[60] The sisters see transparent figures or the walls of the convent become like glass. In several entries, sisters' bodies are described as becoming clear as crystal, with light shining through them. In one particular instance, a sister becomes transparent after meditating on the beauty of obedience. Her obedience to the rule of Scripture means that she has nothing to hide; her physical transparency is a manifestation of her moral purity.

The language of transparency could also be linked with longing. In another story, a nun yearns to be with her biological sister who is not in the convent. One day after worship, she has a vision in which the walls of the cloister turn to glass and she can see a heartbroken woman standing on the other side. Christ tells her that this sorrowful woman is her sister in the forest. Her grief stems from the fact that while she can see Christ through the glass walls of the convent, she is still distant from him, unlike her cloistered sister. In this account, transparency allows visual but not physical access.[61] It gives and it withholds. It both incites and perpetuates desire.

Given the theme of transparency in the *Sister Book*, the crystal bellies in *The Visitation* begin to make a bit more sense. There's some evidence that tiny paintings of Jesus and John the Baptist might have originally been pinned behind the crystals, allowing viewers to see these miraculous babies while still remaining distanced from them.[62] Even without such images, the material qualities of the crystals—solid yet allowing light to pass through—reinforce these lessons of obedience and yearning.[63] Mary and Elizabeth are obedient to God's call, even in extraordinary circumstances. Their transparent wombs are material evidence of their faithfulness; they have nothing to hide. But they also reiterate that both women are longing for a redemption—a rescue—that has been promised but has not yet materialized. Centuries later, the sisters of Katharinenthal likewise desire to be obedient and to be in the presence of Jesus. The sculpture enacts a perpetual reaching for that which they long to fully grasp.

We should also pay attention to the implications of the text wrapping around Elizabeth's shoulder on a narrow banderole. The words are a quote from Luke 1:43: "Who am I, that the mother of the Lord should visit me?" When we, as viewers, say this out loud or even read the text silently, the first-person voice becomes our own.[64] Who am *I*, a sister at Katharinenthal or Elissa Yukiko Weichbrodt, that the mother of the Lord should visit me? I, like Elizabeth, actively behold the incarnation.

And this is how *The Visitation* offers a new story about vision for women. Rather than simply functioning as objects of a desiring gaze, Mary and Elizabeth offer a different way of looking altogether. With linked hands framing their crystal wombs and gazes turned toward each other, they see what others—including Elizabeth's husband, Zechariah, and Mary's betrothed, Joseph—struggled to accept. They see God's favor. They look at each other with love, dignifying and testifying to the other's experience of both longing and belief. They bear witness.

A Loving Look

To witness is to attest to the reality of a claim, to affirm that something is true and genuine. We might associate bearing witness with the courtroom, but more recently the term has been connected to trauma theory and even made its way into pop psychology. In some ways, "bearing witness" has become so elastic that it can be hard to know what we mean. Is it listening to the testimony of survivors of violence? Is it watching a video circulating online of a man's unjust death? Is it reposting that video? Is it just documenting ourselves crying in the car? Can bearing witness lead to secondhand trauma? Philosophers, historians, theologians, and psychologists will continue to disagree on the ethics, biology, and measurable impact of bearing witness.

Still, when I look at *The Visitation*, I am struck by the deep resonances between the sculpture itself, the biblical narrative it depicts, and the *Katharinenthal Sister Book*. As we have already seen, the sculpture's material and form invite our slow, longing gaze. The looping composition, the shifting glow of the crystals, and the curling banderole of text all prompt us to be curious and active viewers. We cannot see or know everything about the artwork with a quick, initial glance. It asks for our extended attention, and the nuns of St. Katharinenthal responded by using the sculpture as a guide for meditating on their own spiritual callings.

As part of their contemplation, the sisters would recall what they already knew about the depicted biblical narrative. They would have been familiar with the text of Luke 1; perhaps some of them had even memorized that Gospel passage. As a result, they would know that this particular scene of greeting takes place after both women, Mary and Elizabeth, have received

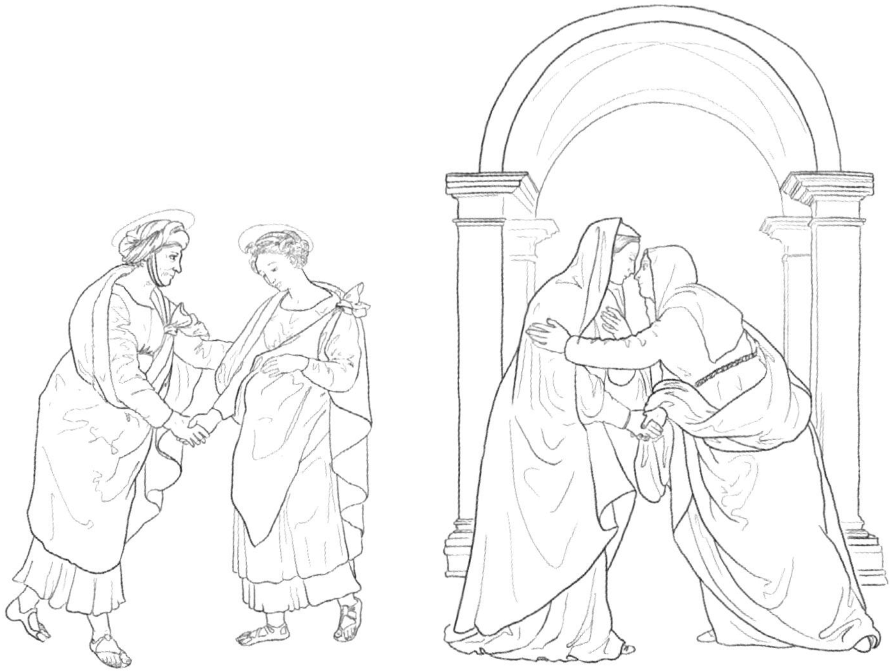

Figure 1.9. Details drawn from visitation paintings by (left to right) Raphael (ca. 1517), Albertinelli (1503), Ghirlandaio (1491), and Pontormo (ca. 1529)

life-altering news. Elizabeth, barren for decades, is now pregnant with John the Baptist, the one who will prepare the way for the long-awaited Messiah. Mary, meanwhile, is told by the angel Gabriel that she will be the mother of Jesus, the rescuer, God himself. Stunned, she asks how this will be possible since she has not had sex with a man. Gabriel reiterates that this child will be divinely conceived, and he offers another miracle as proof of what Mary cannot yet see: "Your relative Elizabeth—even she has conceived a son in her old age . . . her, who was called childless. For nothing will be impossible with God" (Luke 1:36–37). At this, Mary consents: "May it happen to me as you have said" (1:38).

Luke's narrative continues with Mary leaving her hometown and hurrying to visit her cousin. She trusts the angel's words and rushes to give attention to, to *see*, this grace bestowed on her relative. Perhaps, along the way, Mary wonders if her cousin will believe her own news of a divine pregnancy.

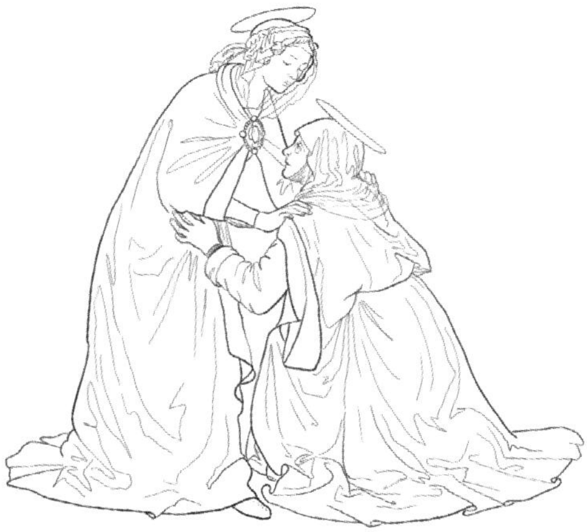

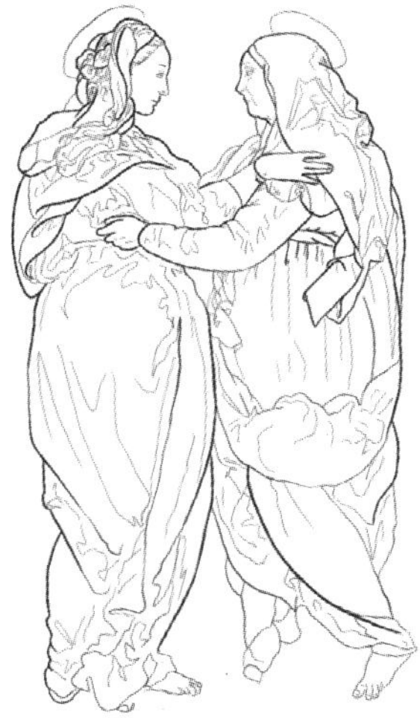

But Elizabeth and her unborn child say, "Yes! It's real!" I imagine that Mary's delight for Elizabeth was increased because she knew of her cousin's barrenness in the preceding years. The women strengthen and multiply each other's joy and anticipation. Like the strange but beautiful crystals, transparent and solid, so much remains mysteriously unknown and out of reach for them. And yet, they bear joyful witness.

This engagement with *The Visitation* echoes the aim of the *Sister Book*. The stories there do not celebrate the achievements of individual sisters, like superlatives in a yearbook. Instead, the book serves as a means of instruction through bearing witness. The entries are written not by the nuns who had the visions or performed the acts of obedience but by other sisters who remain anonymous but describe what they saw. The book encouraged the women to "teach one another by example and take one another as models."[65] As Elizabeth and Mary bear witness to each other's obedience in *The Visitation*, so the sisters are urged to do the same.

This reciprocal witnessing is present in many other, later representations of the biblical narrative. The story was especially popular among Italian Renaissance painters, who crafted dramatic, poignant scenes of the two women embracing (see fig. 1.9). In Domenico Ghirlandaio's 1491 *Visitation*, Elizabeth kneels on the ground as her cousin bends to embrace her. Two other women—traditionally believed to be Mary the mother of James and Salome—stand in the background, witnessing the encounter with awe. In Raphael's ca. 1517 *Visitation*, Mary and Elizabeth focus intently on each other, but we find a small depiction of Jesus's baptism in the background. This tiny, additional scene points to their sons' future relationship and the fulfillment of the promises that the women are already claiming. In Pontormo's 1528 *Visitation*, Mary and Elizabeth seem almost to levitate with joy, weightless in their delight at their encounter. I particularly love a 1503 *Visitation* by Mariotto Albertinelli, likely made for a chapel dedicated to Elizabeth in Florence. The large, luminous painting depicts both women in profile, their noses almost touching as Elizabeth gazes into Mary's eyes and begins to pull her into an embrace. The visual story of women-as-witness is not unusual. But what makes the St. Katharinenthal *Visitation* especially compelling is that it, along with the *Sister Book*, specifically offered this counterstory to *women* with the expectation of an active response.

Crucially, this kind of witnessing is not an end in itself. It makes something else, something *more*, possible. When the women lay eyes on each other, Elizabeth, filled with the Holy Spirit, prophesies. She speaks of what Mary has not yet told her. She gives words to what remains concealed, calling her cousin "the mother of my Lord" (Luke 1:43). Mary is carrying their long-awaited rescuer, and when Elizabeth bears witness to Mary, Mary's own joy can spill forth. In her song, the Magnificat, Mary is exultant. Her initial confusion over and subsequent acceptance of the annunciation now bubble over in wonder-filled poetry: "My soul magnifies the Lord, and my spirit rejoices in God my Savior, because he has looked with favor on the humble condition of his servant. Surely, from now on all generations will call me blessed, because the Mighty One has done great things for me, and his name is holy" (1:46–49).

Rather than being objects of a consuming gaze, the women look at each other with liberating, generative love.

The visitation narrative is not the only place in Scripture where we see such witnessing take place. In fact, Luke bookends his account of Jesus's life with stories of women attesting to his divinity. Women bear witness to the incarnation in Luke 1, and then in Luke 24, women also become the first witnesses of Christ's resurrection. But perhaps most importantly, this loving, freeing look is one modeled by Jesus himself. Jesus's gaze affirms the value of children (Mark 10:13–15). He witnesses Zacchaeus's repentance (Luke 19:5). He acknowledges the crowd's hunger (John 6:5). He insists on seeing the bleeding woman who would prefer to stay hidden (Mark 5:25–34). He looks at a grieving Martha and Mary through his own tears (John 11:35). He directs his disciples' gaze to the woman who anoints his feet (Mark 14:8–9). Jesus pays attention. Of course, Jesus—God humbled in human flesh—bears witness in places where no one else can. As theologian Tish Harrison Warren writes, "There is no darkness into which he has not descended," not even death.[66] Still, even in our finitude, we follow Jesus's example when we inhabit the story of Witnessing.

A Grace to Receive

So what does this counterstory—"I bear a witnessing gaze"—make possible for me? The Venus story teaches me that the best compliment I can give another woman is that she will find favor as an object of desire. *The Visitation*, on the other hand, offers a loving, responsive presence.

> "I see you laboring in quiet obedience, and I'm here."
> "I see you wondering why, and I'm here."
> "I see your aching body, and I'm here."
> "I see you raging against injustice, and I'm here."
> "I see your joy, and I'm here."
> "I see you weeping, and I'm here."

Instead of consuming another person for pleasure or power, instead of furthering competition or comparison, witnessing offers dignifying acceptance. But witnessing also does not demand complete understanding. As with the crystal cabochons, we can acknowledge the limits of what we can see, and we might also find ourselves changed in the process. As we bear witness, *we* become more tender, more resilient, more open to ache, and more certain of our dependence on others and God. Though we may not have visions like the sisters of St. Katharinenthal, we can find new intimacy with Christ by giving our creative, caring attention to those he cares for.

Bearing witness is also a *mutual* gift. Mary and Elizabeth both give *and* receive the grace of each other's regard. Mary offers her physical presence to her cousin, witnessing her long-awaited pregnancy. But then, remember, it is Elizabeth's affirmation of Mary's experience that prompts her overflow of praise. In the Venus story, receiving another's look results in objectification. But in the counterstory of Witnessing, we do not need to resist the gaze. Instead, the loving look makes us more human.

The last time I visited the Metropolitan Museum of Art, I was exhausted. Blow after blow of traumatic deaths, crippling depression, and catastrophic injury had pummeled my family for almost a year. Overwhelm and dread were frequent companions. My ability to be the kind of spouse, mother, professor, and friend that I expected myself to be felt utterly compromised. I was grateful for this opportunity to see art, though, and when it was time to leave, I traced my familiar exit route through the museum's medieval wing. There, as usual, I found *The Visitation*, golden and glimmering in its rectangular glass case.

Previously, I had treated the sculpture as a reminder of the importance of bearing witness to *others*. But on this day, as I traced the looping arms and gazes of Mary and Elizabeth and repeatedly tried to catch a glimpse inside their bellies, I understood the inverse to be true. I needed others to bear witness to *me*. And they had. Friends gifted me beauty when I struggled to find any of it myself. They remembered the dates of doctors' appointments and checked in. They sent text messages with morning prayers when they knew my fears were darkest. And at the very same time, they also attested to my joy. They celebrated the fulfillment of long-held dreams and cheered for tiny victories. When it felt like my delight could be only a sputtering flame, they coaxed it into a warming fire.

I imagine the sisters of St. Katharinenthal, looking at Mary and Elizabeth, recording each other's stories of yearning on behalf of each other, and I tell myself that I belong in that same linked chain of mutual gazes. I can see, and I am seen.

2

Vessel

Girl Power?

After the church service concludes, I fish a slightly worn green paper folder out of my canvas tote bag and rush over to my friend. We have combined our deeply romantic, fourteen-year-old imaginations and overstuffed vocabularies to cowrite a serial novel, passing sheaves of notebook paper back and forth each week. Our story is a vaguely medieval fantasy that features a quick-witted heroine destined to unravel familial intrigue and save her people. "I didn't write too much this week," I admit to my friend, "but I drew something." I pull out an illustration of our protagonist, carefully outlined in black ink and filled in with my Prismacolor Premier seventy-two-count colored pencil set. The young woman is dressed in a long, flowing dress with a high waist and fluttering sleeves. Her dark-brown hair swirls around her as she steps forward boldly, a sword in one hand and a billowing flag in the other.

The woman is my own creation, but I also want to *be* her. She radiates virtuous strength and intelligence, and her physical beauty is, to my mind, a reflection of her inner goodness. But why do I think that *this* is what a powerful woman looks like? I haven't studied portraits of Isabella of Spain or Elizabeth I. My heroine isn't modeled on Queen Liliʻuokalani, the beloved last monarch of the Kingdom of Hawaii whose statue stands outside our state capitol, and I don't even know yet about women like Christine de Pizan and Eleanor of Aquitaine. If my illustration isn't based on a historical woman who was virtuous and loyal and intelligent and wielded authority, where does this visual story come from?

At fourteen, I hadn't given much consideration to how images make meaning. I wasn't paying attention to how repeated pictures carve mental grooves that allow for quick categorization of the good guy and the bad guy, the heroine and the whore. I hadn't wondered why I could find paintings of historical kings and dukes and generals gesturing grandly from atop rearing horses while Queen Elizabeth I simply stood there, ensconced in unimaginably large lace collars.

I did, in fact, copy some older images as the model for my fantasy heroine and personal avatar. But the visual stories I knew of active, heroic women weren't actually images of women at all. Wrapped in flowing, draped robes, these women perched atop capitol buildings, hovered above memorials, and sat like guardians outside famous museums. One heralded the beginning of *Karate Kid* and other movies with her glowing torch. Another stood in New York Harbor.

Like the virtuous Venus of the previous chapter, these women were not really *human*. They were smooth, perfect, idealized symbols. They personified disciplines like history and literature, abstract ideas like justice and liberty, or geographic and political entities like the continent of Asia and the nation of France. And women have been so ubiquitous in these roles that now they don't seem like roles at all.

This is the story of the Vessel: women as containers for others' meaning and messages. The history of this visual script offers a helpful insight into how images and objects both reflect and shape women's lived experiences. Some actual historical women used the story as an opportunity to assert their talents and interests. For others, the opposite proved to be true, and the symbol of their bodies obscured the reality of their labor.

Before I could learn any of that, though, I had to realize how *unnatural* this story actually is.

Washington's Wardrobe

"Yeah, like that naked sculpture of George Washington." This passing comment from a friend in my first year of graduate school sent me on a furtive

Wikipedia search. I had been to Washington, DC, just a couple years earlier, and I was fairly certain that all the representations I had seen of our first president included appropriate eighteenth-century clothes, but my friend was right. The online encyclopedia entry for "*George Washington* (Greenough)" included a photograph of a larger-than-life-sized marble sculpture of the founding father—recognizable by his curly wig and strong brow—seated on a throne and wrapped in nothing but a sheet. He raises one muscled arm while displaying his literally rock-hard pectorals and abs (see fig. 2.1).

I double-checked the date, halfway wondering if this was a joke by a contemporary artist. But, no, the sculpture had been made by the American Neoclassical artist Horatio Greenough and commissioned by Congress for the centennial celebration of Washington's birth. The work was completed in 1840 and installed in the rotunda of the US Capitol and then on the Capitol grounds until 1908, when it entered the Smithsonian Museum of American Art.

I giggled. I had never seen anything else like this: the first president seemingly cosplaying as a Greek god. Was it a historical romance fever dream? It seemed like anything *but* serious art, even though that's what Greenough thought he was making. Why was it so funny?

I mentally ticked through sculptures I remembered seeing in the nation's capital. There was the stately—and clothed—Abraham Lincoln in his eponymous memorial. There were plenty of bronze sculptures of historical men whose names I could not recall but who were all dressed in period-appropriate clothing.

But what about women? Women wearing Grecian robes, much like Greenough's Washington, flutter about the Capitol building as pediment sculptures, tucked into the triangular frames above major entrances. America, Justice, and Hope pose above the east central entrance (see fig. 2.1). Another figure of America, swathed in classical drapery with her attendant eagle, welcomes visitors to the Senate wing of the Capitol. Lady Peace guards the entrance to the House of Representatives wing. And on top of the Capitol dome, Lady Freedom, silver stars glinting on her feathered helmet, surveys the National Mall, sheathed sword in hand.

Certainly, men are also included in some of these sculptural arrangements. In his *Progress of Civilization*, which fills the pediment over the

Senate entrance, Thomas Crawford flanks the female figure of America with smaller male figures. A Native American boy and chief are both nude, evoking classical statues. But the men of European descent all wore eighteenth-century clothing. Admittedly, this can lead to some interpretive confusion. Is the man holding a sword in Thomas Crawford's *Progress*

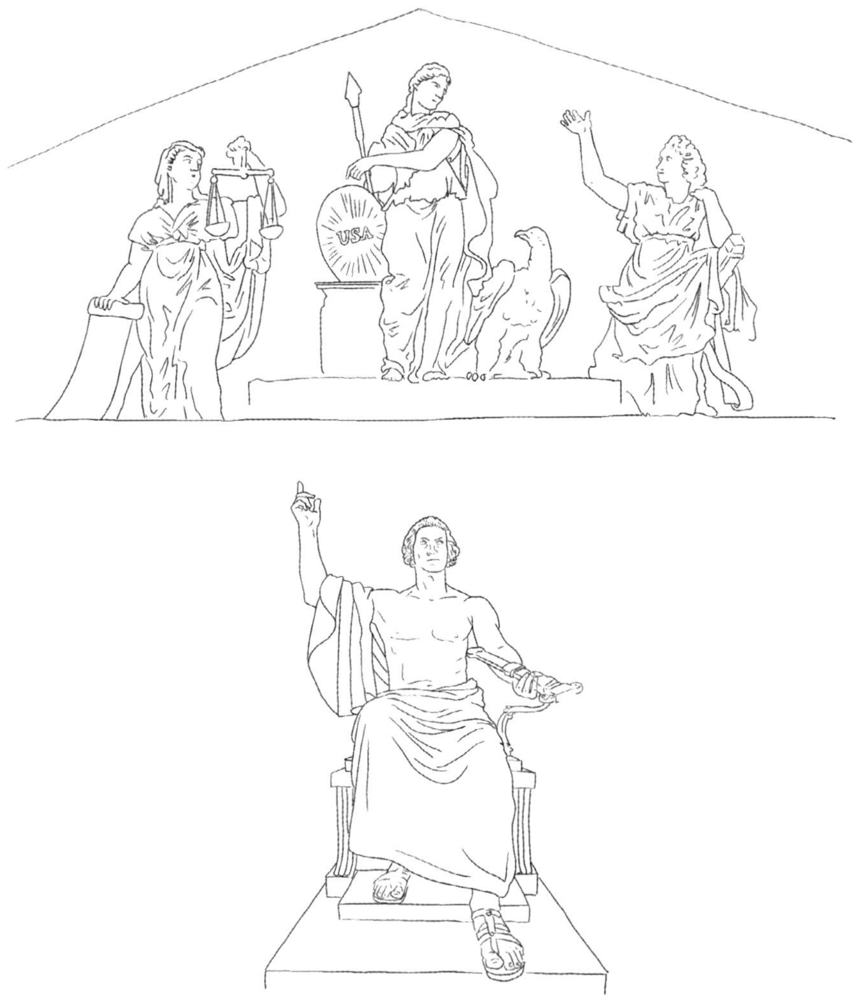

Figure 2.1. Drawn from Luigi Persico, *Genius of America* pediment, 1825–28, and Horatio Greenough, *George Washington*, 1840

of Civilization supposed to be George Washington? Or just a generic soldier? Is the woodsman Davy Crockett? Is the seated scholar Thomas Jefferson?

Of course, I never wondered if the helmeted woman on top of the Capitol was Deborah Sampson, who disguised herself as a man and fought in the American Revolution. I accepted her as a symbol, a personification of the *idea* of freedom rather than a historical figure who fought for that reality with her own body. But why? Why could I so easily accept a woman in simultaneously clingy and billowing robes as a public sculpture while laughing at George Washington in sandals?

Virtues, Vices, and Vixens

Literary scholars, philosophers, and historians have all weighed in on the origins and significance of personification in Western art and visual culture.[1] Many point to ancient Greece and Rome as the originators of representing virtues as women, and they suggest that the reason has to do with language.[2] In both Greek and Latin, most abstract nouns are gendered feminine. You would speak of "victory" using the same grammatical constructions that you would use when talking about your aunt. When celebrating victory in public monuments and buildings, *nike* and *victoria* became Nike and Victoria, deities whose feminine bodies echoed feminine language. Victory personified also had specific "attributes" to make her identity clear to viewers. If a woman had wings and carried a wreath or palm branch, she wasn't an *actual* woman; she was Victory.

Later, Roman Christian writers adapted this practice. In his early fifth-century poem *Psychomachia*, the writer Prudentius weaves an epic battle tale between vices and virtues, all of whom are personified as women. Throughout the medieval era, visual representations of these characters appeared in illustrated manuscripts and as a part of church architecture. As theological and philosophical writings circulated through Western Europe, audiences could begin to expect a standard, recognizable set of attributes. For example, Prudence often held a mirror and a snake, indicating self-knowledge and wisdom, while Temperance is shown diluting wine with water, representing moderation and balance.

Soon, women's bodies were also being used to represent scholarly disciplines of the liberal arts.[3] In the church of Santa Maria Novella in Florence, Italy, images of the virtues and the liberal arts combine in a large, complex fresco painted by Andrea da Firenze near the end of the Middle Ages, between 1366 and 1367. Known as *The Triumph of Thomas Aquinas*, the fresco celebrates the spiritual and intellectual commitments of the Italian priest and scholar. Aquinas is seated on an elaborate golden throne, holding an open Bible. He is flanked by biblical figures, including Moses, David, and the four Gospel writers. Floating above the throne are the seven virtues personified as angelic women, all identifiable by their dress or the objects they are holding.

The bottom half of the fresco consists of a long row of fourteen thrones. A woman sits on each throne, while a man sits on the ground below her. While every woman is a personification of a scholarly discipline, every man is a portrait of a particular historical figure who practiced that discipline. For example, Astronomy is represented as a young woman with long, blond hair wearing a burgundy gown (see fig. 2.2). She holds an astrolabe, a kind of ancient star chart, and she gestures up toward the heavens with her free hand. Below her, a bearded man in brown robes looks up at the sky while taking notes. But he's not another personification of astronomy. He is, instead, an actual astronomer, Claudius Ptolemy from second-century Alexandria, Egypt.

How would original viewers distinguish between personification and portrait? Repeated symbols, like the star chart, would help. But ultimately this recognition hinged on the absence of actual women within the disciplines. The painting couldn't be a portrait of a particular female astronomer because the existence of a female astronomer was laughably impossible.[4] It's not that women were incapable of being scientists; rather, it's that male-oriented cultures typically did not offer such an education to women. Why? The answer is more complicated than just "because they hated women."

In Western medieval Europe, social class, not sex, was the most powerful determiner of one's lived experience. You were who you were because of who your parents were and where they fell in a rigid social hierarchy. Thus, a noblewoman would have more in common with a nobleman than with a peasant woman.

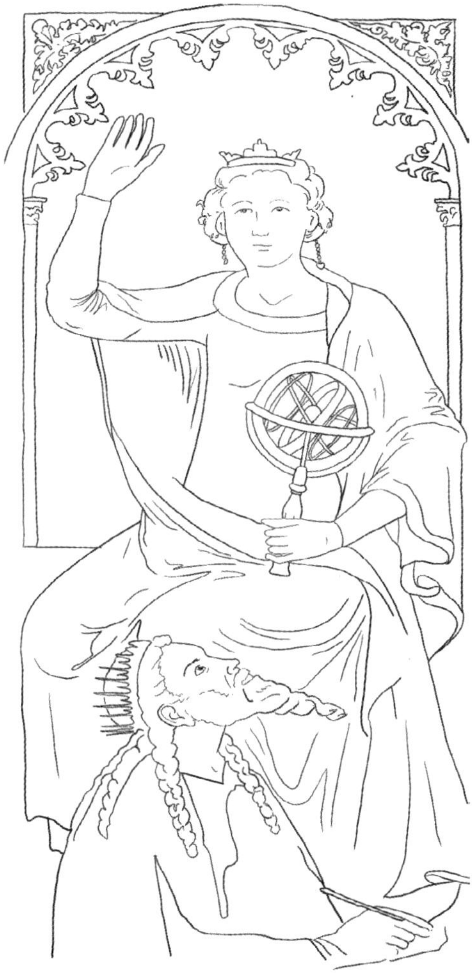

Figure 2.2. Detail of Astronomy and Ptolemy drawn from Andrea da Firenze, *The Triumph of Thomas Aquinas*, 1366–67

Still, the Vessel story developed from and shaped attitudes toward women and their lived experiences. Unlike women in ancient Greece or Rome, most medieval women were not confined to their home. There were no clear boundaries between public and private spaces, and women expected to play a role in the economic life of the family. For peasant women, this entailed working in the fields alongside men. Especially during the High Middle Ages (1000–1300), women participated in familial trades like brewing beer or weaving and embroidering textiles. The divisions between men's work and women's work or public and private spaces didn't harden until much later.

We can also sketch out some generally held beliefs *about* women from the period. In Western Europe, the Christian church largely controlled education and the preservation of knowledge. Most theologians of the period adopted Aristotle's view of women as deformed men. In this "one-sex" model, female bodies were just male bodies that had failed to develop properly in the womb.[5] Furthermore, in medieval theology, women's physical inferiority to men also had a moral dimension. Women were believed to be morally weaker than men. They were more prone to deception—a trait they supposedly inherited from the first woman, Eve—and more likely to succumb to their animalistic lusts. (We'll learn even more about this view of Eve when we examine the Monster story in chapter 5.) Therefore, we can dismiss the idea that the virtues were represented as women because European society believed actual women to be actually virtuous. A gulf emerged between real women and symbolic women.

Some medieval women recognized that gap. And they found it to be a portal.

A Feather on the Breath of God

If my fourteen-year-old self had known about medieval women like Hildegard of Bingen, my fantasy stories would have been based in convents rather than castles. Born in Mainz, Germany, to a noble family, Hildegard entered a monastery as a young girl. Joining a religious order was common for medieval girls of higher birth, and it often benefited their families' political position while providing an education. Over the course of her eighty-one years, most of them spent as a nun, Hildegard compiled a mind-bogglingly long list of accomplishments. As the abbess of three convents, two of which she founded, Hildegard wrote works of theology, philosophy, and natural history and oversaw their illustrations. She corresponded with royalty, theologians, bishops, and popes. She composed sacred music and one of the oldest liturgical plays. She invented her own language. Her first, and most influential, theological work—*Scivias* (Know the Ways of the Lord)—consists of twenty-six visions that deal with creation, the fall, salvation, the church, the sacraments, and the kingdom of God. She did all this while struggling with chronically poor health, including persistent migraines. With that résumé, it's no wonder that I can now read a profile about her on a feminist website or buy a T-shirt emblazoned with her colorful, pop art portrait from an online store celebrating historical female icons!

But Hildegard did not understand her work as evidence of personal ambition, natural intelligence, or careful study. Instead, she attributed her theological insights—and influence—to God himself.

Hildegard recounted being troubled by intense visions of creation, the apocalypse, and the history of salvation. Only her mentor Jutta and her tutor, a monk named Volmar, knew of them. When she finally began to write them down and share them with others, she emphasized what she fervently believed was the divine origin of her theological knowledge.[6] Over and over again, Hildegard positioned herself as merely a conduit of God's message. "I always tremble in fear," she writes in one of her letters, "since I know that I cannot safely rely on my own innate capacity. But I stretch out my hands to God so that He might raise me up like a feather, which, having no weight of its own, flies on the wind."[7] By emphasizing her own weakness and passivity, Hildegard embraced the story of woman as Vessel.

She also reiterated this story visually.

Hildegard's writings are full of bright illuminations, likely made by women in her convent but closely directed by Hildegard herself.[8] They follow the text of her divine visions, resulting in images that often look more like a pastiche of incomprehensible internet memes than recognizable images from an illustrated Bible. The very first miniature in *Scivias* is an image of Hildegard herself (see fig. 2.3).

The portrait is set within a simply rendered, dollhouse-like building on a yellow background. Two tall, narrow towers, capped with red domes, flank a larger, central space. Hildegard sits in this main room, dressed in a long robe with a veil covering her hair. Her feet are propped up on a red

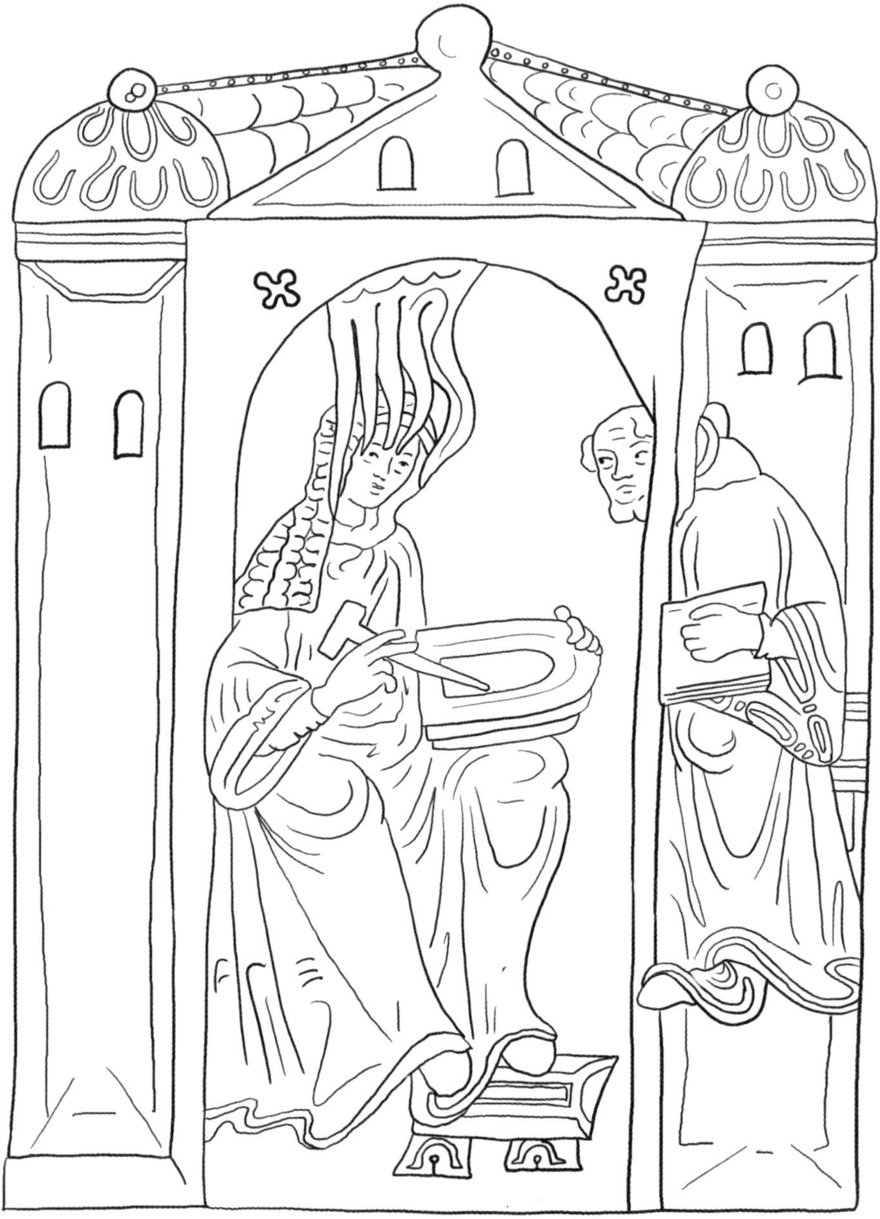

Figure 2.3. Drawn from the frontispiece of Hildegard of Bingen, *Scivias*, 1151

footstool, and she holds a wax tablet and a writing implement on her lap. A comically small, bearded man—dressed in a brown friar's robe—appears to be perched on a floating bench in the smaller tower room to the right. While his body is contained in that separate space, his head pokes into Hildegard's room. He, too, has a tablet on his lap.

Hildegard takes up the most visual space in the illumination. Her body fills the central room, and her right arm even extends beyond the outlined wall. Her dark robe contrasts sharply with the yellow background. The monk's smaller body is mostly squeezed into a much narrower space, and his brown robe does not contrast as strongly with his sage-green background.

But while Hildegard is given visual priority over the monk, something else in the illumination literally overshadows *her*. Bright-red, tentacle-like flames descend from the arched ceiling of her room. They partially obscure Hildegard's face, licking at her veiled head. The red of the flames is the same color as the two tower domes, Hildegard's tombstone-shaped tablet, and her footstool. Visually, the scarlet hue creates a unifying funnel that ends with Hildegard.

The image echoes Hildegard's own words in the prologue to *Scivias*. She writes that in 1141, when she was forty-two years old, "heaven was opened and a fiery light of exceeding brilliance came and permeated my whole brain, and inflamed my whole heart and my whole breast, not like a burning but like a warming flame, as the sun warms anything its rays touches."[9] The result of this light was spiritual illumination. "Immediately," Hildegard continues, "I knew the meaning of the exposition of the Scriptures."[10] Just as her words downplay her agency in favor of her being a messenger of the divine, so her portrait visually emphasizes that she is a carrier for—not the originator of—the ideas.

None of this means that Hildegard was uneducated or operating in an intellectual vacuum. While she attributes her ideas solely to her visions, scholars can recognize the influence of theologians like Augustine of Hippo as well as contemporary Neoplatonic thinkers.[11] Hildegard's visions also spoke directly to the sorry state of the church in the early twelfth century. The obvious passion and presumed purity of Hildegard's message struck a nerve among religious orders and laypeople upset over corruption and lax morals among the clergy. Hildegard also reaffirmed orthodox positions on specific doctrines that were under attack at the time.

Hildegard shared her theological visions only after receiving permission from male clergy, including the revered abbot Bernard of Clairvaux. Around 1148, Pope Eugenius III read a portion of *Scivias* and authorized Hildegard to speak publicly about her visions. And she did so, embarking on a series of preaching tours and speaking to religious houses of both nuns and monks, as well as to laypeople.[12]

Scholars have wrestled with how to understand Hildegard's words. Can she really speak freely when all church doctrine has to be assessed by and sifted through a male church hierarchy? Does she really believe, as she writes in her letters, that she is but "a poor little woman"?[13] Despite pop feminist claims to the contrary, Hildegard did not seek gender equality in the church. By claiming to be "only" a vessel, Hildegard effectively worked within dominant beliefs about women's inferiority to make herself heard.

I find myself thinking about Hildegard at a most unexpected moment: a keynote lecture on women in American evangelical ministries at a conference of Christian historians. From the front of a Christian college chapel, church historian Kate Bowler gives a witty, careful account of how women in conservative evangelical spaces negotiated public mega-ministry from the 1970s to the early 2000s. The most well-known, influential women in popular Christian ministry emerged, Bowler notes, from theological traditions that did not ordain women. Women like Victoria Osteen and Beth Moore found tremendous success because they identified and utilized public roles that were deemed acceptable for women in those conservative spaces.[14]

On one level, this seems unextraordinary. Women in Hollywood, politics, and public life more broadly all do versions of the same thing, But when Bowler starts talking about "hot mess" Bible teachers, I hear an echo of Hildegard. "By the 1990s," Bowler writes later in her book *The Preacher's Wife*, "the most famous Christian women in ministry were famous not for what they had accomplished, but for what they had endured."[15] A woman might be deemed trustworthy to speak *because* of her chronic pain, her dead child, or her unfaithful (but now repentant) spouse. She may—or may not—have formal theological or clinical mental health training, but such credentials pale in comparison to the presumed power of trauma that transforms her into a conduit of authentic, unquestionable wisdom. In her book, Bowler connects this phenomenon to that of trusted advice columnists from the nineteenth century who supposedly pulled from their vast store of experience. Perhaps, though, it's a story that's even older.

Our contemporary "industry of disclosure" seems like a new iteration of Hildegard's medieval negotiation of her own painful visions.[16] We trust the results of a woman's suffering as something pure and unassailable rather than being curious about the ways she is both shaped by and chooses to manage the multiple, converging currents of personal and professional experiences, training, and relationships. She is a container for trauma and intuition, her agency obscured and the possibility of healing and growth foreclosed. And yet, telling the Vessel story is a way for her to be heard by those who might otherwise discount or ignore her.

I didn't know Hildegard's story as a teenager, though. So instead, I looked for women—even imaginary ones—who seemed to be doing anything at all.

A Leading Lady?

As soon as I flip the page in my eighth-grade history textbook and see the glossy illustration, the rousing battle cry from my beloved *Les Misérables* soundtrack clicks on in my head:

> Do you hear the people sing?
> Singing the song of angry men?[17]

Unencumbered by the knowledge that Victor Hugo's novel and the hit musical actually refer to the later Paris Uprising of 1832, I can practically hear the ragtag figures in Eugène Delacroix's *Liberty Leading the People* (1830) singing in lusty harmony as they emerge from a smoke-filled background and spill over a barricade already littered with dead bodies (see fig. 2.4).

The painting is full of contrasting shadows and highlights, and all my attention is immediately fixed on the woman near the center of the painting.

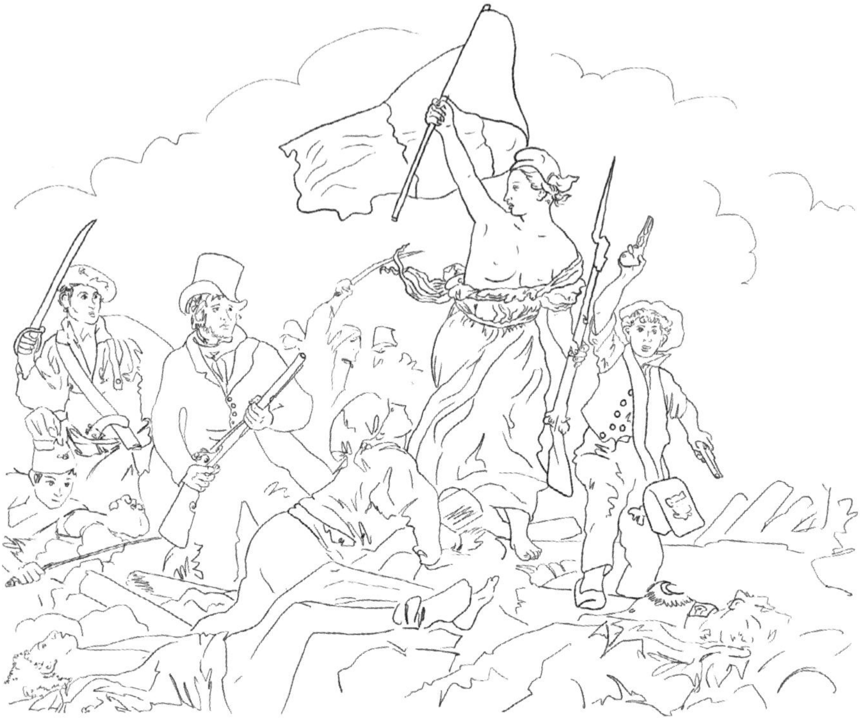

Figure 2.4. Drawn from Eugène Delacroix, *Liberty Leading the People,* 1830

She strides forward boldly, clutching a musket with a gleaming bayonet in one hand and looking over her shoulder to ensure that others are following. Her right arm sticks straight into the air, lifting a fluttering French tricolor flag as a beacon for the oncoming battle. Her body forms the apex of Delacroix's triangular composition, and the light seems to glow on her pale skin and butter-yellow garment.

I look a little more closely and realize that the woman is bare-breasted, her dress puddling around her waist and dropping off one shoulder as she marches into battle. I briefly try to maintain my secret hope that this woman is a *real* woman, a valiant, historical heroine that I will read about in the coming textbook chapter. After all, who has not struggled with an errant bathing suit strap while romping on the beach? Eventually, though, I have to acknowledge that this woman—though dynamic and flushed from her efforts—is a Vessel.

The caption informs me that the woman is *Liberté*, also known as Marianne, the symbol of the French Republic. The men and boys around her are representative of different types of Parisians who participated in the July Revolution of 1830 against the Bourbon monarch. We see a scruffy factory worker, a well-dressed upper-middle-class man, an adolescent revolutionary, and a young schoolboy. But instead of representing a class of Frenchwomen, Marianne is the personification of an abstract idea. We know this, the book says, from her peculiar, pointed hat. The Phrygian cap—given to freed slaves in ancient Rome to signify their new status—served as a symbol of liberty in Europe and North America in the eighteenth and nineteenth centuries. Meanwhile, her bared breasts alert us to her allegorical function. This is not a wardrobe malfunction; it is her symbolic name tag.

I find the personification of *Liberté* to be thrilling. Before Disney princesses were wielding swords or bows and arrows, *Liberté* offered the tantalizing visual story of an active, inspiring female leader. Once I ditch her Phrygian cap and artfully rearrange her dress, it's Delacroix's symbolic woman who serves as the model for my teenage, coauthored fantasy novel. The fact that she is "just" an allegorical figure doesn't bother me. Perhaps it even feels safe. Sealed off from the filth and dysfunction of real-world politics, I imagine a tale in which I—or at least a symbol that looks like me—inspire right thinking and right doing by sheer force of my moral fortitude. What I don't realize, however, is that Delacroix's *Liberté* isn't "only" a symbol. Her existence actually conceals the stories of actual women from sight.

Delacroix's painting has been the subject of copious historical scholarship. Despite its present-day popularity, it initially received mixed reviews and then fell in and out of favor in the subsequent decades of French political turmoil. Finally, in 1874, it was displayed in the Louvre, becoming a beloved symbol of the French nation decades after the political violence it references had passed. In some ways, Delacroix's painting dramatically broke with tradition. His fluid brushwork and his decision to depict a contemporary event with the pomp of an epic classical battle signaled a shift away from his more conservative rivals. Yet Delacroix's use of a woman's body to symbolize both the abstract concept of liberty and the French nation perpetuated a much older practice.

Allegory Imitating Life Imitating Allegory

We've already seen that, by the end of the medieval period in Western Europe, women's bodies served as personifications or "allegories" of abstract virtues and academic disciplines. This symbolic visual language became increasingly uniform throughout the sixteenth and seventeenth centuries, and Cesare Ripa's immensely popular handbook, *Iconologia* (1593), provided a catalog of symbols that artists could pull from.

During the sixteenth and early seventeenth centuries, also known as the Age of Exploration, women's bodies began to serve as an additional set of symbols. Female allegories of the continents decorated maps, travel narratives, hanging tapestries, and the ceilings of churches and palaces.

In Ripa's first illustrated edition of *Iconologia* (1603), the personification of Africa wears a loose kaftan with a dramatic slit and an elephant's head as a crown (see fig. 2.5). Her attributes suggest Europeans' fascination with Africa's bounty and danger: She stands between a lion and a double-headed snake, holding a cornucopia of wheat in one hand and a scorpion in the other. What may be especially surprising to us is that the woman's face and body are rendered according to classical norms. She looks like a woman of European descent. Later illustrations do depict Africa as a dark-skinned woman. However, this early version makes it abundantly clear that personifications don't need to resemble the thing they represent.

These allegories of the continents both reflected and shaped European beliefs about unfamiliar people and lands. For example, a popular engraving produced by a Dutch publishing house around 1600 depicts the Florentine explorer Amerigo Vespucci encountering the personification of America. Vespucci stands on the banks of a wooded shore, his ship anchored in the background. He holds a staff with a crucifix in his right hand and a navigational tool in his left as he gazes at a young woman who seems to have just awakened from a nap in her hammock. The woman is almost entirely naked; she wears a feathered headdress, a skimpy loincloth, and some jewelry, but her legs, arms, stomach, and breasts are all bare.[18] Her sexualized body, available to both Vespucci and the viewer of the print, justifies the actions of European explorers: The land and resources of

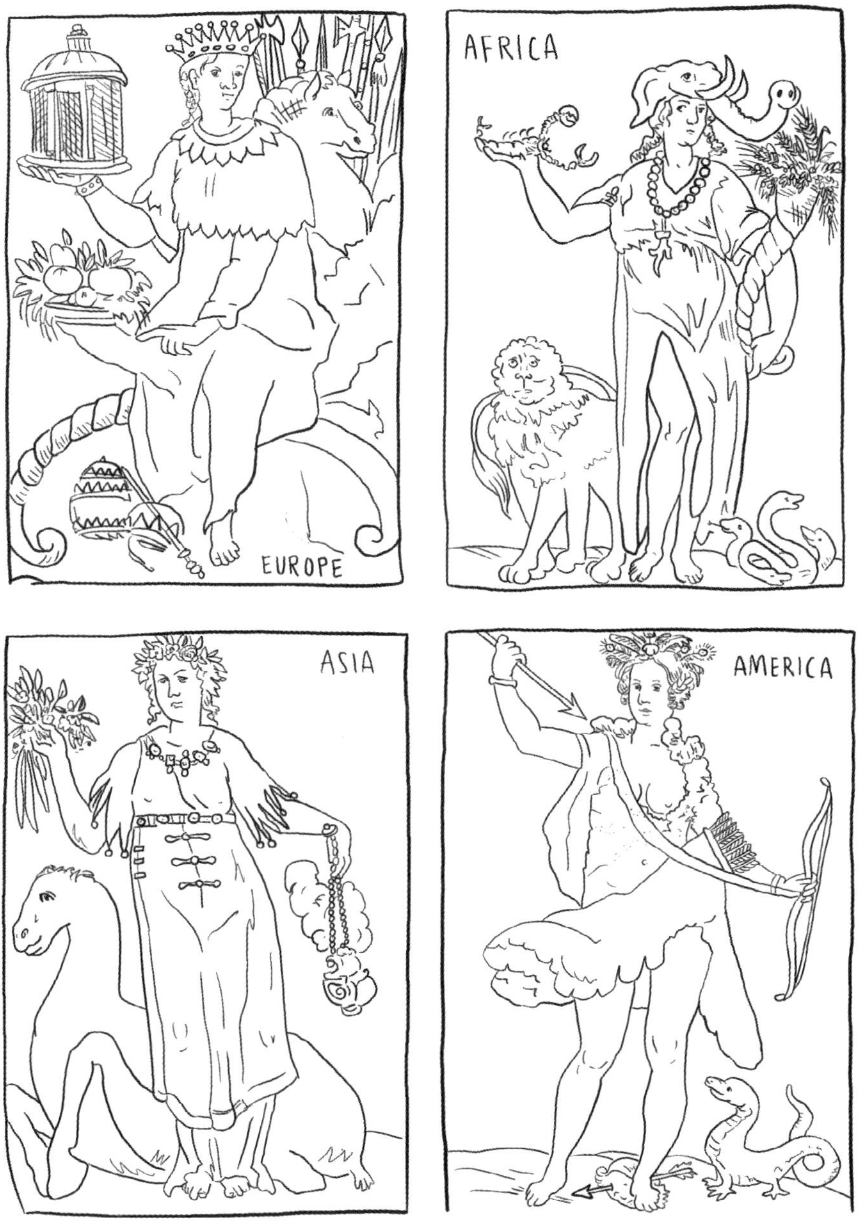

Figure 2.5. Drawn from Cesare Ripa's allegories of the continents in *Iconologia*, 1603

America are available for European political and economic conquest just as a naked woman is available for sexual pleasure and plunder.

It's little wonder, then, that as the transatlantic slave trade grew, allegorical representations of Africa also became increasingly sexualized. A troubling feedback loop developed. Belief, representation, and action reinforced the same story. That story said that Africa—and African people, especially women—existed to be possessed by Europeans. It's a devastating irony that representing a continent as a human actually supported the *dehumanizing* of the real people who inhabited that place.

At the same time, European nations increasingly used noble, pale-skinned women as personifications of new national identities. The Dutch maiden—in classical drapery, accompanied by a lion and a pole topped with a hat—emerged as a visual rallying point during the Dutch revolt against Spanish rule in the sixteenth century. Shortly thereafter, Britannia—a helmeted maiden holding a trident and shield—revived an ancient Roman personification of the British Isles. Germania, also a Roman symbol, reappeared as the mother of the Holy Roman Empire. And while North America was represented as a Native American woman in the seventeenth century, the more classically European figure of Columbia—usually dressed in white with a Phrygian cap—came to represent the new republic of the United States. Looking at the preponderance of female figures on maps and coins from the seventeenth century, one might be excused for thinking that the known world was entirely populated and run by women!

Liberty Is a Lady

France, however, was something of an outlier. Until the late eighteenth century, the idea of French national identity was inextricable from the monarchy.[19] The king was the literal head of the body politic. Thus, revolutionary printmakers in the late 1780s and early 1790s often distorted or destroyed the monarch's body to convey their political displeasure.[20] As the French Revolution progressed, however, Republicans sensed the need for a new visual identity. They increasingly used images of the goddess *Liberté* to represent the new nation they were trying to forge. By the early 1790s, a woman wearing a Phrygian cap and a slipping drape could be called

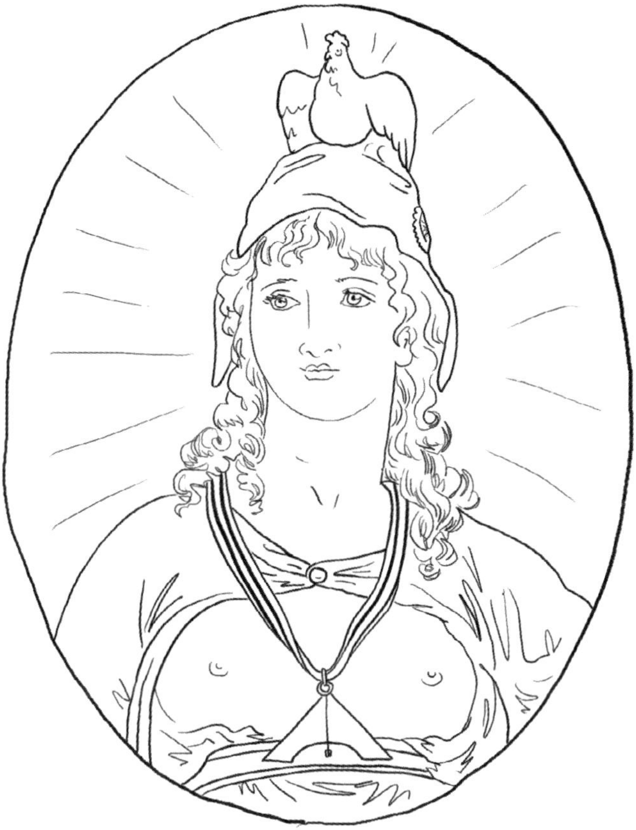

Figure 2.6. Drawn from Alexandre Clément, *Republican France: Offering Her Breasts to All French People*, ca. 1792–93

either *Liberté* or Marianne (see fig. 2.6). The bared breast was important. First, it signaled that she was a symbolic figure rather than a real woman. Second, *Liberté*-as-France was admittedly erotic. The hope was that the same passionate desire a man might have for a beautiful woman could be applied to the service of a new nation.[21] Patriotism and eroticism—a longing to possess and protect—twined together. However, as historians Joan Landes and Lynn Hunt have demonstrated, *Liberté*'s attitudes or poses shifted according to the political needs of the Revolution. She could be a calming influence in the midst of violent upheaval, but she could also be radically violent herself.[22] In various forms, *Liberté* was everywhere.

But how did women see *Liberté*? How did the new representations of the French nation—an imagined superwoman—relate to the lives of actual women? In the early, optimistic days of the Revolution, the ideals of liberty and equality were extended, at least in theory, to women and to enslaved people in French colonies. Women of different social classes understandably saw the possibilities and priorities of the Revolution differently. For some, universal suffrage and expanded educational opportunities took precedence.[23] For others, the impossibly high cost of bread was the most pressing concern. Women like Sophie de Condorcet used their social position to advocate for women's legal rights in writing and at intellectual gatherings known as salons. Others, like the working-class activist Pauline Léon, proposed that women should arm themselves and form their own militias. Indeed, Léon participated in the Storming of the Bastille in 1789, carrying her own pike, and she led hundreds of women in protest marches and even violent demonstrations to advocate for a secure, affordable supply of bread.

Decades later, when Delacroix painted his *Liberté*, women of different social classes and with different convictions were still negotiating a tumultuous political reality. One woman, the laundress Marie Deschamps, reportedly participated on the front lines of the July Revolution, picking up a discarded musket and firing on the royal guards. The art historian T. J. Clark has actually argued that Delacroix was celebrating Deschamps's heroism in his iconic painting, not representing a symbolic *Liberté*.[24] And yet, though Delacroix seems to have been aware of Deschamps's actions, the bared breast and the Phrygian cap firmly locate the woman as a vessel—the personification *of* liberty, not an agitator *for* liberty.

Actual women were everywhere, laboring with their bodies and minds throughout the successive waves of the French Revolution. But in the end, the early ideals of the Revolution were never fully realized. According to historian Lynn Hunt, "The proliferation of the female allegory was made possible, in fact, by the exclusion of women from public affairs. Women could be representative of abstract qualities and collective dreams because women were not about to vote or govern."[25] Just as we saw with allegorical representations of academic disciplines, the absence of actual women from the halls of government made it possible for a symbolic woman to be present. Perhaps counterintuitively, the popularity of the Vessel story—the ubiquity of a woman's body in a symbolic role—concealed the role that real women were playing in the new nation.

Even though women did not gain the right to vote through the Revolution, they did negotiate a different social role. While *Liberté*'s bare breast could serve as an impetus for erotic patriotism, it also pointed to a new emphasis on motherhood—and breastfeeding—as a *civic* virtue. The new nation might be represented metaphorically as a nursing woman, but literal breastfeeding mothers would suckle and sustain France's new citizens.[26]

The Mother story will be investigated more thoroughly in chapter 4. But this particular blurring of allegorical and actual women was made possible through a significant change in how European thinkers understood the category of "women." Instead of the one-sex model favored by the medievals, Enlightenment naturalists stressed the differences, rather than the similarities, between male and female bodies. In the two-sex model, biology determined destiny. For example, women's smaller frames were interpreted as proof that they were more childlike, and their smaller skulls meant they were not as intelligent as men.[27] A woman's body increasingly dictated her role in the world; her identity and her reproductive function were inseparable. This "natural law"—not religion—dictated that women remain in the private sphere, where their emotional, nurturing bodies were most needed. Men, on the other hand, were suited for public life because of their inherent rationality and strength.

Thus, in the new French nation, women could participate by fulfilling their role in this supposedly natural order: creating, sustaining, and educating its future, virtuous citizens. Some scholars have rightly pointed to women's active agency in assuming this position with pride.[28] But the point of the visual story was to emphasize the distinction and *distance* between public and private spheres, active and passive roles, and male and female bodies.

Echoes and variations of this patriotic Vessel became popular throughout Western Europe and in the United States. The draped, calm, powerful women I saw atop buildings in Washington, DC, were the sisters and daughters of France's *Liberté*. Because the story was told over and over again, it became normal for blank-faced vessels to occupy public spaces that largely excluded actual women. A seeming celebration of women's bodies functioned as a means of limiting or concealing the contributions of real, embodied women to the public good.

There's another kind of exclusion at work too. It seems that in order to be a universally appealing symbol, you must have a particular kind of body, one of European descent that aligns with vaguely classical ideals. Women outside that narrow confine run the risk of being reduced to *only* their bodies.

"That Kind of Praise"

At yet another graduate school panel, I nervously approach the raised platform and take my seat up front alongside several other participants. "Oh good, I'm not the only one," another woman whispers conspiratorially. She's smiling, and her tone is light, but I suspect that we're both wondering the same thing.

Am I here to be a body that checks a box?

As a biracial, white-Asian woman, I sometimes feel like I can *only* be my body, and other times I feel like my body is what makes me invisible. If I focus my research on Asian American women artists, am I a narcissist, insisting that everyone pay attention to *my* identity? Or does my body somehow make me authentically authoritative in that discourse? At times I wonder if navigating both conservative evangelical and progressive academic spaces would be easier if I studied something that felt more distant from my visible identity. Maybe researching male Italian Renaissance painters would be the key to peace and success, allowing me to be both "disinterested" and "subversive" simultaneously? Eventually, though, studying representations of race and gender in nineteenth- and twentieth-century art is precisely what helps me identify and name another iteration of the Vessel story.

On the first day of Black History Month in 2017, I let out a small cheer when I open my browser and see the day's Google Doodle. A Black woman with a hammer and chisel chips away at a large marble sculpture. Google's name is written in glowing, yellow-and-orange script, with the woman and her sculpture suggesting the shape of the second *g*. I recognize the reference immediately. After all, I'm teaching a course called Race in American Art and Visual Culture, and later in the semester my students will read an article on today's featured artist, Edmonia Lewis.

At first, I'm elated. Far too few people know about Lewis, a sculptor of Afro-Haitian and Mississauga Ojibwe descent who spent much of her career as an expatriate in Rome and London. But the final sentences of Google's explanatory tribute give me pause: "Today, we celebrate her and what she stands for—self-expression through art, even in the face of adversity."[29] From what I know of Lewis's work, however, "self-expression" is hardly an accurate descriptor.

I think about *Forever Free* (*Morning of Liberty*), a three-foot-tall white marble sculpture Lewis made in 1867 depicting two interconnected figures (see fig. 2.7). On the right, a shirtless man stands tall, gazing up toward the heavens. His left foot rests on a ball and chain, while he triumphantly raises his left arm, displaying a broken shackle. His other hand rests on the shoulder of his companion: a kneeling woman in a long, simple dress whose hands are clasped in prayer. Upon closer inspection, we see that her left foot is chained to the base of the statue. Lewis made the work two years after the Emancipation Proclamation and a year before the Fourteenth Amendment was ratified.

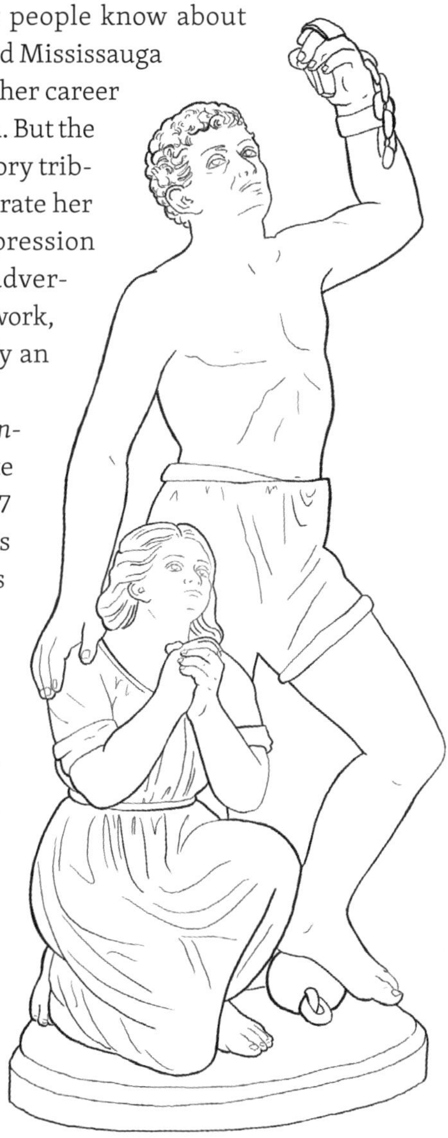

Figure 2.7. Drawn from Edmonia Lewis, *Forever Free*, 1867

We might assume that Lewis, as a Black woman, is expressing her personal jubilance over the abolition of chattel slavery in the United States. We might even wonder if she used herself as a model, inserting her own body into this historic moment. But there are two reasons to question this interpretation. First, Lewis was never enslaved. Second, and perhaps even more disorienting, is the fact that the woman in *Forever Free* looks *white*. Yes, the actual material of the sculpture is snowy white, but the woman's hair falls in soft waves over her shoulders, and her facial features mimic those of a Neoclassical Venus with a narrow nose and rosebud mouth. While the man has tightly coiled hair and a wider nose, the woman does not have any physical characteristics commonly associated with people of African descent. This means, of course, that the sculpted woman certainly does *not* look like the photographs we have of Edmonia Lewis. What's going on?

We have scant verifiable details of Mary Edmonia Lewis's early life. Her mother was African American and Mississauga Ojibwe, while her father has often been described as an Afro-Haitian valet. Lewis was orphaned as a child, and she claimed to have lived with her mother's family near Niagara Falls, making Ojibwe handicrafts like baskets and moccasins to sell to tourists. Lewis's half brother Samuel then helped pay for her to attend Oberlin College in Ohio, one of the few institutions in the United States at the time that enrolled students of all races. While there, Lewis began studying art in earnest, but she also became the target of racialized animosity and violence. Lewis was accused of poisoning two white female students, and though she was acquitted in court, she was harassed and then physically attacked by white vigilantes in the town.

Unable to continue at Oberlin, Lewis made her way to Boston in 1864 and then Rome in 1866. There, working alongside a group of white Neoclassical American sculptors also living and working in the ancient city, Lewis was able to build a career. Her life-sized sculpture *The Death of Cleopatra* was a popular draw at the 1876 Centennial Exposition in Philadelphia, and she was chosen by President Ulysses S. Grant to sculpt his portrait in 1877. She enjoyed regular publicity through the 1880s but died in relative obscurity in London in 1907.

A list of Lewis's most famous sculptural subjects seems to reinforce the importance of race in her biography. In addition to celebrating Black emancipation with *Forever Free*, she sculpted portrait busts of the abolitionist John Brown and Colonel Robert Gould Shaw, the white leader of an all-Black Civil War regiment. She carved characters from Henry Wadsworth Longfellow's poem *The Song of Hiawatha*, which was based on Ojibwe legends, as well as the sculpture *The Old Arrowmaker and His Daughter*. She depicted African subjects such as Hagar and Cleopatra as large-scale free-standing sculptures.

In our contemporary society—where race, gender, and sexuality are deemed primary components of individual identity—it is tempting to narrate Lewis's life as the story of a hidden talent who overcame racism and sexism and proudly represented individuals who sympathized with or shared her marginalized status. This is essentially the approach taken in the 2017 Google Doodle tribute. Lewis is heroized as a model woman of color, paving the way for future generations of Black and Indigenous artists. In a sense, we still want her to be a vessel, a symbol of Black identity and achievement.

But then, what do we make of the fact that all of Lewis's sculptures of Black and Native American women—not just *Forever Free*—have European features? Why would Lewis select subjects obviously related to her personal heritage and then render them as idealized white bodies? How do we account for Lewis playing into stereotypes about Native Americans in her early interviews, embellishing and emphasizing her "wild" childhood among the Ojibwe? Was her relationship with abolitionist patrons born from a self-identification with enslaved African Americans, or was it a savvy business decision, as they were the people most likely to buy her work? Did she sculpt Native American and Black subjects because she wanted to or because she thought they would appeal to patrons who saw her as an exotic curiosity? Did she give her figures European facial features because she had uncritically absorbed the prevailing standards of Neoclassicism? Or did she do so because she wanted to *prevent* her work from being read as a simple reflection of her own identity? Is the kneeling woman in *Forever Free* a direct expression of Lewis's ongoing experience of subjugation as a Black woman, even after emancipation?[30]

Edmonia Lewis was acutely aware that her race and gender would impact her desired career as a sculptor. The racially motivated attacks against her at Oberlin made that clear. However, as she began to build relationships with abolitionist patrons on the East Coast, Lewis also learned that her visible identity might have another effect. In an 1864 account of her first meeting with the white abolitionist Lydia Maria Child, Lewis states vehemently, "Some praise me because I am a colored girl, and I don't want that kind of praise."[31] As a young artist, Lewis longed for her work to be judged according to what she believed were objective standards of aesthetic and technical quality. She didn't want to be condescended to or valued on account of only her race. She did not want to be a Vessel for abolitionists, however noble their cause.

Yet Lewis's professional choices also reveal the double bind she needed to navigate. In order to attain supposedly universal standards of quality—to be deemed a great artist, not a great Black artist or a great woman artist—Lewis needed to account for her body in other ways.

In the mid- and late nineteenth century, American Neoclassical sculptors in Italy typically followed a shared set of practices. They would begin by modeling a sculpture out of clay, building it up on a metal armature. Then they would hire professional mold makers to cast a plaster copy, which would be sent in turn to a local craftsman or given to specialized assistants. These craftsmen copied the plaster sculpture in marble, using specialized tools to transfer the original design to a new stone block. This process allowed established artists like Hiram Powers to have multiple marble copies made from a single plaster cast.[32] Along the way, expatriate American artists were often in conversation with each other, making studio visits and recommending improvements. They also opened their studios to the visiting well-to-do American tourists who wanted an "authentic" experience overseas. Often, these visits might turn into the opportunity to acquire a portrait commission.[33]

Lewis, however, adopted a different set of practices. First, she worked almost in isolation, fearing accusations that other artists were making sculptures for her.[34] Second, she learned how to carve marble herself, not because of some lofty ideals of artistic purity but because she didn't want the public to suspect that a craftsman had improved upon her model.[35]

Doing so, however, also meant that each sculpture took much longer to make than those of her white counterparts. And while most American sculptors worked on commission—that is, they didn't invest in expensive blocks of marble and the cost of labor until after they had a contract—Lewis frequently made sculptures first, then sent them to potential buyers with an invoice attached.[36] In an effort to effectively transcend her body—to be neither praised nor condemned for being a Black female artist—Lewis had to forge a new way of making altogether.

In *Forever Free*, Lewis carves a subject that she thinks will please her potential abolitionist patron, and she does so in a way that aligns with prevailing ideas about gender and female beauty. Remember, the woman's kneeling body joins with her husband's to form a single, solid, pyramidal composition. Nineteenth-century viewers would have seen the pose as one of submission and piety, traits associated with the virtuous woman, while the standing man's protective hand and active stance reflected his cultural role as provider and protector. In context, the message is that emancipation freed African Americans to fully participate in the ideal gender roles of the period.[37] For some viewers, the notion of a virtuous Black woman would be a conceptual oxymoron. Thus, in order to signal that the freedwoman is a *good* woman, Lewis chose to represent her according to the physical ideal of the moment. She looks more like the classicized models popular at the time than a woman who has endured chattel slavery.

Forever Free was one of the sculptures that Lewis sent to a potential patron without first securing a commission. It was also a source of tension between her and her early abolitionist supporter, Lydia Maria Child. Child had cautioned Lewis against taking up large-scale marble sculpture, suggesting that smaller works would be better suited to her abilities. Lewis, it seems, ignored that advice. In a frank letter to a friend, Child criticizes both the sculpture and the artist. "The limbs were like sausages," she writes bitingly. "I do not think it is either wise or kind to encourage a girl, merely because she is colored, to spoil good marble by making it into poor statues."[38] Child refused to publicly support *Forever Free*, though she also refrained from publicly condemning it. Again, confiding to a friend, she excuses what she sees as Lewis's poor judgment by blaming her racial heritage. "How could it be otherwise," she writes, since Lewis was born to a poor Black family and spent "her youth with wild Indians?"[39] Child's condescending attitude toward Lewis—excusing the young woman's underdeveloped skills as an artist while insisting that her career advice be followed—reiterates the difficult terrain that Lewis needed to traverse.

In both the nineteenth and twenty-first centuries, viewers have wanted Lewis to be a Vessel, a receptacle for their ideas about Black and Native achievement and authenticity. We long for her body to be an icon, a symbol, rather than an actual *body*. But Edmonia Lewis was—like all of us—a human full of contradictions and complications. She was a woman who longed for public approbation but wanted to forge her own way, a woman who reiterated dominant notions of feminine submissiveness and passivity in stone while largely doing the opposite with her own active, independent body. I need help telling a better story about Lewis, one that celebrates her humanity in all its paradoxical, elusive wonder.

I need help telling a better story for myself too.

COUNTERSTORY:

Being

Reusable Containers

In 1886, even as Frédéric Auguste Bartholdi's monumental bronze sculpture, *Liberty Enlightening the World*—now better known as the Statue of Liberty—was being dedicated in New York Harbor, critics identified and decried the limitations of the Vessel story. Suffragists welcomed the depiction of Liberty as a woman but were incensed that actual women weren't allowed to be present at the statue's official unveiling. A group of them chartered a boat and sailed through the harbor during the ceremony in protest.

Editors of an African American newspaper in Cleveland, Ohio, meanwhile, offered another scathing critique: "'Liberty enlightening the world,' indeed! The expression makes us sick. This government is a howling farce. It can not or rather *does not* protect its citizens within its *own* borders."[40] They proposed that the statue's torch not be lit until a Black man could "earn a respectable living for himself and family, without being ku-kluxed, perhaps murdered, his daughter and wife outraged, and his property destroyed."[41]

Still, Lady Liberty was quickly identified as a flexible symbol. For European immigrants entering New York Harbor in the early twentieth century, the woman with the torch, crown, and broken shackle functioned as an icon of welcome.[42] During World War I, images of the statue featured regularly in advertisements for war bonds.[43] Other posters featured attractive young women dressed as modern-day Liberties, begging the audience to help protect them by enlisting in the military, buying bonds, or rationing materials. Their vulnerable, beautiful bodies perhaps served as a better conduit for that message than the sturdy, draped giant in the harbor.

At the same time, Liberty also appeared in advertisements for cigars, soap, binoculars, and pencils. In fact, a cartoon published in the satirical magazine *Puck* in the 1880s poked fun at how commodious of a vessel the statue had become. The illustration depicts Liberty as a kind of patchworked scarecrow, covered in advertising stickers and holding a bottle of champagne and umbrella in place of her tablet and torch. Today, Liberty still sells insurance policies and serves as a basketball team mascot.

Contemporary artists also continue to use the personification of Liberty as a means of political critique. Some artists use the recognizable trope to highlight histories that have often been concealed. For example, Lili Bernard transformed Delacroix's *Liberty Leading the People* into *Carlota Leading the People* (2011). In her large painting, she replaces the allegorical figure of Liberty with Carlota, an enslaved, African-born woman leading a rebellion in Matanzas, Cuba, in 1843. Carlota, dressed in a bright-yellow dress, her breasts bared, wields a bloodied knife, gesturing for others to follow her.

In the summer of 2020, following nationwide protests over the killings of Ahmaud Arbery, George Floyd, and Breonna Taylor, artist Kadir Nelson painted *American Uprising* for the cover of *Rolling Stone* magazine's July 2020 issue. Using Delacroix's painting as a model, Nelson depicted a Black woman, wearing a T-shirt emblazoned with George Floyd's face, stepping onto a low wall and punching her fist up into the sky. A young Black boy follows her lead, and a multiracial crowd of protestors carrying homemade signs stands in the background. Also in 2020, Polish-British artist Sebastian Burdon reimagined the Statue of Liberty as a graffiti-style stenciled print. But instead of standing solemnly, Liberty lunges forward, preparing to hurl her torch.

Are these most recent images inversions of the Vessel story or simply new iterations that use women's bodies to communicate new political ideals?

In many ways, the Vessel story seems inescapable. Human figures make easy, relatable symbols, and we seem apt to fill those bodies with our preferred meaning like we might fill a glass jar with our favorite candy. I want something else. I want a visual script that pushes me toward the kind of generous regard that I hope to receive from others. I need reminders of both our shared humanity and the value of our particular experiences. We are all image bearers of the triune God, yet God knows each of us by name. I want a story of Being, not just carrying meaning.

An Artist in Action

A murmur of appreciation rolls through my darkened classroom as I click to the next slide. A dark-haired woman seems to burst out of the flat screen and into our classroom. Wearing an iridescent green dress with a golden mask pendant and working against a warm-brown background, the woman tilts toward us, utterly absorbed in the act of painting an unseen canvas. In her left hand she grasps a palette and several brushes. Her right hand is raised, and the brush she holds touches the edge of the actual canvas (see fig. 2.8).

Artemisia Gentileschi's *Self-Portrait as the Allegory of Painting* (ca. 1638–39) sends a thrill through me every time I show it to my students. Part of the finger-tingling delight comes from the fact that this unconventional image is a picture of the painter herself. It is the great-great-grandmother of today's candid selfie rendered in oil paint. But no small part of our pleasure also stems from Artemisia's visual virtuosity. She uses light to attract and direct our attention, while line keeps us moving through the composition, and she plays with space in a way that creates a teasing puzzle.

Our eyes immediately find the painting's main subject, ostensibly Artemisia herself. Light from an unseen source streams in from the left-hand side of the painting, illuminating her face, décolletage, and outstretched arm. Thicker dabs of white paint highlight her forehead, the tip of her nose, and the sparkle in her dark eyes. The brightness of her face contrasts strongly with her dark brows and the tendrils of deep-brown hair that seem to be escaping from her bun as she paints. Our eyes follow the glimmering creases of her sleeve down to the bottom left corner of the canvas, or they trace her elevated, bare arm that reaches toward the top left.

Artemisia's limbs also create visual momentum that loops us perpetually through the composition. Beginning with her raised right hand, we slide down the smooth arc of her arm and across the canvas. Our velocity increases as we reach the apex of that curve—the artist's head and shoulders—then we

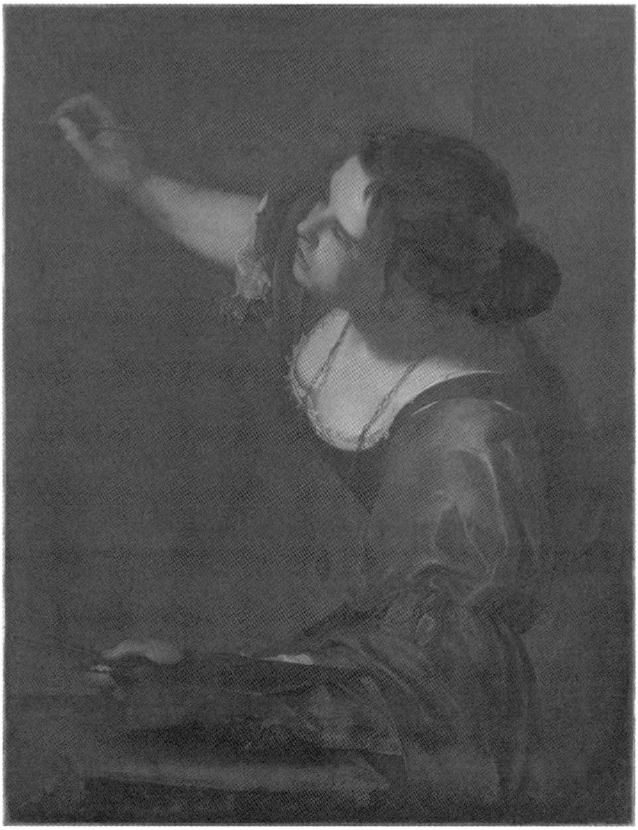

Figure 2.8. Artemisia Gentileschi, *Self-Portrait as the Allegory of Painting (La Pittura)*, ca. 1638–39, oil on canvas. A full-color image of this painting is included in the color insert section.

slingshot back around, down her other arm, past the paint palette, and up the vertical edge of the canvas until we're back where we started. And the circuit begins again. Although the woman's image remains perfectly still, Artemisia's use of line evokes energetic bursts of action.

Then there's the artist's depiction of space. The woman's body fills most of the actual canvas, and it's hard to get a sense of whatever room she might be occupying. Most of the background is a mottled golden brown, but a darker vertical strip runs down the right-most quarter of the canvas. Is she in a corner? Standing in front of a corner? The background is largely unimportant since Artemisia refuses to sit neatly inside an illusion of receding space. Instead, her whole body tips toward us, the viewers, breaking through the imagined fourth wall of the canvas as she paints.

But what exactly is Artemisia painting? For that matter, *where* is the painting she is presumably working on? It's a spatial brainteaser. We do not clearly see an easel or canvas in the depicted space. Some observers understand the lighter-golden-brown rectangle behind the woman to be a prepped canvas, though it seems to be parallel to us rather than at a more believable angle. We might reason that the work in progress is perpendicular to us and just barely cropped out of our view. Yet the way that Artemisia's right hand hovers just inches from the left edge of the actual canvas is tantalizing. Might she actually be at work on the very painting we are looking at? The represented and the real twist together like a Möbius strip, an infinite loop of visible action and invisible results.

There's another seeming opposition that Artemisia weaves together. In a single figure, she appears to be representing both the female personification of painting *and* herself, an actual female painter. It's a dynamic painting, but not a straightforward one. In fact, the ways that this painting has been interpreted over time reiterate the double pitfalls of the Vessel story. But as I've continued to learn more about the artwork and the artist, I've grown increasingly convinced that Artemisia's painting offers us a counterstory of the marvelous work of Being. *Self-Portrait as the Allegory of Painting* neither ignores Artemisia's embodied experience nor reduces her to it.

Whose Artemisia?

Artemisia Gentileschi (1593–1653) was a seventeenth-century Italian painter. While female artists in the period were uncommon, a handful of women—including Marietta Robusti, Elisabetta Sirani, and Lavinia Fontana—achieved relative renown for their paintings in their own time. Artemisia's father, Orazio, was an established painter in Rome. Because his work was more well-known in art historical circles for centuries, most scholars still refer to him by his surname—Gentileschi—and call Artemisia by her first name. After the death of his wife, Gentileschi trained his sons *and* his daughter in his workshop. Artemisia evidenced more talent than her brothers, and by the time she was in her teens her father boasted that she had no peer, even among well-known male painters.[44]

Artemisia went on to have a successful career, first as a court painter for the Medici family in Florence, then supported by wealthy patrons in Rome, Venice, and Naples. In 1638, she spent time in England, joining her father in the court of Charles I. Though records from her later years are sparse, most historians believe that she continued working until her death in Naples around 1656. She was connected to important artist guilds in Florence and Rome, where she was feted as "a miracle in painting, more easily envied than imitated."[45] In addition to prestigious commissions, Artemisia also garnered lavish literary praise at the height of her career. The well-known Neapolitan poet Girolamo Fontanella called her *pittrice famosissima*, or "the very famous female painter," and compared her to the mythical ancient Greek painter Apelles.[46] Fontanella also connected Artemisia's handling of color in her paintings to the handiwork of Aurora, the goddess of the dawn.[47]

After her death, Artemisia—like other female artists from the period—quickly fell into obscurity. Some of her paintings were attributed to male artists, including her father. Others languished in storage, out of sight of historians and the public. Artemisia's first mention in modern art historical scholarship came in 1916, when the Italian art historian Roberto Longhi published an article on Orazio and his daughter. Artemisia, Longhi stated, was "the only woman in Italy who ever understood what painting was," but she was also just a footnote to her father's career.[48]

But in the early 1970s, Artemisia became the focus of a new kind of attention. In addition to unearthing Artemisia's paintings, second wave feminist scholars shone a light on a particular aspect of her early biography. In 1611, when Artemisia was in her late teens, her father hired Agostino Tassi, a fellow artist, to teach his daughter how to render perspective and landscape in her paintings. But one day, upon finding Artemisia without a chaperone, Tassi forced her to have sex with him. Artemisia resisted, loudly. To quiet her, Tassi promised marriage. Having accepted this commitment, Artemisia continued to have a sexual relationship with Tassi for months. However, nine months after the initial assault, Orazio Gentileschi took Tassi to court, accusing him of taking his daughter's virginity and thus damaging the family's honor.

Roman court documents from the trial read like confessional interviews from a contemporary reality TV show. Everyone involved—Orazio, Tassi, Artemisia's supposed chaperone, and Artemisia herself—all work to narrate the events in a way that preserves their own reputation. Artemisia's truthfulness is verified through torture. Cords are wrapped around her fingers and pulled tight as the judges ask questions. Did she experience pain when she had sex with Tassi? Was there blood? Did she cry out for help? "I have told the truth and always will," Artemisia cries.[49] Once freed from the torture device, she lifts her now-damaged hands, turns to Tassi, and declares, "This is the ring that you give me and these are your promises."[50]

At the end of the trial, Tassi is sentenced to five years of exile from Rome, a punishment he never serves. Orazio, meanwhile, quickly marries his daughter off to a little-known painter, who moves Artemisia to Florence. Sometime in the midst of the trial or shortly thereafter, Artemisia paints her first version of *Judith Slaying Holofernes*, a large, dramatically lit painting of the apocryphal Jewish widow and her maidservant decapitating a sleeping Assyrian general (see fig. 2.9).

When the famous painter Michelangelo Merisi da Caravaggio paints the same narrative around 1599, Judith appears as a disquieted young woman, queasily cutting into Holofernes's neck with the uncertainty of a vegetarian slicing a ham. In Artemisia's version, however, Judith and her maidservant are full-figured women actively restraining and violently executing the enemy general. All three figures emerge from a dark, almost black background, as if spotlit on a stage. Their bodies create an inverted, slightly tipped triangle that animates the canvas. At the bottom of the composition, rivulets of blood stream from Holofernes's neck as his mouth gapes and his eyes roll back in his head. Judith's maid, dressed in red, pins the man down on the bed, while her mistress, clothed in blue, leverages her entire body to hack through the bone and gristle of the man's neck. The gory, visceral scene could be pulled from a Quentin Tarantino film.

This painting and a subsequent version made around 1620 were my introduction to Artemisia. I was in my early twenties and simultaneously enthralled and horrified by the artworks and by the artist's history. It felt so easy to interpret *Judith Slaying Holofernes* as an emotional catharsis for the young female artist. Perhaps Artemisia could not exact revenge on Tassi in person, but she could in paint. I imagined Artemisia as an avenging angel, punishing the man who violated her and the father who failed to protect her.

I was hardly alone in this impulse. Popular novels imagined Artemisia's suffering—physical, psychological, and emotional—as the underlying motivation for her work. Scholars, too, argued that Artemisia's rape—and her experience as a woman in a misogynistic society more generally—fundamentally and

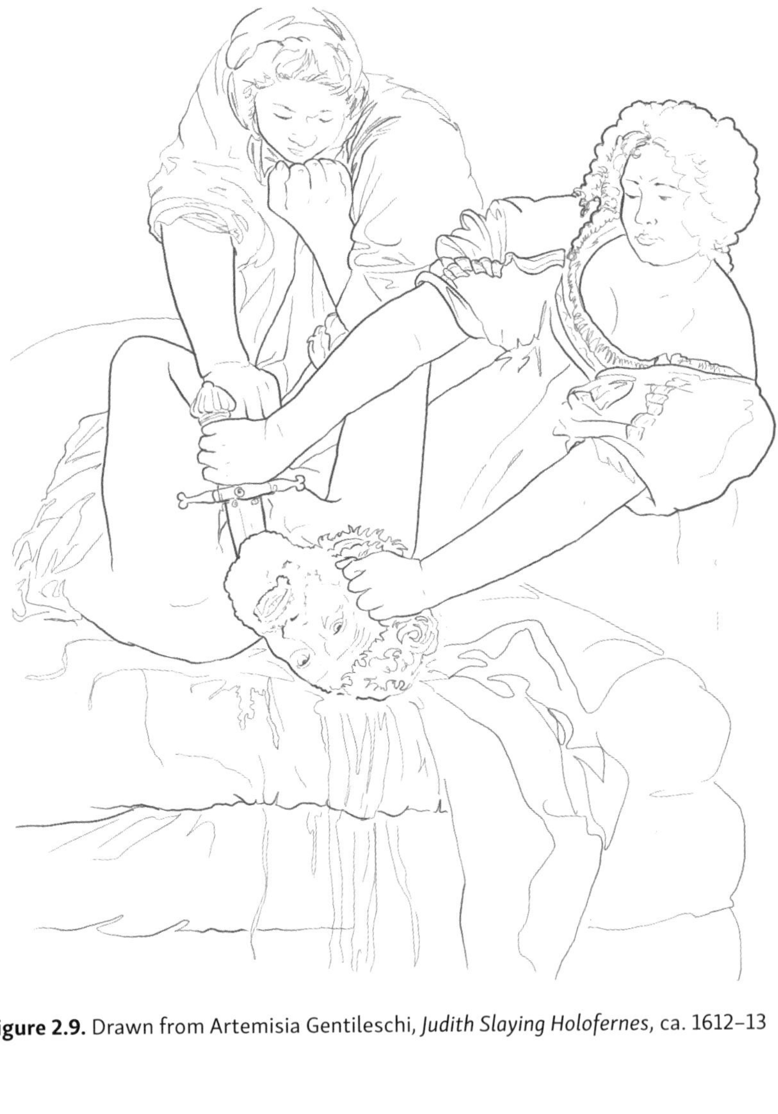

Figure 2.9. Drawn from Artemisia Gentileschi, *Judith Slaying Holofernes*, ca. 1612–13

visibly shaped her entire artistic career.[51] More recently, Artemisia has become the cover girl for potent female rage in a post #MeToo era. "You don't have to be a psychotherapist," one journalist writes, "to be able to read this painting as an obvious declaration of psychic revenge and empowerment against the injustice and humiliation perpetrated on female victims by would-be sexual predators."[52] In these interpretations, the painted Judith serves as a stand-in for Artemisia, and Artemisia becomes a stand-in for women in general.

As much as I sometimes want that story to be true, my training as a historian gives me pause. I can't just conflate the artist and subject with my own contemporary experiences and expectations for art making. Today, we often expect artists to make art that reflects something of their inner lives. We imagine that all visual art is a kind of release, an externalization of an artist's hopes, dreams, sorrows, and experiences. Yet as we noted earlier, most art prior to the modern era was made on commission or for a very particular religious or social purpose. When we compare the subjects of Artemisia's paintings with what we know of her actual life after the trial in Rome, there is very little overlap.

She had five children with her husband, but we see no paintings of motherhood. Only one of those children, her daughter Prudentia, lived to adulthood, yet Artemisia does not paint the grief of losing babies to death. From letters, we know that she carried on a romantic affair with a powerful Florentine nobleman and that her husband tolerated it, perhaps because of the financial stability it afforded. We don't see *that* in her paintings either.

And so, when we look at *Judith Slaying Holofernes*, we can't glibly assume that it is an artistic response to a deeply felt trauma. A historian needs to ask hard questions. How did women in seventeenth-century Italy understand the relationship between their bodies, gender, sex, and marriage? What were the laws and traditions that governed sexual behavior? Was it an extreme act to subject Artemisia to torture, or was this a common practice for certain kinds of testimony?

In my early encounters with the Judith paintings, I wanted to say that those particulars really didn't matter. Obviously that culture was misogynistic and therefore *bad*, and trying to understand that context seemed an awful lot like excusing an obvious injustice. What I wanted was a strong critique and a call to do better in our present.

But if I did that, I'd be engaging in what my historiography professor called "presentism," assuming that *my* diagnosis of a historical situation, *my* emotional responses, and *my* imagined solutions could transcend my own moment and be seamlessly applied backward. If I turned Artemisia into a twenty-first-century, proto-feminist heroine, I'd be denying something of both her humanity and my own.

Empathetic thinking demands careful collection and assessment of historical evidence alongside honest acknowledgment of the distance between self and subject. No historical record is transparent; we have to allow for friction, or even contradiction. Certainly, it matters that Artemisia was a painter who was a woman, but it also matters that she was a woman in seventeenth-century Western Europe, making work in a particular context, for a particular clientele, and with a particular understanding of the job of an artist.

Allegory as Artist

The same care needs to be applied to *Self-Portrait as the Allegory of Painting*.

When I first saw the painting, I wanted it to be a straightforward self-portrait or at least as straightforward as a self-representation can be. I imagined that if I had walked into Artemisia's studio in 1638, I would have seen her vigorously addressing her canvas, her disheveled hair an indicator of her frenzied inspiration. Many other artists' self-portraits from the seventeenth century seemed staid and boring. They followed the same format: a three-quarter pose with the artist holding a palette and paintbrushes and wearing dark clothing, a bland expression, and, on occasion, a gold chain to signal his status. If those self-portraits were corporate headshots, Artemisia's seemed more like personal brand photography, representing something true and essential about her individual identity.

It did feel like a bit of a betrayal when I learned that Artemisia was presenting herself as the *character* of Painting. To an educated seventeenth-century viewer, the reference would have been clear, even without a title. Artemisia precisely references Cesare Ripa's *Iconologia*, the standard manual for symbolism in seventeenth-century Italy. According to Ripa's 1611 edition, *Pittura*, the Italian word for "Painting," should be represented as a beautiful woman with dark, wavy hair in slight disarray and arched eyebrows that "show imaginative thought."[53] She should wear an iridescent dress that seems to change color and a golden chain from which hangs a theatrical mask while holding a brush in one hand and a palette in the other. Artemisia's painting follows Ripa like an assignment checklist. Is this just another Vessel story?

There is, however, one significant difference. Ripa says that *Pittura* should have her "mouth covered with a cloth tied behind her ears."[54] But Artemisia's *Pittura* is not gagged. In fact, her lips are slightly parted, almost as if she is about to speak.

For one well-respected Artemisia scholar, this self-portrait is nothing less than a woman artist's brilliant, deliberate subversion of the misogynist status quo.[55] According to art historian Mary Garrard, the discipline of painting was not even deemed worthy of personification until the early sixteenth century. The famous Italian artist Leonardo da Vinci—who of course had no small stake in this debate—argued that painting should be considered one of the liberal arts because it required imagination.[56] That is, painting required the use of the mind, not just the hands. This claim helped raise artists' social status in Renaissance Italy from that of laborer to that of intellectual. Soon, the female personifications of painting and sculpture, along with architecture and poetry, decorated the private homes of leading Italian artists and noblemen. But—Garrard points out—while male artists could decorate architectural spaces with the allegory of painting, it was harder to use that figure to elevate their personal status in self-portraits. Giovanni Domenico Cerrini's *Allegory of Painting with Self-Portrait of the Artist* (ca. 1639) offers one awkward attempt. The painting depicts a partially nude, blond woman, swathed in billowing strips of pink, yellow, and blue fabric. She holds a palette and brushes in one hand while holding up a small canvas with the other. The painting-within-the-painting is a portrait of Cerrini himself, staring back seriously at us. Cerrini takes more liberties with Ripa's recommended symbolism for *Pittura* than Artemisia does, but the bared breast makes it clear that we're looking at an allegorical figure rather than a portrait of an actual historical painter who was a woman.

Meanwhile, in her *Self-Portrait as the Allegory of Painting*, Artemisia does what no male painter can do. Instead of depicting herself in the presence of Painting, she presents herself *as* Painting, "a statement that was at once more humble and more profound."[57] Garrard pushes her argument further, suggesting that each of the artist's visual choices is a deliberate statement about the very nature of painting. Artemisia, according to Garrard, engages in contemporary philosophical debates about color versus line and theory versus practice. In this interpretation, Artemisia is a shrewd, subversive intellectual and the painting is a proud manifesto.

This neatly triumphant inversion of the Vessel story was appealing and invigorating to me. *This* Artemisia was the ideal heroine: Smart, savvy, talented, and beautiful, she overcame great personal trauma and celebrated her own distinctiveness. History's subsequent intrusion on this pleasant state of affairs was, quite frankly, very annoying.

The more I studied, the more multiple complications became evident. First, by cross-referencing Artemisia's letters with her patrons' and collectors' inventories, a number of historians concluded that this painting was likely made when Artemisia was in her mid-forties.[58] That meant that the artist probably did not, at least at the time, look like the flushed, smooth-faced woman in the painting. Some scholars also questioned the accuracy of calling the painting a "self-portrait" at all. There is nothing in the painting itself that announces that we are looking at an artist's *self*-representation, and the paper trail is inconclusive. What if Artemisia, middle-aged and working for a new patron, Charles I of England, was just painting an allegorical figure that was popular at the time? What if the current title was a modern misreading? And finally, was there enough evidence that Artemisia was actually aware of and participating in such high-minded philosophical debates? Or were we simply seeing what we wanted to see? Were we choosing to see such clever, intellectual statements in her work just like others had seen evidence of her sexual trauma?

Artemisia's painting is still part of the British Royal Collection, and the Royal Collection Trust continues to identify the artwork as *Self-Portrait as the Allegory of Painting*, dating it to Artemisia's brief time in England with her father in the late 1630s. But as scholar Elizabeth Cropper writes, "Self-identification with a work has little to do with resemblance."[59] Artemisia signs the painting "AGF," which stands for "Artemisia Gentileschi fecit," or "Artemisia Gentileschi did it." The painting can even represent Artemisia without documenting her *physical* appearance.

The Contradictions of Being

I now see Artemisia's *Self-Portrait as the Allegory of Painting* as an invitation to hold multiple kinds of tension. There is the visual tension of the painting itself: the play of dark and light, the precarious balance of her tilting body and outstretched arms. There is also the historical tension of all that we want to believe we know and all that we must acknowledge we simply *cannot* know. Then, too, there is the complicated, conflicted reality of Artemisia's own life, where her hasty marriage after the public trial is what gives her the respectability and thus the freedom to pursue her unlikely career.

A few years ago, while preparing to teach about Artemisia again in class, I realized that something about the *Self-Portrait* was still vexing me. I had just looked at one of Artemisia's less popular paintings, an image of Bathsheba at her bath while King David spies on her, painted in the late 1630s or early 1640s, around the time of the *Allegory of Painting*. While Artemisia's most well-known works—her *Judith Slaying Holofernes*, *Self-Portrait as the Allegory of Painting*, and *Esther Before Ahasuerus*—all have spare, sometimes almost blank backgrounds, this painting of Bathsheba is full of contextual detail. We see David's palace and a verdant garden rising up behind the stone balustrade that separates Bathsheba's courtyard. But those background elements were not painted by Artemisia. Instead, another artist specializing in architecture painted David's palace, and an artist specializing in landscape likely added the garden. Such collaborations among artists grew increasingly popular in the seventeenth century and could be seen as evidence of Artemisia's solid reputation as a figurative painter. It would be an honor for these younger male painters to collaborate with someone who had the status and patronage of Artemisia.

But there might be an additional reason for this joint venture.

What if Artemisia just wasn't very good at painting scenery?

Historian Patricia Simons points out that when young Artemisia paints her first major canvas in 1610, *Susanna and the Elders*, she locates the protagonist in a minimal, shallow space.[60] Male artists painting the same subject around the same time tend to paint Susanna in a plant-filled garden, often with architectural features. Artemisia, still at the beginning of her career, does not have the knowledge to render a believable, deep space. And so, Orazio hires his assistant, Agostino Tassi, to teach his daughter *prospettiva*, "the illusion of perspective." As we have already learned, in the course of instructing Artemisia, Tassi also assaults her. When Orazio takes Tassi to court, it is likely that Tassi had failed to deliver on both his promise to marry Artemisia and his promise to tutor her. Simons points to the later Bathsheba painting as additional evidence that Artemisia never gets to complete that part of her education.[61] She doesn't paint elaborate backgrounds because she *can't*. Her opportunity to learn how to do so was taken away.

Decades after her assault and the truncating of her artistic education, Artemisia renders a convincingly foreshortened human figure in *Self-Portrait as the Allegory of Painting*. But the depicted space that her figure inhabits is strangely flat and abstracted. I do not think that Artemisia was making some grand, therapeutic statement about embracing her past self by fudging on the perspective system of this painting. I do know, however, that recognizing this limitation in her work reminds me of her distinct personhood, her *Being* in a particular story.

There's resonance, actually, between the way that Scripture tells stories about women and what I see in Artemisia's self-portrait. The Bible's women are complicated and contradictory too. I think about women like Miriam, who is described as a courageous young heroine (Exod. 2:4–8), a jubilant prophetess (15:20–21), *and* a jealous older sister (Num. 12:2). There's Ruth, an immigrant and widow who essentially makes the first move on her second husband, Boaz (Ruth 3:6–9). And there's Tamar, who, when denied the protection of the law, dresses like a prostitute but is deemed more righteous than her father-in-law, Judah (Gen. 38:26). Their individual stories matter enough to be told.

I think, too, of Jesus meeting the Samaritan woman at the well. He makes a point of telling her that he knows her life experience. "You've had five husbands," he tells her, "and the man you now have is not your husband" (John 4:18). Then he gives her good news for her future that directly addresses her particular past and her ethnic identity. The living water he offers is specifically for *her*, even as it quenches the thirst of the world.

Throughout his ministry, Jesus treats people as individuals with unique experiences *and* a shared need for his restoring grace. Artemisia's *Self-Portrait as the Allegory of Painting* bolsters my courage to tell my own story in a way that maintains complexity, celebrating real achievements while acknowledging real hurts. Instead of ignoring my body or being reduced to my body, I can tackle the gift and grief of being alive with honest care. And perhaps even more beautifully, I can extend that same possibility to others.

3

Maiden

A Lady in Waiting

I lay my colored pencil down and carefully examine my handiwork. A raven-haired woman with pale skin, blushing cheeks, and full, pink lips stands in front of a gothic window on a stone balcony. Looking sadly off into the distance, she wears a sweeping, peacock-blue dress while clutching a single pale rose to her chest. Ivy twines around the stone railing, and maple leaves fill the top left corner.

My high school portfolio is full of women like this, women with elegantly hunched shoulders, sharp, high cheekbones, and yearning expressions, swathed in abundant hair or drapery that emphasizes their delicacy. Many of my drawings are based on paintings by Dante Gabriel Rossetti and his nineteenth-century cohort, the British Pre-Raphaelites. Others, however, are copies of designer fashion campaigns I pull from my aunt's stack of magazines. I draw a slumped Kate Moss swathed in a black, lace veil, a woman slouched in a chair wearing a Givenchy sequined gown, and a gloomy Prada model lounging in the bow of a rowboat on a foggy lake. They are all achingly gorgeous, even in their apparent distress.

It's not that I lack visual stories of active, sporty, defiant women. The Spice Girls are singing about girl power; Buffy is slaying vampires; Xena is a warrior princess. I sketch a jubilant Mia Hamm mid-kick, her ponytail streaming behind her as she prepares to strike a soccer ball. Mostly, though, I keep drawing the sloped shoulders and hollowed chests of Pre-Raphaelite muses and fashion models. Athletic, sassy girls seem fresh and modern, but somehow both conservative purity culture *and* high fashion tell me that enduring, alluring beauty is found in the story of the Maiden.

There's more to being a maiden than simply being unmarried. She is the woman waiting in the tower before being breathlessly snatched up by the hero. Whether due to sleep, capture, or even illness, her body is exquisitely pliable. If tragedy has befallen her, she may be hysterical or self-destructive, driven to madness by lost love. She rouses men to action through her obvious need for outside assistance. At the same time, she also makes women's pain seem inevitable.

I can tell that I'm not doing a particularly good job of inhabiting this story with my own body. After all, I'm regularly informed—by peers, older women, and my pastor—that I am "intimidating." I'm too serious and too curious, too quick to both answer and ask questions. So, I bite my tongue in Sunday school and try to smile more.

Decades later, even in a new world of Pixar protagonist princesses, the story of the Maiden continues to reemerge. It's a story we tell not just in children's books and movies but on social media and in music videos, political news coverage, and health and beauty advertising. Over and over again, we see this tale: The Maiden is contained, captured, and maybe even a bit consumptive—that is, she's beautiful because she's dying.

A Butterfly in a Box

"Ladies cross their legs," the white-haired woman tells me kindly but firmly. I'm visiting extended family in Virginia, and the Sunday school teacher is correcting my sitting posture. I'm mortified but also a little confused.

"But I'm wearing shorts under my dress," I whisper.

I'm seven or so, and my mom had taught me that the reason to be aware of how I move and sit in a dress is to keep my "private parts private." Wearing bike shorts under my skirts addresses that concern while still allowing me to run around the church yard after the service and, most importantly, flip over the railings like a gymnast.

This woman, however, seems to suggest that it is my gender, not the practicality of my clothing choices, that should dictate how I sit. I'm already tall and gangly, and as I fold myself up into a more compact position, I begin to wonder if a contained body is the best body I can be.

While the Venus is on display, unwillingly or otherwise, the Maiden is praised for being inaccessible. The dignified, constrained bodies of the Three Graces in Botticelli's *Primavera* offer an allegorical model of appropriate feminine behavior, but Domenico Ghirlandaio's half-length *Portrait of Giovanna Tornabuoni* (1488)—made around the same time as Botticelli's painting—demonstrates how actual women can also be pressed into shallow boxes (see fig. 3.1). The portrait is a two-and-a-half-foot-tall tempera painting on wood. A pale, elaborately coiffed woman, dressed in a richly decorated, red-and-orange dress, sits in perfect profile facing to the left. Immediately behind her we see a shelf that holds a brooch, a prayer book, coral rosary beads, and a small piece of paper with a Latin inscription. Particularly in its use of space and texture, Ghirlandaio's painting reminds me of a specimen pinned behind glass.

Though Giovanna practically fills the composition, her body seems like a flat cutout, pressed between the viewer's gaze and the dark shelf behind her. It seems impossible that there is enough space for a real body to fit in the shallow space. Furthermore, the tempera paint that Ghirlandaio uses makes every edge—the slope of Giovanna's nose, the curve of her long neck, the ringlets that frame her face—sharp and crisp. The intricate textures of Giovanna's dress and jewelry and the individually painted strands of hair all attract our attention without creating an illusion of depth. Again, we have the sense that we are admiring a decorative surface, like a patterned butterfly wing.

Ghirlandaio's painting of Giovanna Tornabuoni is one of hundreds of portraits made in fifteenth-century Italy. Unlike the medieval age, early modern Europe increasingly emphasized the identity and achievements of individuals, and portraits—as representations of particular, recognizable people—reflected and reinforced this interest. However, not all portraits necessarily served the same social function.

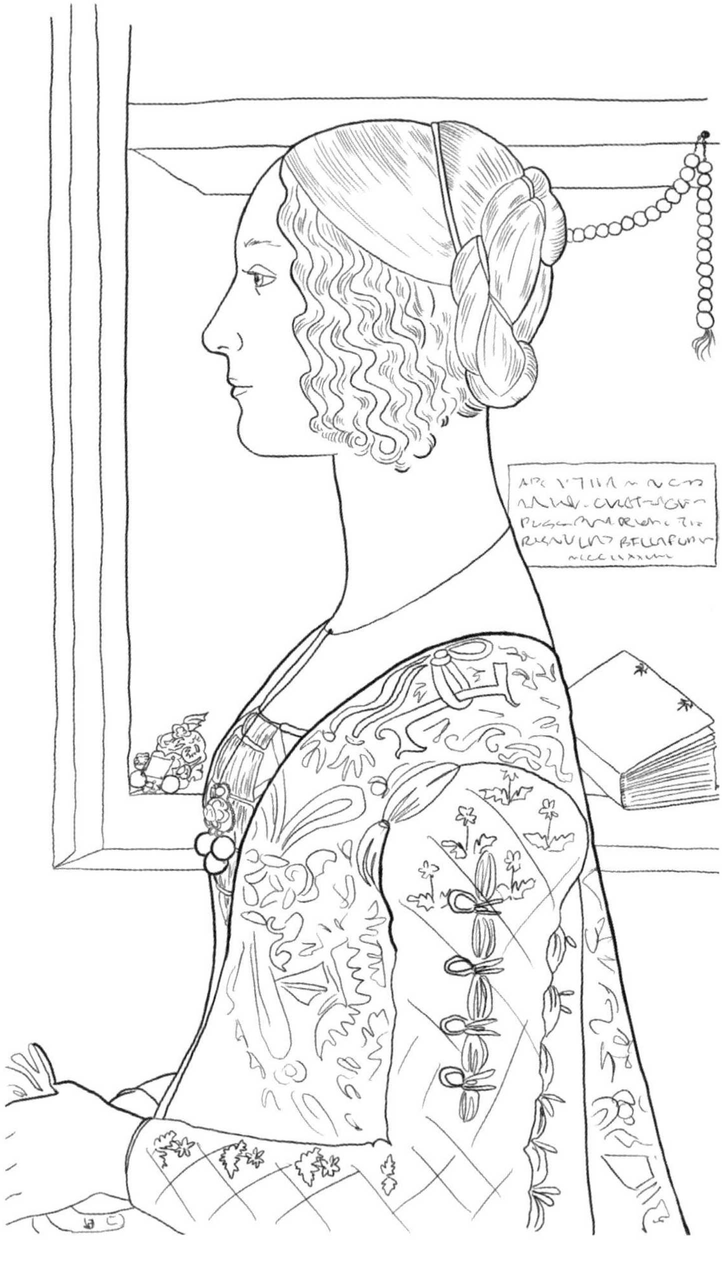

Figure 3.1. Drawn from Domenico Ghirlandaio, *Portrait of Giovanna Tornabuoni*, 1488

In the early 1400s, most stand-alone portraits made in Florence, Italy, were of men and depicted the sitter from the side. The profile view was reminiscent of coins and medallions from ancient Rome, a culture with which the Florentine merchants and ruling families wanted to align themselves. The profile also provided the most precise physiological information about a particular person's unique facial features and proportions. Beginning around 1440, however, male portraits increasingly adopted the three-quarter view, a pose still common today for school photos and business headshots.[1] By 1450, nearly all portraits of men used this new pose that created the illusion of an actual body in actual space. Yet during that same period, profile portraits became and remained popular for another set of people: well-to-do Florentine women.

The portrait of Giovanna Tornabuoni is just one of the dozens of still extant paintings of *women* made during that forty-year period. When viewed together, clear similarities emerge (see fig. 3.2). The profile view always renders the sitter static, more of an object than a vital being capable of dynamic action. The women appear even more fragile due to their elongated, spindly necks, sloping shoulders, and hollowed, slouching chests. The women stare straight off the edge of the panel, refusing to meet the viewer's gaze. The unseeing eyes underscore the women's objecthood. We can stare at their smooth faces, elaborate dresses, and intricate hairstyles without worrying that they will catch us mid-inspection. Again and again, women's profile portraits follow the same template, long after men have abandoned the format.

Historian Patricia Simons argues that a profile portrait was often made when a woman became engaged or married and was then displayed in her new home. The paintings emphasized women's value to their husbands by visualizing both wealth and virtue. In a culture where marriages were arranged primarily to increase familial social and economic standing, paintings like Ghirlandaio's were announcements of a groom's successful achievement rather than his romantic passion.

But like the woman in the Virginia Sunday school classroom, fifteenth-century women also participated in containing maidenly bodies. Mothers reinforced and sometimes even expanded standards of virtue for their daughters, pointing to their own portraits as guidelines. We know from

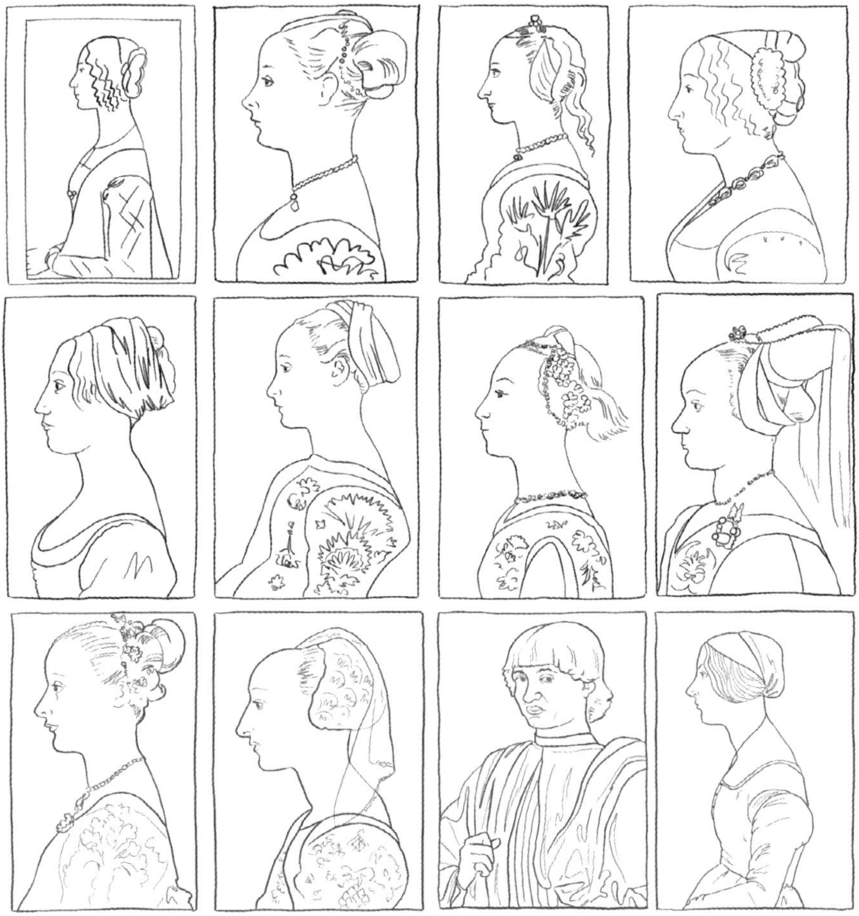

Figure 3.2. Drawn from fifteenth-century Italian profile portraits of women and Andrea del Castagno, *Portrait of a Young Man*, ca. 1450

sharply critical letters that they also assessed other women's daughters as brides for their sons.[2]

What were they looking for?

Giovanna's portrait gives us clues to why she was a desirable bride. In addition to the physical charms of her high forehead and long neck, the accompanying rosary and prayer book suggest her piety. Her averted eyes also signaled her moral goodness. According to fifteenth-century handbooks like Francesco Barbaro's *On Wifely Duties*, loose women looked men in the eye, while lowered eyes signaled a woman's modesty.[3] The card pinned to the back wall of the painting reiterates these assertions. It reads, "Art, would that you could represent character and mind! There would be no more beautiful painting on earth." Giovanna's physical beauty is equated with her moral excellence.

Notably, Giovanna's clothing and jewelry do not indicate the wealth she brought into the marriage. Instead, they demonstrate how she became a valuable object through her marriage. Her sumptuously decorated garments—a butter-yellow damask vest and intricately slashed and embroidered sleeves—are not just a fashion statement. Two *L*'s worked into the fabric of her dress on her shoulder refer to her husband, Lorenzo Tornabuoni, while the repeated triangular pattern is a Tornabuoni family emblem. The jewels in the painting—large pearls and rubies—are Tornabuoni family jewels. Giovanna, like the gems in the painting and the painting itself, is a precious object, made even more valuable because she is sealed off from others, her chastity and purity assured.

After all this, we might be surprised to learn that Giovanna was no longer technically a maiden when this portrait was made. In fact, she was no longer even alive. Her husband commissioned the painting two years after she died giving birth to their second child. He kept the portrait on display in his "room with the golden ceiling" in the family palace, a private parlor where he hosted his guests, even after he remarried.[4] Giovanna's portrait joined other prized artworks and medallions honoring Tornabuoni family members, signaling that she, too, had been an exquisite possession, a rare butterfly in a box. And there, contained and controlled, she remained in waiting.

"You Must Be My Tree!"

Purity culture gurus in the 1990s did not shy away from using the language of maidenhood to describe what they saw as biblical femininity. I even had a book titled *Of Knights and Fair Maidens*, which promised "a radical new approach to a very old way of developing relationships," where men acted and women responded.[5] Likewise, the oft-cited Elisabeth Elliot chided women who expressed romantic interest in men rather than allowing the men to pursue them.[6] Books specifically aimed at young men, like John Eldredge's *Wild at Heart*, reiterated the same point: "Deep in his heart, every man longs for a battle to fight, an adventure to live, and a beauty to rescue."[7] In my conservative evangelical world, such language fit into a larger framework of male headship and female submission.

Ironically, the notion that men want only women they have to pursue was also a story occasionally echoed back to me on the covers of *Seventeen* and *Cosmopolitan* in the grocery store checkout line and in a newspaper review of the book *The Rules*.[8] The bestselling 1995 book by Ellen Fein and Sherrie Schneider offered advice like "Don't talk to a man first (and don't ask him to dance)."[9] While the Spice Girls were telling men what they want (what they really, really want), other cultural bedfellows continued to tell the Maiden story, in which a woman's worth was measured by the extent of a man's determination to pursue her.

The romance of the tale could also obscure or even condone violence. Both *The Rules* and *Of Knights and Fair Maidens* claimed that the modern era had wandered astray when it came to romantic relationships. They wanted to return to the tried-and-true techniques of an imagined, undefined "past." Yet when I actually examined art

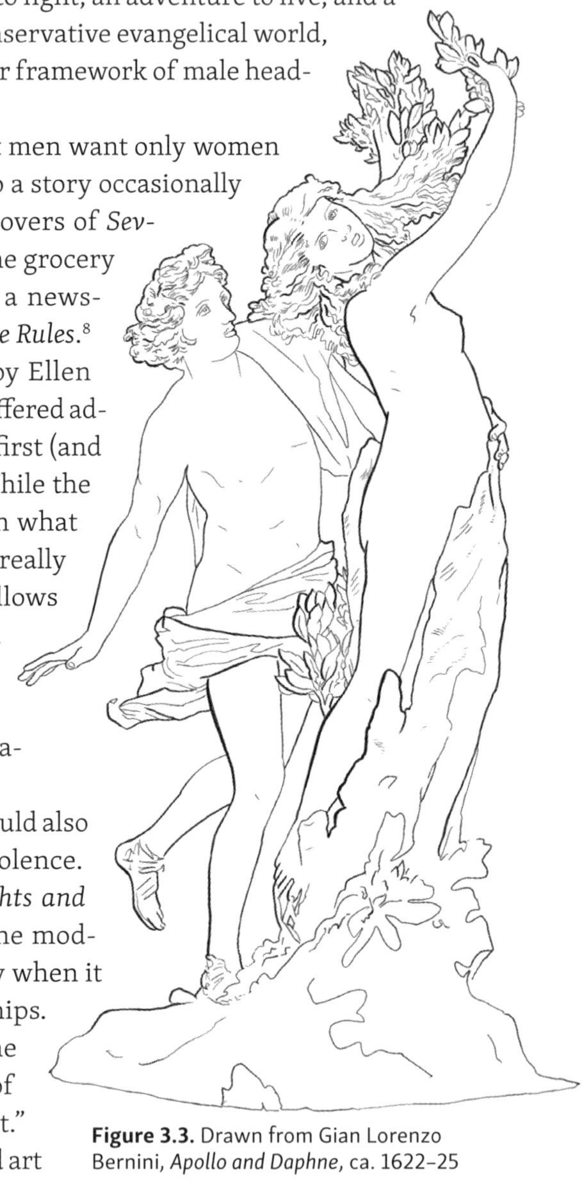

Figure 3.3. Drawn from Gian Lorenzo Bernini, *Apollo and Daphne*, ca. 1622–25

history, the Maiden story I found was chilling. Returning to the past forced me to grapple with my capacity to remain blind to things happening right in front of my eyes.

I first see Gian Lorenzo Bernini's *Apollo and Daphne* (ca. 1622–25) in my art history survey textbook. Despite having only a single view of the eight-foot-tall marble sculpture, I am captivated.

Bernini has frozen a split second in marble for our extended perusal (see fig. 3.3). The two figures are caught mid-action; their bodies seem about to twist together like two threads. Apollo—a shirtless, handsome youth—is sprinting forward. His drape swirls about his body as he lunges forward, one arm reaching out to clasp Daphne's waist and the other outstretched to counterbalance his movement. Apollo's right arm creates a sharp diagonal to his yearning gaze that continues up and across to Daphne's raised arms. Meanwhile, Daphne steps up on a rocky outcropping, her entire body stretched up as she looks over her shoulder at the pursuing god. In contrast to Apollo's open, billowing robe, tree bark appears to wrap around Daphne's legs like a stiff skirt. The two bodies seemingly meld together, and sprays of tender leaves sprout from Daphne's reaching fingers.

While the entire sculpture is carved from a single block of white marble, Bernini creates varying textures. My eyes slide easily across Apollo's and Daphne's smooth, polished skin and loop up and around the rippling folds of Apollo's drape. I note the contrast between Daphne's soft flesh and the rougher tree bark. I get caught in the tangle of Daphne's windswept ringlets and marvel at the delicacy of the leaves that cover her fingertips.

It is, I think, the most beautiful sculpture I have ever seen, and I desperately want to see it in person so I can walk around the elegant figures and see Bernini's detailed effects up close.

Instead, I content myself with tracing the outline of the figures, then painstakingly filling in a delicate network of curving, overlapping lines to add shading and volume to the flat outline. Short, repeated pen strokes fill in the swell of Apollo's thigh and suggest the twisting movement of Daphne's torso. I am especially pleased with my precise rendering of Daphne's windswept hair and Apollo's billowing drapery.

Yet despite how much time I spend on my drawing, I fail to register the implications of a crucial feature. Daphne's expression is one of terror. Her mouth is open not with delight but because she is begging for help.

To Bernini's educated, seventeenth-century viewers, his subject would be clear. He is depicting the climactic moment of a Greek myth recounted in Ovid's *Metamorphoses* (1:450–567). Apollo, the sun god, spies the beautiful wood nymph, Daphne, and is overcome by desire, but Daphne—who has vowed to remain unmarried—flees from him. Eventually, about to be caught by the pursuing Apollo, Daphne calls out to her father, the river god Peneus, and begs him to destroy her beauty. Immediately, she transforms into a laurel tree. This is the moment that Bernini's sculpture represents. Ovid's poem, however, continues. Apollo embraces and kisses the tree, even as it shrinks away from his touch. Still, he persists. "Since you cannot be my bride, you must be my tree!" Apollo crows, explaining that the laurel tree shall become the wood for his lyre and bow and its leaves will be his crown. And thus, Apollo gains possession of Daphne anyway, as the laurel tree becomes his emblem.

I am so astonished by the sculpture's formal qualities and technical finesse that Ovid's narrative recedes into the background. My hefty art history book takes the same approach. After briefly summarizing the myth, the textbook authors turn to celebrating Bernini's skill: "The fidelity with which the softness of female flesh; the lithe body of Apollo; the textures of hair, bark, and leaves are rendered is no more dazzling than Bernini's craftsmanship in carving the scores of minute and slender projections from fragile marble. He has reached in his mid-twenties the height of his ability at pictorial sculpture."[10] I cannot see the violence lurking beneath the surface. In fact, I'm so blinded by the "dazzling" craftsmanship that I perceive the sculpture as a dramatic, ideal romance.

Apollo and Daphne was one of several sculptures that the young Bernini completed for his patron, Cardinal Scipione Borghese. Borghese had built a new villa and pleasure garden outside Rome, and he wanted to fill his home with beautiful art and rare collectibles. In addition to a handful of portrait busts, Borghese commissioned Bernini to make several large marble sculptures depicting biblical or mythological narratives.

By the time Bernini completed *Apollo and Daphne*, he had already carved another dramatic scene from Ovid's *Metamorphoses* for his powerful patron. Pluto, the muscular, bearded god of the underworld, accompanied by his three-headed dog Cerberus, lunges forward, lifting a flailing Proserpina in his arms. The young woman twists away from her captor, pushing her left hand into Pluto's face as carefully carved tears stream down her marble cheeks. Cardinal Borghese gifted the sculpture to his political rival and then requested that the young artist make another statue along a similar theme. Bernini obliged with *Apollo and Daphne*.

Artist and patron mutually reinforced each other's reputations: Bernini's as a dazzling prodigy, the next great Roman sculptor, and Borghese's as a sophisticated patron of the arts. The pagan subject matter was justified through the addition of a Latin couplet to the base: "Those who love to pursue fleeting forms of pleasure, in the end find only leaves and bitter berries in their hands." Now, the sculpture could be presented as a warning against chasing carnal delight.

When I see the sculpture in person, visiting Italy for the first time as a thirty-six-year-old woman, I'm halfway dreading the encounter. In the intervening years, I've learned new ways to look at *Apollo and Daphne*. Instead of seeing a romance, I recognize a terrified woman being pursued by a man who won't take no for an answer. I'm also struck by the realization that, while Daphne may serve as the visual focal point of the sculpture, she is essentially erased from her own story. Apollo's name comes first in the title. Apollo is the one driving the action. Even the attached couplet assumes a male viewer who will naturally align himself with Apollo rather than Daphne.

Now, standing in the Borghese Gallery, I want to scream in frustration. The sculpture is even more beautiful than I imagined and more terrifying because of it. I want to pull apart form and function, to hold Bernini's technical finesse in one hand and the horror of a woman trying to resist unwanted sexual attention in the other. But their entanglement is part of the work's power. The Maiden story is told with such aesthetic skill that I find myself longing—just for a moment—to be as beautiful as Daphne. Indeed, I want to believe that this sculpture can just exist in a bubble of beauty, untouched by my twenty-first-century concerns about consent and floating above the cultural realities of its own seventeenth-century world.

I know that's impossible. Artworks are always forming viewers, giving us stories that shape our lives. And the story of the captured Maiden was never just locked inside Cardinal Borghese's home. It was performed on a public, political stage.

Fortune Is a Woman

My breath catches the first time I see Giambologna's sculpture in person. I'm rushing to get my tickets to Florence's Uffizi Gallery, and I don't realize that I'm walking through the famed Piazza della Signoria until I'm halfway across it. The south end of the square is marked by a long, covered platform framed by a set of arches, known as the Loggia dei Lanzi. Erected in the late fourteenth century as a stage for public ceremonies, the loggia also houses an impressive array of public sculpture. I don't have time to stop and stare the way I want to, but even from a distance, the thirteen-and-a-half-foot-tall sculpture under the far right archway demands attention.

Three larger-than-life figures weave together into a vertical corkscrew (see fig. 3.4). At the bottom, an older, bearded man crouches on the ground. Twisting to look up at the two figures above him, he raises one hand in horror. A

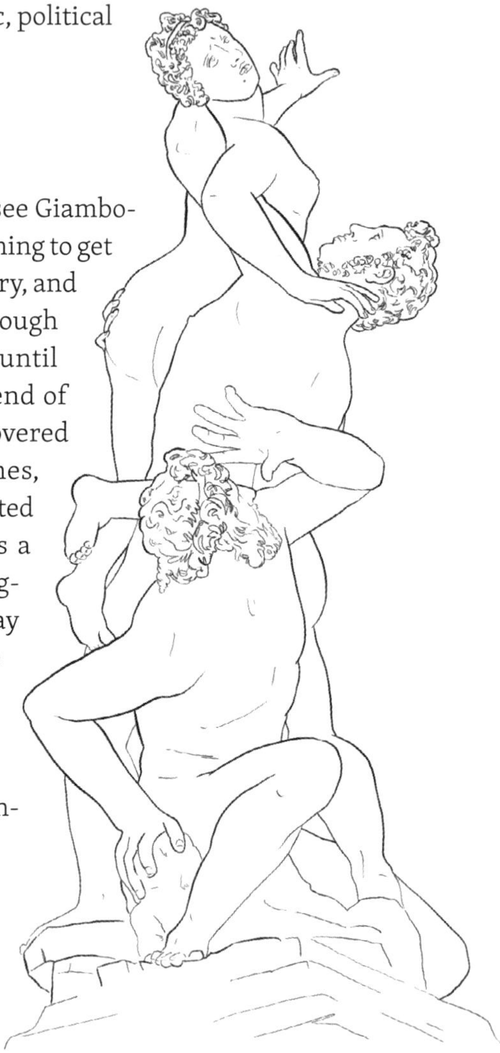

Figure 3.4. Drawn from Giambologna, *Abduction of a Sabine Woman*, 1579–83

young, muscular man with curly hair sandwiches the older figure between his legs. This man, in a move akin to a figure skating lift, effortlessly lofts a maiden in his arms. But the woman arches away from her captor, arms outstretched like a vine's unfurling tendrils. The three figures intertwine in a sinuous, dynamic spiral that can't be fully appreciated from a single angle.

Later, as I walk around the sculpture, I find one particular view that makes me pause. The young man gazes up at the maiden, eyes wide, mouth beginning to part as if to speak. He looks enthralled. I want to say that he's in love.

Is this a *love* story?

But if so, why does the woman look terrified?

The bronze relief panels on the sculpture's base tell me that this is the *Abduction of a Sabine Woman*, made between 1579 and 1583 by Giambologna, a Flemish sculptor who had relocated to Florence as a young man. Another name for the sculpture—and the story it tells—is *Rape of a Sabine Woman*.

Greek and Roman mythology abound with stories of women—usually mortals—being pursued, abducted, and sexually violated by men—usually gods. Zeus often uses disguise to achieve his ends, appearing as a woman's husband (Cassiopeia), golden coins (Danae), a white bull (Europa), or even another god (Callisto). Some women in ancient mythology are known *only* because they were raped by a god and thus birthed a half-mortal son. Such is the case for Alcmene and her son Hercules. The popular tale Giambologna tells—the same one told on the marriage chests discussed in the Venus chapter—is that of Rome's founding, when Romulus's men violently kidnap the neighboring Sabine women to marry them and start families. In most of these stories, gods and demigods pursuing and procuring that which they desire is a virtue. Later Italian Renaissance artworks likewise represented these narratives as heroes' tales, celebrating physical strength, intellectual cunning, and honorable perseverance.

Today, the legal term "rape" denotes sexual penetration without consent. In ancient Roman law, *raptus*—from the word *rapere*, "to snatch, to carry off"—was the crime of kidnapping a woman, and it sometimes involved sexual violence with the intent to force a marriage. But in the ancient world, women were always understood to be under the care of a man, whether that be their father or their husband. Thus, if a man committed *raptus*, his crime was against the man he stole from, not against the woman he assaulted.

Some scholars have suggested that it is unfair for us to apply our modern understanding of sexual identity to the past, suggesting that premodern women did not conceive of rape as the personal violation that we understand it to be today. Yet early fifteenth-century women like Margery Kempe and Christine de Pizan condemned the act and spoke of their own fear of rape as "the greatest possible sorrow."[11] And how, too, should we understand the obvious fear in the eyes of Giambologna's maiden? Why does the artist create this deliberate tension between the man's apparent devotion and the woman's terror?

On the one hand, Giambologna's *Abduction of a Sabine Woman* reflects some then-new ideas about men, women, and sex. Beginning in the early sixteenth century, as Italian society began to make more allowances for men's sexual activity outside of marriage, a new kind of imagery emerged. In depictions of classical mythology, the maiden tangled with her would-be rapist not just to illustrate a story but to arouse the presumed male viewer. Even before the creation of dark internet hovels, images of sexual coercion and violence were used as erotica. Part of the supposed appeal was found in the woman's initial resistance, a sentiment supported by Ovid when he wrote that Daphne's beauty was "enhanced by flight" (*Metamorphoses* 1.525–35).

The other insight that Giambologna's sculpture offers us may be more surprising. The work is also making a political statement and is connected to another shift in the early sixteenth century: the rise of absolutist rulers. Italian princes claimed increasing authority for themselves as absolute, or total, rulers. Some even claimed to be like the god Jupiter, standing above human law.[12] Political theory of the period increasingly celebrated violence as crucial to a ruler's success.[13]

The most famous summary of this position is found in *The Prince* (1532), written by the diplomat and philosopher Niccolò Machiavelli and dedicated to Lorenzo de' Medici, the Duke of Urbino. In one of his concluding chapters, Machiavelli urges rulers to be forceful and take risks. This is his reasoning: "Fortune is a woman and if you wish to keep her under, it is necessary to beat and ill-use her; . . . she allows herself to be mastered by the adventurous rather than by those who go to work more coldly. She is, therefore, always, woman-like, a lover of young men, because they are less cautious, more violent, and with more audacity command her."[14] Machiavelli deploys the story of the Vessel, personifying Fortune as a woman. How he imagines Fortune to act, however, reflects his beliefs about actual women. In his mind, a maiden loves being violently overtaken and "mastered." Thus, you should control a country the same way you control a woman: total subjugation.

The visual story of the maiden—captured and conquered—reiterated this point in a variety of public or semipublic spaces. In Florence, the main government building was decorated with narrative paintings of Jupiter. Each one symbolized a particular political achievement by the powerful former ruler of Florence, Cosimo de' Medici. For example, Jupiter's abduction of the Phoenician princess Europa represented Cosimo's conquest of the city of Piombino. So it's no surprise that another, later ruler of Florence, Francesco de' Medici, would install Giambologna's *Abduction of a Sabine Woman* right outside that same building, in front of the Loggia dei Lanzi stage.[15]

Giambologna's maiden remains in the public square to this day, outlasting the artist, the patron, and even the political system it was made to support. Yet the danger remains the same. Art has the power to represent a moral travesty with such aesthetic finesse "that we may be seduced into accepting the image as one worthy of imitation in our own lives."[16] What is at stake if we call violence "beauty"? What do we teach ourselves to ignore?

Bound to Love It

Crucially, not every captured woman can be a Maiden.

I can still recall my immediate shame as a college sophomore when I see the advertisement. I'm flipping through stacks of magazines, pulling out pages to turn into collages for a studio class, and I suddenly freeze. My neck turns bright red. The ad consists of an overhead view of a Japanese woman in a kimono, lying down and laced tightly onto the tongue of a men's gigantic dress shoe. She gazes up at the viewer with coy compliance, the fantasy of the submissive geisha girl. I quickly tear it from the magazine and slip it into my folder. Even though thousands of people have already seen the ad—and perhaps even been compelled to buy the depicted shoes—I can't bear the thought of anyone else running across the image.

Western visual culture tells us that some women are destined for bondage. As we saw in the Venus story, paintings of so-called odalisques—the imagined, nineteenth-century sexual slaves in Turkish harems—reflected contemporary ideas about race and gender. Middle Eastern women were seen as more sexual than women of European descent, and both their bodies and their land were presumed to be available for colonial possession.

In the United States, the actual, historical abduction and assault of Black and Native American women remained conspicuously absent from nineteenth- and twentieth-century visual culture. Artists and illustrators crafted alternative images that told a more palatable version of American history. For example, in the mid-nineteenth century, as Americans of European descent continued to forcibly displace the Indigenous people, a gauzy, reimagined story of Pocahontas gained increasing popularity in poems, novels, and plays. In these retellings, the young Powhatan girl who interceded to save the British colonist John Smith from death became a beautiful "Indian princess." As in the later Disney feature film, Pocahontas and Smith were often represented as star-crossed lovers. Depictions of Pocahontas—often with her breasts exposed—flinging herself onto John Smith abounded. In other visual culture, Pocahontas's conversion to Christianity and her marriage to the colonist John Rolfe were used to suggest the peaceful transition from Native to European rule.

What we rarely remember—and what is never represented—is that Pocahontas literally was a captured woman. In 1613, English colonists kidnapped her, held her for ransom, and pressured her to convert to Christianity. But that experience is never told as a Maiden story. Her seizure as a Native woman is not romanticized or aestheticized; it is just assumed to be inevitable.

For enslaved women of African descent in the United States, sexual coercion received no window dressing at all. The seizure of women and their containment in the system of chattel slavery were almost entirely absent from images because the reality of their situation did not need a visual excuse.

Throughout the twentieth century, women of Asian descent were increasingly depicted as docile, passive dolls. The stereotype of the geisha or the "Lotus Blossom" emerged in earlier travel accounts of Western explorers who described East Asian cultures as eager to please.[17] Chinese women's bound feet and Japanese women's tightly wrapped kimonos were interpreted as an inherent desire to be sexually submissive. During World War II, the Korean War, and the Vietnam War, the US government even encouraged this view of Asian women in its internal propaganda.[18]

When I hear the news in March 2021 that six Korean women working at spas and a massage parlor in Atlanta have been shot and killed, my mind jumps back to the shoe advertisement. While the murderer claimed to be motivated by self-hatred over his addiction to pornography and not racial contempt, thousands of Asian American women—myself included—doubted that those factors could actually be disentangled.[19] We had seen the story of our fetishization told over and over again. Yet we told ourselves not to worry, to keep working hard, and, above all, to be polite.

These killings were anything but beautiful. Yet for much of Western art history, the Maiden story also aestheticized white women on the brink of death.

Death Becomes Her

"Ugh," my college friend exclaims in mock exasperation, "you're like so anorexic." She spins me around and continues, "When you turn sideways, we can't even see you."

I don't suffer from an eating disorder, but I do have a very thin, tall frame. And in the early 2000s, in the world of low-rise jeans, rail-thin supermodels, zero-calorie snacks, and so-called heroin chic, "anorexic" seems like a synonym for "gorgeous." We compliment each other's protruding hip bones and talk about food like its presence—rather than absence—will kill us. It's a dangerous, devastating state of affairs, but it's hardly a historical anomaly.

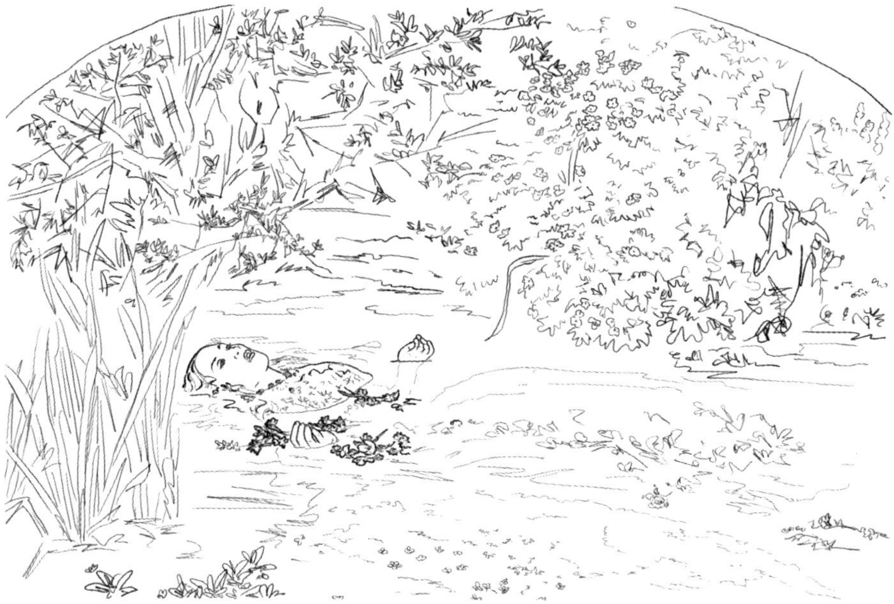

Figure 3.5. Drawn from Sir John Everett Millais, *Ophelia*, 1851–52

The maiden is not only contained and captured. She's also, to use a Victorian term, consumptive, dying from tuberculosis.

I cannot talk myself out of the aesthetic pleasure of looking at John Everett Millais's most famous painting, *Ophelia* (see fig. 3.5). Just shy of four feet across, the luminous oil on canvas painting sits in a golden, arched frame. Ophelia—deathly pale, with eyes and mouth slightly open—floats on her back, partially submerged in the dark river, hands raised helplessly to the sky. Her hair and dress fan out around her sinking form, and the flowers she holds in one hand begin to drift across the water's surface. Millais packs the canvas full of detailed foliage, but my eyes keep returning to the contrast between Ophelia's porcelain face and the smooth void of inky water surrounding her head and torso.

At the same time, Millais unifies Ophelia with the natural surroundings. The elaborate embroidery on her silvery dress mimics the delicate network of weeping willow leaves and dying nettles on the bank. As she sinks, her dress and hair merge with the water, painted with looser brushstrokes than the tight, precise depiction of surrounding plants.

The painting is luminous and heartbreaking all at the same time.

The vision of this beautiful, dying maiden is so firmly lodged in our collective imagination that we forget that such a scene doesn't exist in Shakespeare's *Hamlet*. In the play, young Ophelia descends into madness after Hamlet, her lover, kills her father. The last time Ophelia appears on stage she is disheveled and seemingly incoherent. She sings as she hands out flowers to different characters, each with a symbolic meaning. Two scenes later, Hamlet's mother tells Laertes, Ophelia's brother, that his sister has drowned, having fallen into a brook while picking flowers but "incapable of her own distress."[20]

When Millais made his painting in 1851–52, Ophelia was seen as an example of women's supposedly natural emotional weakness. Psychiatrists used Ophelia as a case study of "hysteria," a condition that affected only women.[21] Actresses whose own biographies echoed Ophelia's lovesick decline were particularly celebrated.[22] Likewise, part of the mythos surrounding Millais's painting was the recognizability of his model, Elizabeth Siddal.

Siddal and Millais were both connected to a circle of English artists and writers known as the Pre-Raphaelite Brotherhood. Officially formed in 1848 by three men—John Everett Millais, Dante Gabriel Rossetti, and William Holman Hunt—the group rejected what they saw as the mechanical classicism of the British academy. As their name suggested, they preferred the clarity of detail and intense color found in earlier, fifteenth-century art. Fueled by a romantic belief in individualism, Pre-Raphaelite painters sought to express "genuine ideas" in a serious and heartfelt way. To do so, they turned to the direct study of nature. Their artworks, like Millais's *Ophelia*, combined precise naturalistic detail with medieval or Christian narratives. Pre-Raphaelites favored tragic heroines: a sorrowful Persephone, an anguished Penelope, a doomed Beatrice, and a resigned Lady of Shalott, preparing to meet her death.

Siddal was a painter in her own right, but her biography has been entangled with the character of Ophelia and the expectation of a maiden. Siddal, who had been working at a hat shop in London, began modeling for the Pre-Raphaelite painters in 1849. Her tall frame, striking face, and copper-colored hair appear in numerous artworks by artists working as part of the Brotherhood. Quickly, though, she attracted the particular attention of painter and poet Dante Gabriel Rossetti. The two became engaged, and Rossetti encouraged Siddal in her own poetry and painting. She even exhibited with the Pre-Raphaelite Brotherhood in their 1857 exhibition.

The story of Siddal posing as Ophelia for Millais has been frequently recounted. Because of the Pre-Raphaelite commitment to working only from observation, Millais had Siddal float in a tub of water while he painted her partially submerged. Lamps were supposed to keep the water warm, but Millais became so engrossed in his work that he didn't notice when the lamps ran out of fuel and the water grew frigid. Siddal, at least in Millais's telling, was likewise so committed to her role as muse that she suffered silently. She caught a cold that developed into pneumonia. Her father threatened legal action until Millais agreed to pay for Siddal's medical bills. Siddal's health seems to have never fully recovered.

Ophelia was the last painting she posed for before her then-fiancé Rossetti banned her from modeling for anyone besides himself. That tumultuous, volatile relationship culminated with him rushing to her sickbed in 1860 and carrying her frail form to the church so they could be wed. Still weak, Siddal gave birth to a stillborn daughter in 1861, then died from an opiate overdose in 1862 while pregnant with her second child. Rossetti insisted that her death was accidental, not deliberate, though speculation about suicide abounded. Siddal's otherworldly beauty, physical decline, and tragic end all seemed to mirror the lives of the heroines she had previously portrayed, including Ophelia.

However, when Millais first exhibited *Ophelia* at the Royal Academy in 1852, the painting received mixed reviews. Some critics lauded its high level of detail, while others critiqued Ophelia's unconventional features and linked her drowning death and open mouth to symbols of sexual promiscuity.[23] One complained, "There must be something strangely perverse in an imagination which souses Ophelia in a weedy ditch, and robs the drowning struggle of that lovelorn maiden of all pathos and beauty, while it studies every petal of the darnel and anemone floating on the eddy."[24]

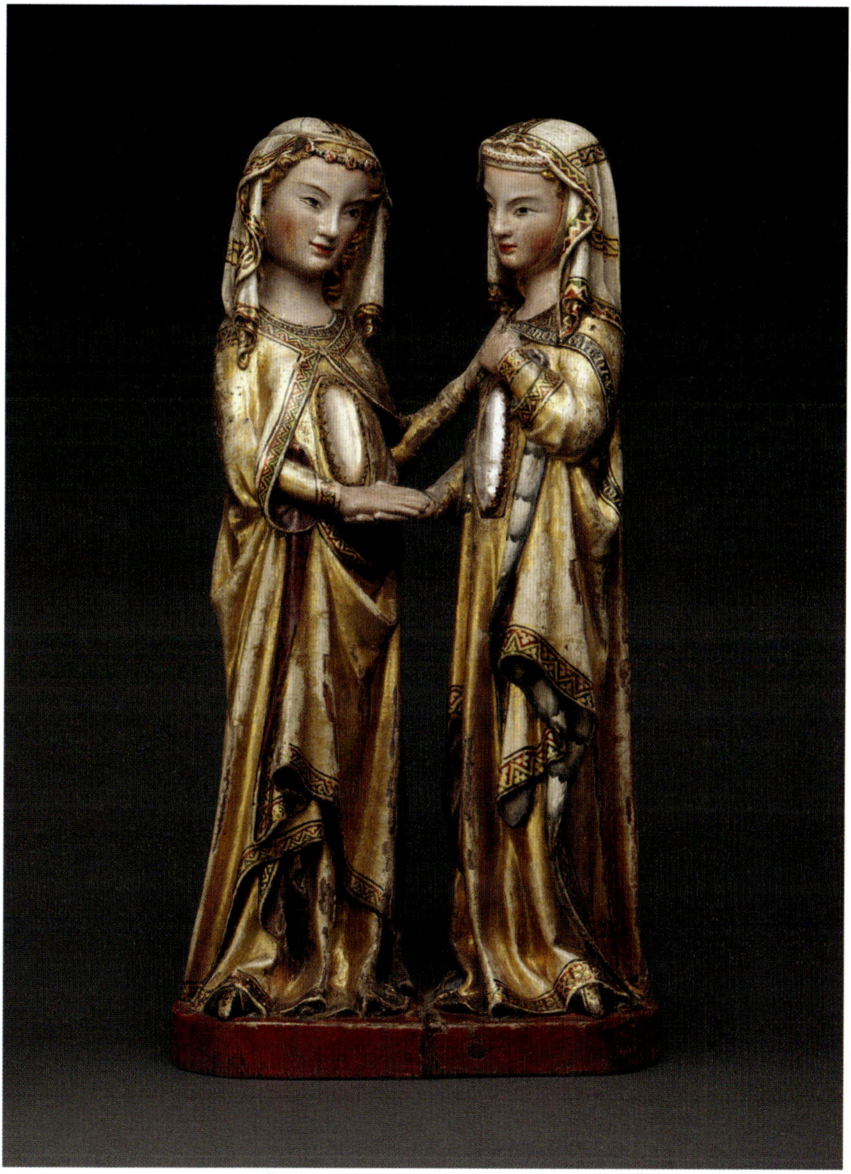

The Metropolitan Museum of Art, New York. Gift of J. Pierpont Morgan, 1917.

Heinrich of Constance, *The Visitation*, ca. 1310–20

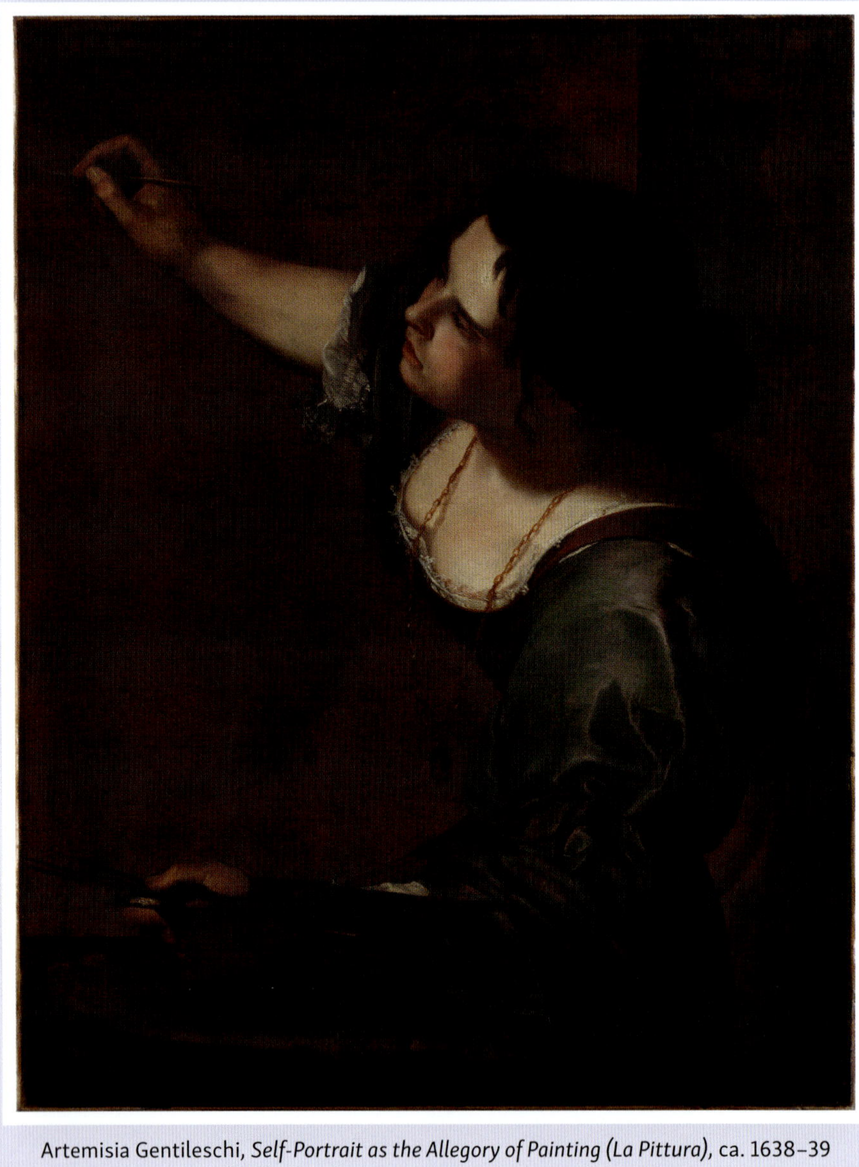

Artemisia Gentileschi, *Self-Portrait as the Allegory of Painting (La Pittura)*, ca. 1638–39

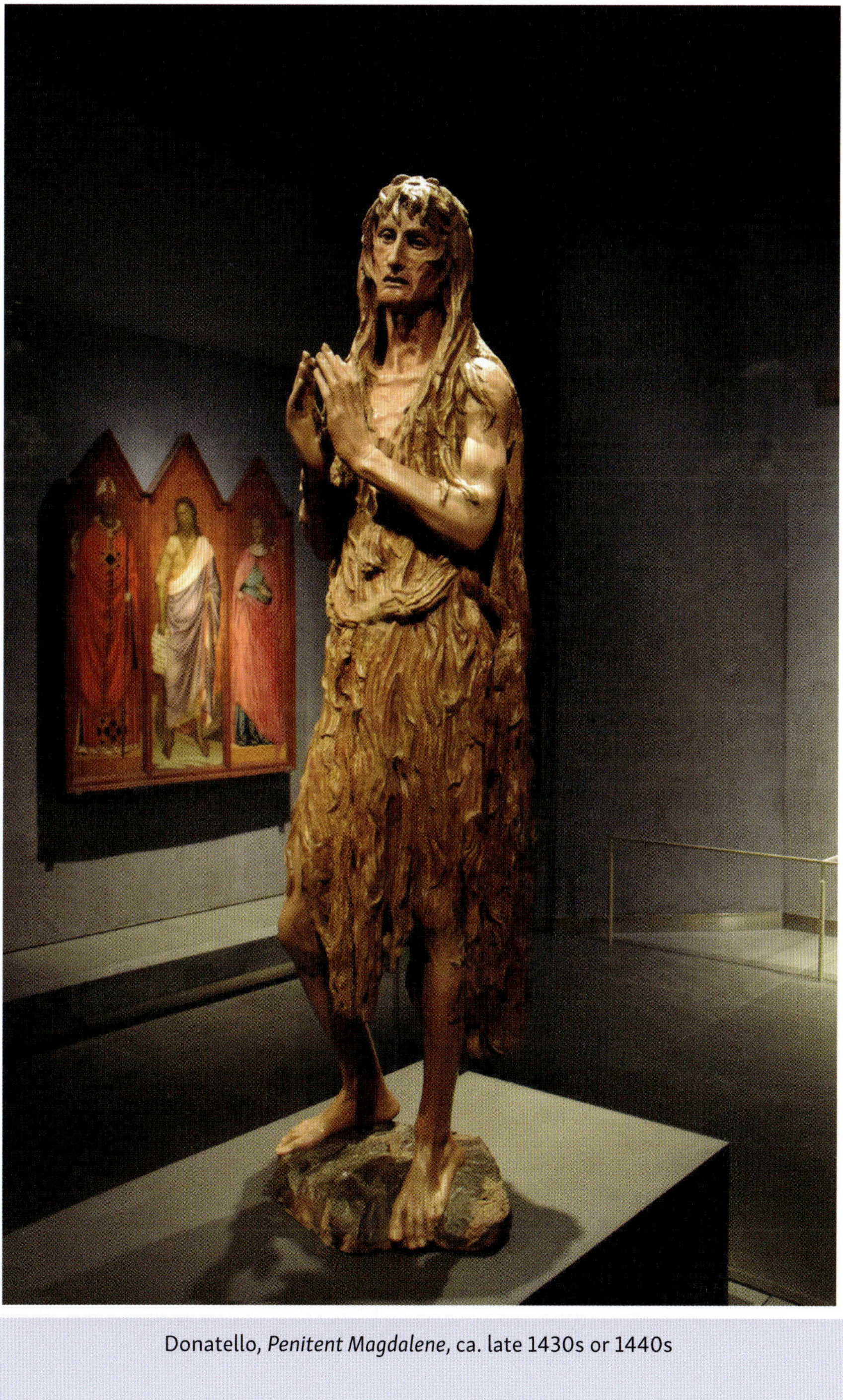

Donatello, *Penitent Magdalene*, ca. late 1430s or 1440s

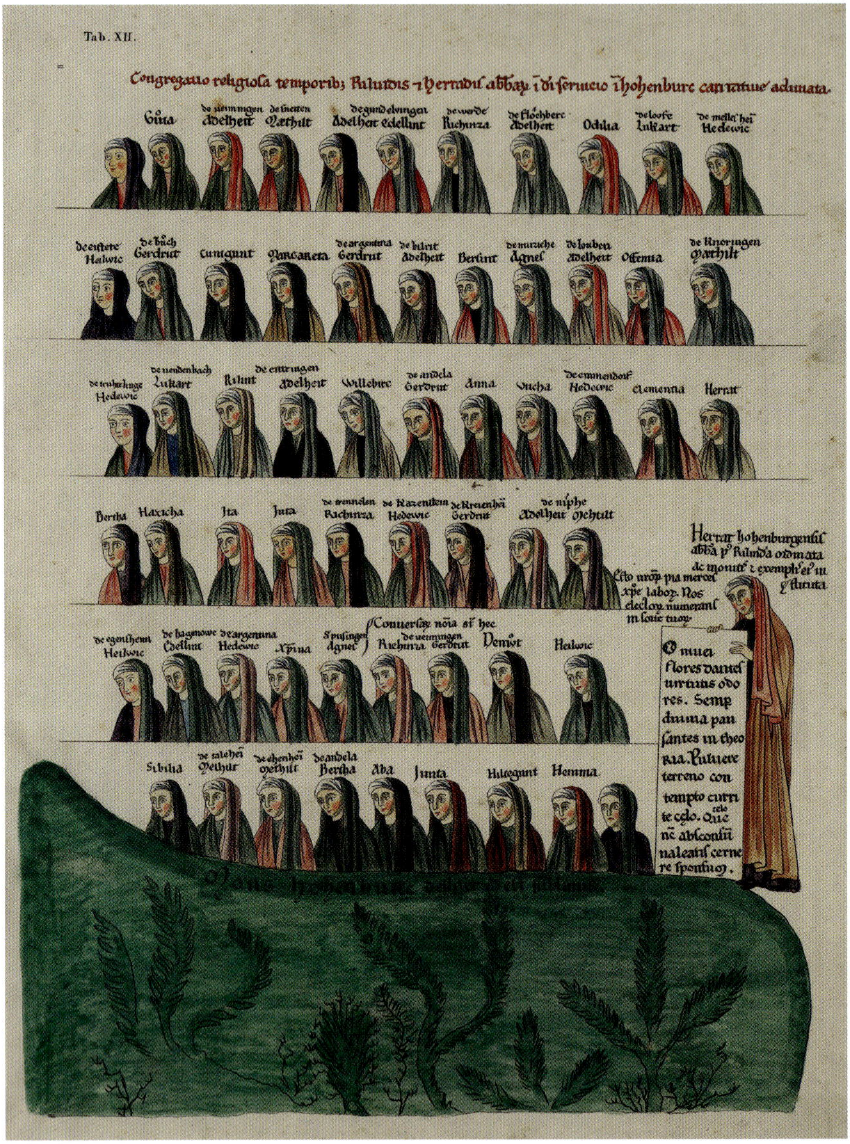

The women of Hohenburg Abbey as depicted in *Hortus Deliciarum*, fol. 323r, ca. 1167–85, from a facsimile made by Christian Moritz Engelhardt in 1818

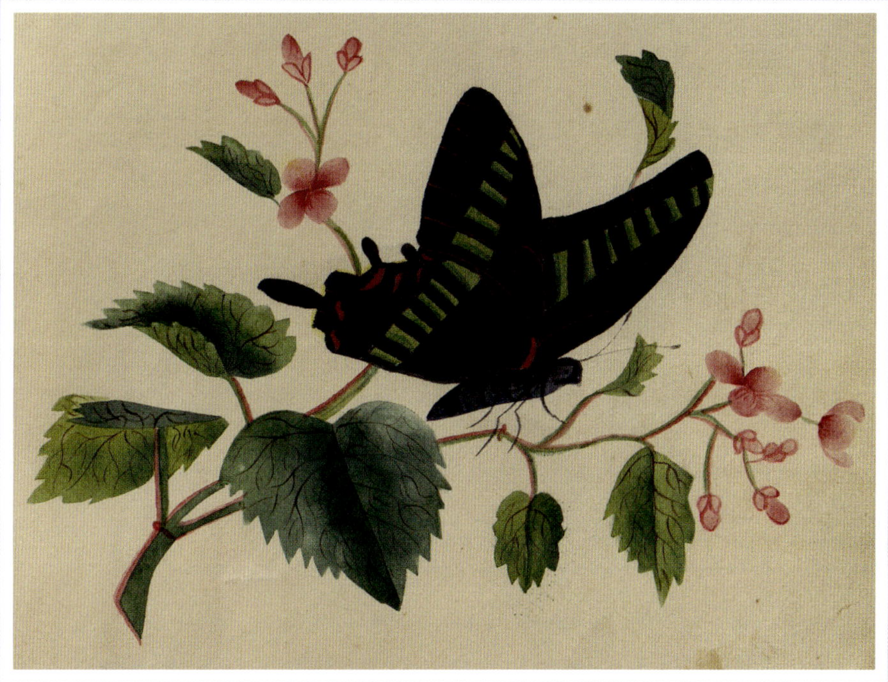

Sarah Mapps Douglass, *A Token of Love from Me, to Thee*, ca. 1833

Author photo

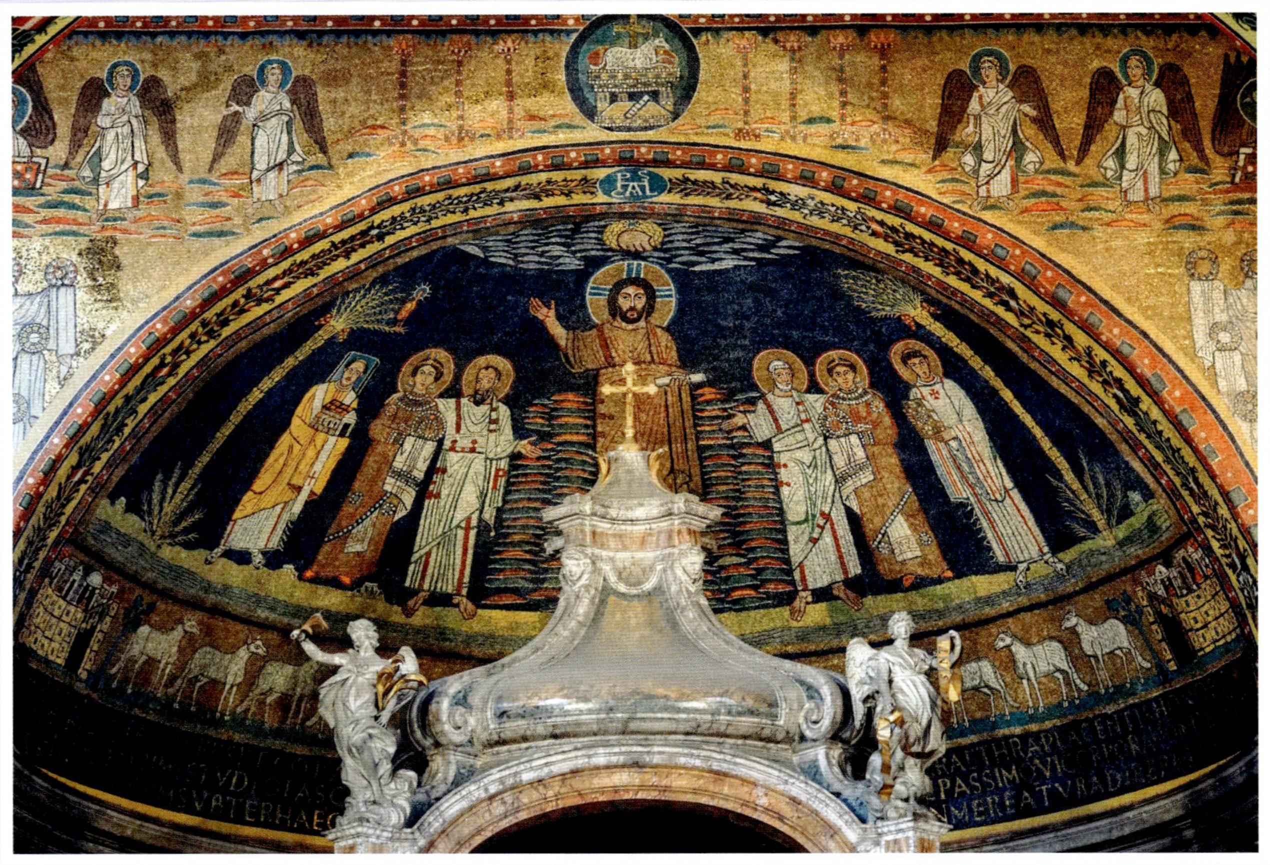

Apse mosaic of Santa Prassede, Rome, Italy, ca. 822

Importantly, the expectation was that a dead woman *should* be aesthetically pleasing. There were, after all, plenty of other women who seemed to be dying beautifully, not just in art but in life.

Beginning in late eighteenth-century England, cultural ideas about beauty became increasingly entangled with tuberculosis, a bacterial infection of the lungs that was often fatal. Called "consumption" at the time, the disease involved coughing up phlegm and blood, as well as other symptoms, such as diarrhea, fever, and emaciation. Yet doctors, poets, novelists, beauty writers, and preachers all described the effects of the illness as enhancing a woman's beauty. Bright eyes, a clear, pale complexion, and rosy cheeks were all seen as attractive qualities.

They also happened to be the symptoms of a progressive tuberculosis infection.

Women's beauty guides, such as *The Art of Beauty; or the Best Methods of Improving and Preserving the Shape, Carriage, and Complexion* (1825), acknowledged that the best way to achieve these ideals was to actually be consumptive. Failing that, the authors offered tips on applying subtle makeup or even making a concoction from the poisonous belladonna plant to enlarge pupils and darken eyelashes for that dewy glow.[25] Even women's posture was affected. Compressed shoulders and a slightly curved back were both fashionable *and* a result of consumption. For those women unfortunate enough to remain healthy, certain sleeve and bodice styles, with a sloping, narrow shoulder line and slender waist, could help them look more wilted or willowy (see fig. 3.6).[26]

This strange conflation of beauty and disease emerged from the Enlightenment reconception of women's bodies and moral nature. As we saw in the Vessel story, the two-sex model came into prominence during the Enlightenment, emphasizing the physical, emotional, and even spiritual differences between men and women. Whereas medieval theologians saw women as deformed males, prone to lust and indulgence, Enlightenment naturalists posited that women's physical weakness necessitated that they be protected from the demands of modern life. Industrialization in Western Europe furthered and expanded upon this belief. The shift from an agrarian, craft-based society to an urban, mechanized one hardened the separation between public and private spheres. While poor and working-class

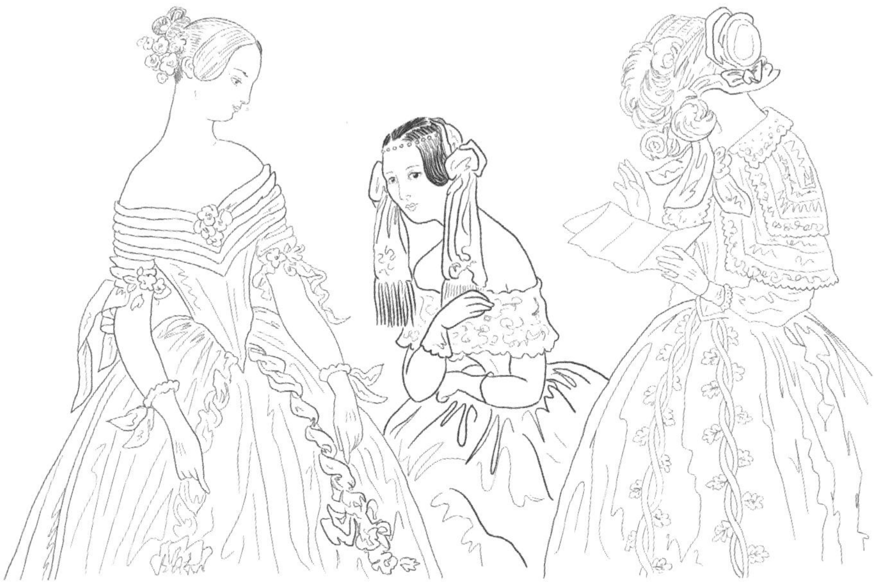

Figure 3.6. Drawn from a ca. 1840 fashion plate

women continued to work outside the home, middle- and upper-class women focused on domesticity as their "true," womanly calling. Associating religion with the home also led to the melding of piety with femininity. Due to their inherent fragility and sensitivity, women were now seen as being more naturally spiritual and morally upright than men, who necessarily spent their days in the cutthroat or even immoral worlds of business and politics.[27] It became the women's job to offer a steadying and uplifting hand to their husbands, sons, and society as a whole.[28]

What does this have to do with consumption? These beliefs about women's essential nature led nineteenth-century doctors to believe that tuberculosis was a *feminine* disease. Women's "sensibility," their capacity to respond to emotion and to beauty, was precisely what made them more susceptible to consumption.[29] In addition, their exceptional moral character also meant that they were expected to demonstrate saintly patience throughout their illness.[30] Femininity was, as medical historian Carolyn Day has pointed out, inextricably tied to suffering.[31] A strange, dangerous feedback loop developed: Women's supposedly superior morality made them more likely to suffer, but it also made them more beautiful, physically and spiritually.

Although the Pre-Raphaelites worked in the decades after consumption was in vogue, those who found Elizabeth Siddal attractive often connected her beauty to possible illness. A fellow artist remarked that she was looking "thinner and more deathlike and more beautiful and more ragged than ever."[32] What starts out seeming like a concern for Siddal's health ends up being a compliment on her appearance. Later, Rossetti's brother wrote that Siddal possessed "a consumptive taint," noting her "pink and white complexion" and "large-lidded eyes."[33] Based on these physical traits, he goes on to praise her character: "One could not have seen a woman in whose whole demeanor maidenly and feminine purity was more markedly apparent."[34] Judging from what we know of her symptoms and the rest of her life, scholars today think it unlikely that Siddal suffered from tuberculosis. But the story she was given—the story that made her beautiful—easily equated deathly illness with beauty and physical fragility with moral might.

As I read about Siddal, I find a reproduction of one of *her* artworks. The pen and ink drawing depicts a young woman in vaguely medieval dress sitting at her loom but turning over her shoulder to look out the window. The figure is doll-like, with the large eyes and heart-shaped face of an anime character. At first, I'm not sure what narrative Siddal is referencing, but the caption tells me this is *The Lady of Shalott* (1853).[35] I didn't recognize the narrative immediately because most other illustrations of Lord Alfred Tennyson's epic Arthurian poem depict the moment when the maiden is dead or on the brink of death, cursed for looking out the window directly onto Camelot.

Siddal, however, chooses a different scene. Instead of being gorgeously dead, admired by Sir Lancelot as she floats down the river, Siddal's Lady of Shalott is active. "Half-sick of chasing shadows," she turns from her mirror and looks directly out the window as Lancelot rides by.[36] Scholar Emily Orlando argues that this artistic selection is purposeful, "suggestive of windows of possibility."[37] Yet for the Lady of Shalott—and for Siddal herself, who dies in physical and mental distress—that window never becomes a door to walk through.

I want to roll my eyes at all this dying-to-be-beautiful business. And yet, excruciatingly skinny women still walk runways or lounge on beds, selling perfume and handbags. Alongside "body positive" content on social media, I am still served tips on how to flatten my belly and look good in a swimsuit. We persist in our obsessive belief that we can control our bodies' appearance if we are disciplined enough. Perhaps we just call it "health content" or "taming the flesh" instead of "consumption." I still tell myself that I *should* suffer on my runs, that there is always some slice of my body that could be whittled away just as there is always some vice or anxiety I should conquer. I may not be trapped in a tower or have been abducted by a lustful god, but I know full well how to contain myself in a tangled trap of deadly expectations.

Maidens to the Rescue?

Now that I am no longer young and single, the tug of the Maiden story seems less insistent. I wonder, for a while, if it's disappeared for good, buried beneath "The Future Is Female" T-shirts and young adult novels full of active female protagonists. But then it reappears in an unexpected place: scattered amid the YouTube advice being given to struggling boys and men.

By numerous measures, young men are in crisis.[38] They are falling behind in educational achievement. Unemployment rates are rising, while the number of men in intimate relationships is dropping. More men than ever report being lonely. Suicide rates for men have risen significantly over the past decade. Everyone from conservative pastors to progressive feminist moms are alarmed.[39] As the mother of adolescent boys myself, I find that the thick blanket of panic can be suffocating.

What's to blame? Some commentators point to economic factors. Others cite the fact that educational institutions have not been designed with boys' needs in mind. A third group argues that boys are purposeless in a society that no longer honors traditional male roles like "protector" and "provider." This explanation can sometimes be framed as a deliberate attack on masculinity by progressive elites.

It's here, in the so-called manosphere, that the Maiden story is told as a solution to the crisis. According to these commentators, women *need* to be dominated.[40] They want to be pursued, even when they say no. They long to be pampered and provided for, captured and contained in a glittering shell. In this telling, women must be maidens or else men will literally lose both their livelihood and their lives.

But why do we assume that our stories must be zero-sum games? To claim that men can be men only if women are maidens is to dehumanize us all. We need a bigger imagination. We need another story.

COUNTERSTORY:
Moving

Go, Girl

If Giambologna's *Abduction of a Sabine Woman* (1579–83) is the epitome of the Maiden story, then Elisabetta Sirani's *Timoclea Kills the Captain of Alexander the Great* (1659) seems like the perfect inversion. The painting depicts a dark-haired young woman in an elegant gown effortlessly tipping a bearded man into a garden well, red cloak billowing and legs flailing helplessly as he disappears. The story comes from Plutarch's *The Life of Alexander*. After pillaging a conquered city, one of Alexander the Great's captains sexually assaults a woman, Timoclea, then demands that she give him any hidden money in her possession. Timoclea lies, telling him there is money hidden at the bottom of the garden well. When the captain leans over to look, Timoclea pushes him in and kills him with heavy stones. But later, Alexander the Great himself clears her from guilt because of her obvious dignity and virtue. By choosing to paint the moment when Timoclea acts, Sirani flips an all-too-familiar story. In Giambologna's statue, the maiden is held aloft, about to be assaulted. In Sirani's painting, the assailant is literally toppled by the woman he just abused.

It's no wonder that when early feminist scholars were doing the hard, necessary work of rediscovering historical women artists, they celebrated paintings like this one by Sirani and Artemisia Gentileschi's *Judith Slaying*

Holofernes (which we discussed in chap. 2). As modern viewers, we interpret Gentileschi's Judith and Sirani's Timoclea as symbols of women's empowerment. The artists—and the women they depict—are heroines, strong, vital, and seemingly unrestrained by society's limiting expectations.

These older paintings align with current inversions of the Maiden story in popular culture. Instead of being contained, captured, or consumptive, girls and women in TV shows, movies, graphic novels, and illustrated books fend for themselves and save others as well. Disney princesses no longer wait patiently for a prince to show up. An emphasis on weightlifting for women and the increased visibility of women's sports in general have also pushed a new ideal of a muscled, capable body into the spotlight. The story of women as ideally passive, physically weak, and in need of rescue has been turned inside out.

But when it comes to Elisabetta Sirani, more recent historians have tempered our impulse to identify her as a seventeenth-century girl-power advocate. While Sirani was immensely successful and popular in her own time, the bulk of her work was still quite traditional, including paintings of the Madonna and child or familiar women-as-allegory scenes.[41] In addition, most of Sirani's paintings of heroic women were made for wealthy, male patrons in Bologna. *Timoclea Kills the Captain of Alexander the Great*, for example, was commissioned by the banker Andrea Cattalani.[42] For Cattalani, like a growing number of secular collectors, a painting *of* an extraordinary woman painted *by* an extraordinary woman was doubly valuable in its rarity. Although Sirani tried to expand the availability of artistic training to women in Bologna, taking on numerous female students, she was still seen as the *exception* rather than the rule. Her paintings of heroines were made for erudite male viewers to treasure as elite prizes.[43] They were not intended as imaginative guides for women in her own time, much less our own.

In our own contemporary, reactive culture, it's not surprising that #girlboss rhetoric is being flipped back again. A new wave of women identifying as "tradwives" or "stay-at-home girlfriends" has used social media to offer serene, lush visions of retreating to the domestic sphere. Rejecting aggressive heroics in the workplace, they celebrate the peace they find in nurturing and cultivating a home and family, often while invoking an imagined past of ruffled dresses and quietly clucking chickens.

The jerking, dramatic swings are predictable but exhausting. What would it look like to be propelled by hope instead?

Magdalene on the Move

The first time I saw a photograph of Donatello's *Penitent Magdalene* (ca. 1440) in an art history textbook, I thought someone had made a mistake in the caption. How could this life-sized wooden sculpture of a bedraggled, toothless woman be Mary Magdalene? And how could it be the work of Donatello, the fifteenth-century Florentine master best known for his sensuous, sinuous, bronze *David* (ca. 1430–40)?

Donatello depicts a woman with sunken eyes, gaunt cheeks, and long, wavy hair that falls to her knees, covering her like a shapeless, shaggy garment (see fig. 3.7). Her mouth opens slightly to reveal broken teeth. She is barefoot and seems about to take a step forward with her large, bony feet. From the side, it seems as if her hands are pressed together in a gesture of prayer, but from the front we can see that her fingertips are not yet touching.

The sculpture is full of contrasting elements. Donatello carves Mary Magdalene's long hair with rough, rippling grooves. At times it almost seems like he is imitating the bark of a tree trunk. Yet the Magdalene's arms and legs are smooth and supple, with particular, lifelike details. We can see the indentation of nail beds on her fingers and the veins and tendons in her feet. There's also a striking contrast between Mary Magdalene's face and limbs. Her

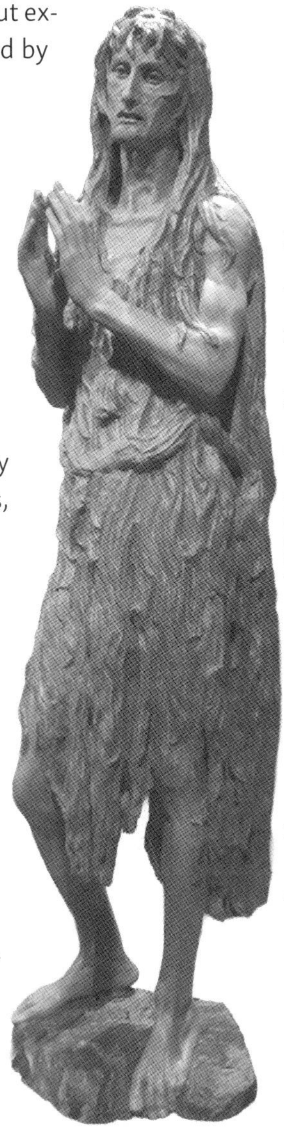

Figure 3.7. Donatello, *Penitent Magdalene*, ca. late 1430s or 1440s, white poplar and gilding. A full-color image of this sculpture is included in the color insert section.

face is lined and haggard; she has the hollow appearance of someone who has not had food or water in many days. And yet, her legs are those of a marathon runner, lean and sinewy. Her arms are visibly, strikingly muscular. We see the ripple of biceps and deltoids as she bends her elbows.

And there's one more surprise. If we look very closely, we can just make out traces of gold leaf highlighting the edges of her hair.

The visual story that Donatello tells is jarring to my modern eyes. This Mary Magdalene is not a sensual Venus. She has too much psychological complexity to be a Vessel for an allegory. She's also not a Maiden. She is not prettily contained, frozen in a frame like the profile portraits of women from the same period. Nor is she captured, like the woman held aloft in Giambologna's sculpture, outside in the nearby piazza. And though she may initially look consumptive with her gaunt cheeks, her muscular arms and legs contradict that impression. In her simultaneous disarray and determination, Donatello's *Penitent Magdalene* offers a counterstory crafted for women of his own time that can still be valuable today. The Magdalene is Moving, and she is moving toward wholeness.

What Mary Is This?

When Donatello carved his sculpture in the fifteenth century, Mary Magdalene was already a popular subject in Italian art and devotional literature. In the Gospels, Mary Magdalene is mentioned by name twelve times. Luke identifies her as a woman healed from evil spirits who then traveled with Jesus and his twelve apostles (Luke 8:1–3). The Gospel writers note her presence at Christ's crucifixion (Matt. 27:56; Mark 15:40; John 19:25) and burial (Matt. 27:61) and acknowledge her as one of the first witnesses of his resurrection (Matt. 28; Mark 16; Luke 24; John 20). In John's account, the risen Christ specifically tasks Mary Magdalene with telling the rest of his disciples the good news (John 20).

But in the sixth century, Gregory the Great—the bishop of Rome—preached a sermon that conflated Mary Magdalene with Mary the sister of Martha and Lazarus (Luke 10:39) and the "sinful woman" who anointed Jesus's feet (7:37–38). Mary Magdalene thus became known as a repentant prostitute, an idea that persists to this day.[44]

In the thirteenth century, a popular French text known as *The Golden Legend* expanded on the lives of numerous biblical figures and saints. According to the account in *The Golden Legend*, Mary Magdalene was an extraordinarily rich and beautiful prostitute who repented to follow Jesus. After Christ's ascension, Mary Magdalene withstood persecution, preached to the inhabitants of present-day France, performed miracles, and then spent the last thirty years of her life living a life of penance, alone in a desert cave. She neither ate nor drank but was sustained by angels who lifted her up daily to hear the songs of heaven.

Around this time, Mary Magdalene's story also absorbed the legend of another saintly Mary. According to a seventh-century text, Mary of Egypt ran away from home as a young teenager in order to slake her physical lust and then traveled to Jerusalem to seduce Christian pilgrims. But after a miraculous encounter with a holy image there, she converted, renounced her sinful lifestyle, and committed to living an ascetic life in the desert. Her formerly beautiful clothing disintegrated until she was covered by only her own hair.

Thus, by the fifteenth century, the woman who taught alongside the apostles and bore witness to the resurrection was an amalgam of many different women's stories. When depicting her in crucifixion scenes, artists typically depicted her with an alabaster jar—referencing the washing of Jesus's feet—and with long, uncovered hair, which could also symbolize her unbound sensuality as a former prostitute. Her time living as a hermit in the desert, when her hair covered her as a garment, was also a popular subject.

Over time, Mary Magdalene also became the patron saint of penitent sinners, repentant sex workers, expectant mothers, gardeners, and pharmacists. As one scholar notes, Mary Magdalene "is a cipher upon whom [people] could project their own concerns, fears, hopes, and spiritual aspirations."[45] I haven't found a "historically accurate" representation of Mary Magdalene in European art. But that's also not what I need. Rather than getting distracted by the biographical inaccuracies of this popular conception of Mary Magdalene, we can ask what we can learn from the stories artists have told about her, and to whom.

A Magdalene for Magdalenes

When Donatello carved his *Penitent Magdalene*, hairy Mary Magdalenes were not unusual. There are numerous thirteenth- and fourteenth-century painted examples in Florence that Donatello likely saw, most of them depicting Mary Magdalene standing in contrapposto like Venus but entirely draped in her own, floor-length hair.[46] There are also other wooden, life-sized sculptures of a hirsute Magdalene. In the earliest surviving examples from the town of Pescia, a town near Florence, Mary Magdalene stands erect, her face placid and her hands pressed together in prayer. Smoothly rendered tresses of blond hair entirely cover her body. To a modern viewer, she looks like Rapunzel awaiting rescue.

In contrast, the hair of Donatello's *Penitent Magdalene* is shaggy and uneven. She looks as if she cut her own bangs over the bathroom sink. She is also in motion. Her bent knee and lifting foot tell us that she is about to step forward, and the narrow gap between her hands suggests that she is in the act of pressing them together in prayer. She is not dramatic, like Artemisia Gentileschi's *Self-Portrait*, but her movement is deliberate.

Her face haunts me. It has haunted others too. The sixteenth-century painter and art critic Giorgio Vasari described her as "washed away by her fastings."[47] Subsequent commentators and scholars followed suit. She has been called a "thin wasted form," "only passive," and "not much more than a skeleton."[48] But these accounts miss the central contradiction of the sculpture. Her gaunt, lined face is coupled with the obvious strength of her body. Her sinewy neck and muscled arms and calves ripple with quiet, potential energy.

In scale and in substance, Donatello urges viewers to identify with Mary Magdalene. On her slightly mounded base, she stands just under six feet tall. Carved from poplar, the sculpture has an inherent softness and warmth. Unlike the cool polish of marble or gloss of bronze, wood seems more akin to actual flesh and hair. Magdalene tugs at our humanity perhaps more intimately and insistently than Bernini's icy cold Daphne.

So for whom did Donatello make this depleted but determined, somber but strong woman, so unlike other depictions of this biblical figure?

Unfortunately, no documents from the fifteenth century have been found that give us the exact date of the statue's creation or its intended location. For a long time, scholars believed that the sculpture was made late in Donatello's career. The expressiveness and psychological intensity of Mary Magdalene's face were seen as evidence of Donatello's awareness of his own mortality or even his repentance over his earlier, more sensuous sculpture.[49] However, some more recent discoveries have prompted a reassessment of this timeline; a number of scholars now accept that the *Penitent Magdalene* was made in the late 1430s or early 1440s, during the height of the artist's career.[50] We know that the sculpture was in the baptistery outside the Florence cathedral in 1500, but strangely it is not included in an inventory of the building's artworks from 1469.[51] So where did the sculpture live for the first sixty or so years of its existence?

Historian Martha Levine Dunkelman argues that Donatello was originally commissioned to make this sculpture not for the baptistery and the general public of Florence but for a very specific audience: *convertite*, or "converted prostitutes," at the convent of Santa Maria Maddalena di Cestello.[52] The convent was founded in the mid-thirteenth century specifically as a home for women who had left sex work. By the mid-fifteenth century, it was one of several such institutions in Florence.

Unfortunately, the church at Santa Maria Maddalena di Cestello has been renovated, rebuilt, and renamed, making a firm attribution impossible. Still, we have a few clues. Other records tell us that Donatello had a relationship with the convent's major patrons. Furthermore, a painting made for the convent in the 1480s contains a depiction of Mary Magdalene that is clearly influenced by Donatello's sculpture, right down to the muscular arms and barely touching hands.[53] Finally, as we've already seen, Mary Magdalene had—by this time—become a patron saint of reformed prostitutes. The subject makes sense for a convent of *convertite*.

What might the *Penitent Magdalene*'s original viewers have been like? In fifteenth-century Florence, prostitution occupied an ambivalent space. On the one hand, sex outside marriage, especially sex for hire, was seen as a clear violation of Scripture. On the other hand, prostitution was also justified as a means of preventing men from taking mistresses or compromising virtuous women of higher social class. Despite the stereotype of the lascivious, libidinous prostitute, most sex workers were economically vulnerable women. Because they were considered "fallen" women, Florentine law contained them to one marginal part of the city lest they taint other women.

Though they tended to be small and poorly funded, convents for *convertite* like Santa Maria Maddalena di Cestello offered a way for cities to reframe prostitutes as not just a necessary evil but a potential audience for evangelism and rescue. In sermons, especially ones specifically aimed at prostitutes during Lent, priests often emphasized that Mary Magdalene's body was the conduit of both her sin and her salvation.[54] The promise to sex workers was that though they may have sinned, they might also find peace with God through vows of renewed chastity and obedience. Though forgiveness and salvation ultimately depended on Christ's sacrifice, their new personal holiness, worked out through their bodies, demonstrated their deep, reciprocal love for Christ.[55]

In the sixteenth and seventeenth centuries, artists like Titian, Caravaggio, and Peter Paul Rubens tended to emphasize Mary Magdalene's physical beauty. Her supposed life as a prostitute gave artists permission to represent her nude or only partially clothed as she contemplates the evils of her past life and dedicates herself to a life of holiness.

Georges de La Tour's *Penitent Magdalene* (ca. 1640) also depicts a very different Mary from Donatello's sculpture. In La Tour's oil painting, a woman with porcelain skin and glossy, dark hair sits in the dark before a small table holding a framed mirror and flickering candle. Her face is turned away from the viewer, toward the candle, and her folded hands sit on a human skull that rests on her lap. The scene is sober but darkly beautiful. Deep shadows contrast with the pool of candlelight, and Mary Magdalene's perfectly smooth skin and hair seem to glow. La Tour's painting suggests that Mary Magdalene becomes *more* beautiful when she turns from her supposed life of prostitution and acknowledges her own finitude. Repentance—moving from one life to another—is like a makeover.

Donatello's *Penitent Magdalene*, however, makes no such promise. His Mary Magdalene may be living a reformed life, but she does not look all the better for it. Repentance is not a recipe for better skin, hair, and nails. The Penitent Magdalene is most definitely not a commercial for self-care. At the same time, Donatello's *Magdalene* neither devalues nor degrades the human body. Instead, the sculpture embraces the vital paradox of living as bodies in a world already and not yet redeemed by Christ, combining "terrible stress and enduring power."[56] Donatello gives the converted prostitutes—and now us too—an image of both perseverance and struggle.

Even if Donatello's *Penitent Magdalene* was not made for a convent, other evidence suggests that his sculpture would still have been understood as a call for active repentance. By the fourteenth century, images of Mary Magdalene in Florentine churches often included her holding a banner with the words "Do not despair, you who make a habit of sin, follow my example, renew yourself in God."[57] Such a message would also be fitting for a baptistery, where it was later housed.[58] Wherever she is located, the *Penitent Magdalene*—perpetually stepping forward with powerful arms, bent in prayer—asks viewers to follow her example and to move toward restoration.

Strengthen the Tired Hands

Standing in front of the sculpture in the Duomo Museum in Florence, I have to admit that I don't want Mary Magdalene's story. I'd rather be the enthroned Virgin Mary in the previous room or the elegant Magdalene grieving Christ in Michelangelo's nearby, unfinished *Pieta* (1547–55).

I shift my weight from one foot to the other. As I do, I can just make out the traces of gold that still glimmer on the edges of the *Penitent Magdalene*'s long, shaggy hair. This woman, who still seems so unbeautiful to my eyes, is crowned with stunning grace. Salvation does not give her an escape route. It gives her a pilgrim path. But she also does not have to wait for resurrection to be counted as loved and precious.

I'm still not sure that I *like* her, though. That reality suggests that there may be more of me in her than I'd like to admit.

I leave the original sculpture and walk over to a life-sized replica that the museum has on display. They invite visually impaired people and other guests to "see" the art by running their hands over the surface of the copy. Unlike the original, which is elevated on a plinth and behind glass, the touchable replica is just barely raised off the floor. Mary Magdalene's hands are directly in front of my face.

I move. Tilting my head to mirror her pose, I slide my hands in between hers. Our fingers tangle together in supplication (see fig. 3.8).

My story is not that of a reformed prostitute for whom the sculpture was first made, and yet my own body bears marks of living in a broken world. I am not untouched by what I have experienced or by what I have done. But I am also not alone. Gazing steadily at the *Penitent Magdalene*, I roll my shoulders back and feel the crackle in my breastbone as my own anxieties release.

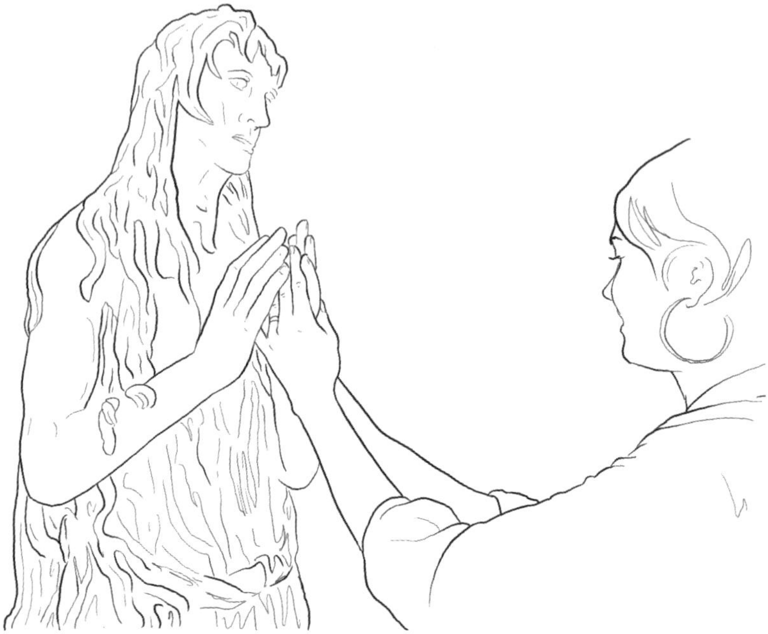

Figure 3.8. Holding hands with a replica of Donatello's *Penitent Magdalene*, drawn from a photograph by Christiana Fitzpatrick, 2018

This may not be the historical figure of Mary Magdalene, but at its core, the visual story that Donatello tells is a biblical one. After all, the Christian life is one characterized by active repentance, not stubborn defensiveness or passively awaiting Christ's return. We are a people on the move. The *Penitent Magdalene* prompts me to action, to acknowledge both my brokenness and my belovedness while walking forward in faith. The *Magdalene*'s muscular arms bring Hebrews 12:12–13 to mind: "Therefore, strengthen your tired hands and weakened knees, and make straight paths for your feet, so that what is lame may not be dislocated but healed instead." She is Moving toward wholeness, in faith, and she invites us to do the same.

4

Mother

Madonna of the Christmas Stamps

Long before I became a mother, I already knew the Mother story. During my short-lived stint as a middle-school stamp collector, I devoted an entire page in my album to Christmas stamps depicting the Madonna and child. Images of the Virgin Mary holding the infant Christ have been a mainstay in Western art history, and most of the stamps featured Italian paintings from the fifteenth through eighteenth centuries. There was Ludovico Carracci's image of Mary cuddling a plump Christ child, Antonello da Messina's placid Mary holding a mischievous toddler, and Antoniazzo Romano's painting of Christ holding his mother's neck with one hand and clutching a goldfinch in the other. But my favorite was the tightly cropped view of Paolo de Matteis's *Adoration of the Shepherds* (1712).

The original painting depicts Joseph, homely shepherds, curious villagers, an ox, a donkey, and an exuberant, floating cherub all clustered around Mary and Jesus in the darkened interior of a stable. The Christmas stamp crops everyone else out and zooms in on the two most important figures (see fig. 4.1). Mary, wearing pale pink and draped in a blue cloak with a white veil, gazes tenderly down at the chubby, curly-haired infant lying on the straw before her. Both figures' luminous peach skin contrasts sharply with the dark background. Importantly, the scene's light emanates not from a candle or a lantern but from the infant Christ himself. A glowing halo surrounds his head and illuminates his mother's face. They look adoringly at each other, their gazes forming an implied line that binds them together. Their pale skin blends together, and their bodies merge to create a stable, triangular composition. Mother and son are a single visual unit; their physical closeness suggests their emotional intimacy and mutual devotion. The only thing that seems to exist in Mary's world is her beloved son.

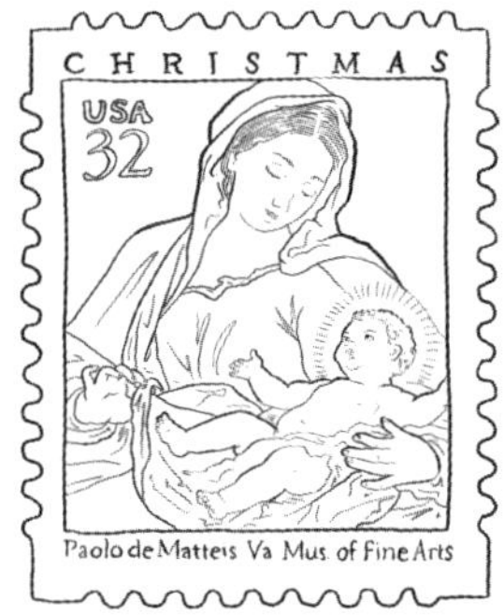

Figure 4.1. Drawn from the 1996 United States Postal Service traditional Christmas stamp

As a young girl, I imagine that motherhood will look this way for me. I will be utterly content just to hold and gaze upon my child for hours on end. Nothing else could possibly matter as much.

But a dozen years later, I'm enrolled in an art history doctoral program and set on a path that tends to expect undivided commitment. Frankly, I'm often fine with that demand. I love my coursework. I adore the thrilling challenges of pulling together the threads of an argument, of explaining a difficult concept to undergraduate students, of finding a connection between objects that no one else noticed before. My brain feels utterly alive, like a plant flourishing under just the right conditions.

I wonder: Will that disappear if I become a mother? Will I no longer find combing through archives to be as thrilling as I do now?

If pregnancy "just happened" in the course of my marriage, I would be excited—even elated. But a visit to the doctor confirms some long-held suspicions: I won't be getting pregnant without some amount of medical intervention. Those treatments come with a myriad of side effects and financial costs but no guarantee of success. "Do you want to put your body through that?" my husband asks gently. My mother—who knows firsthand the sting of infertility and lost pregnancies—cries with me on the phone and reminds me that I'm still worthy of love, regardless of my maternal status.

I feel like I'm caught in an impossible tangle. How do I unwind my own desires from the external expectation that I should be willing to dedicate seemingly unlimited time, emotional energy, and money to achieve motherhood? And what *is* this goal that I would be pursuing, exactly?

Multiple visions of motherhood have existed in Western art for millennia, but one narrow visual script dominates. This Mother is beautiful, placid, and entirely focused on and fulfilled by her child. In evangelical circles, the Mother story carries spiritual urgency. Having children is often synonymous with being a godly woman. Yet a virtually identical Mother story shows up in celebrity portraits, influencers' posts, inspirational calendars, and vaguely Impressionist paintings in the gynecologist's office. She appears in humanitarian ads, imploring us to care for her child's wellbeing with even a fraction of her commitment. To be a Mother is to enact a story of total care for and ultimate devotion to one's children.

Tired Mary and the Old Man Baby

It seems obvious that the many Madonna and child images, like the ones in my stamp collection, are the visual source for this particular script. But the Mary currently projected in my graduate school art history survey course does *not* fit the brief. As soon as the professor flashes the image on the screen, students across the three-hundred-person class begin to giggle quietly. A particularly cheeky architecture student raises his hand. "Did the artist, like, never see an actual baby?" he asks. In the back row of the auditorium, another teaching assistant leans over to me and whispers, "He definitely saw a tired mom, though."

The painting sparking all this debate is a stylized, half-length depiction of the Madonna and child painted around 1230 by Italian artist Berlinghiero (see fig. 4.2). Christ, dressed in red, perches on Mary's left arm, while she gestures toward him with her right hand. Her head and body, draped in a dark-blue robe, seem to curl toward and around her son. The figures are set against a glimmering gold background, with halos etched into the surface.

Jesus, to the students' amusement, seems more like a miniature man than a human baby. His posture is erect, his proportions are closer to those

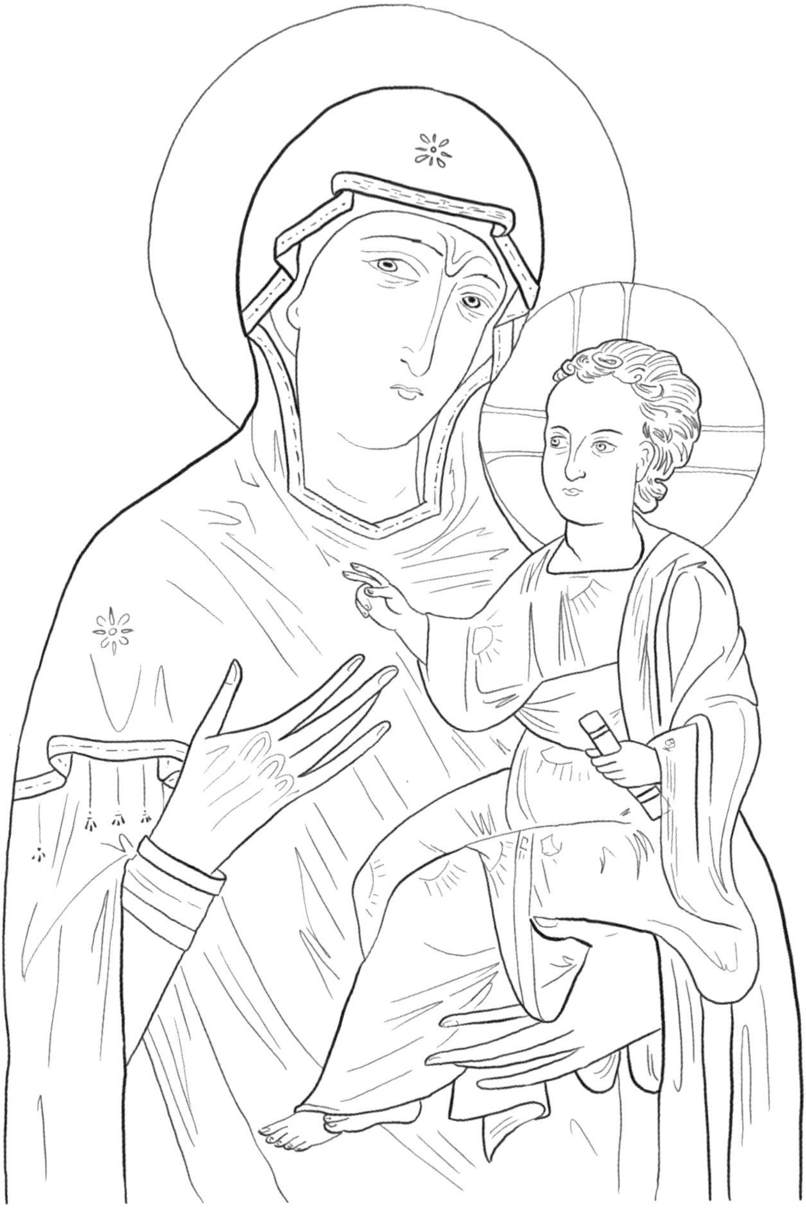

Figure 4.2. Drawn from Berlinghiero, *Madonna and Child*, ca. 1230s

of an adult, and even his hairline seems to belong to a middle-aged man. He holds what seems to be an absurdly large red crayon in his hand, though the professor says that it represents the scroll of the Law. Mary, meanwhile, has impossibly long, spindly fingers with no discernible knuckles. And her facial expression—a tiny, pinched mouth, averted eyes, and a deep pucker between her furrowed brows—reads as either "very stressed" or "constipated." But Berlinghiero's Madonna isn't sad because her son has teething pains or cries inconsolably every time she leaves to use the bathroom. As the professor of our Introduction to Western Art class explains, this image of the virgin and child is an icon, an image intended to direct a viewer's prayer and teach them something about the represented figures.

Depictions of Mary and the Christ child were not common in the earliest days of Christianity. As the church grew, however, representing Mary became a way to emphasize key doctrines such as the mystery of Christ's dual divine and human natures and the necessity of his incarnation.[1] To reiterate these concepts, artists developed a visual theology that could be used to teach the faithful.

This is what we see in Berlinghiero's painting. The gold background indicates that we are looking at a spiritual reality, different from our present, physical one. Mary wears blue to symbolize her purity, while Christ's red garment represents the blood he will shed for the salvation of his people. Christ holds the Law in his hand because he is, according to the apostle John, the Word made flesh. Even his peculiar hand gesture has symbolic significance. His middle and index fingers pressed together remind viewers of his two natures—human and divine—united in one person, and his thumb creating a circle with the remaining fingers references the Trinity.

So then, why does Berlinghiero's Jesus look like a miniaturized man instead of a wiggling infant? The devotional image emphasizes that Christ is *unlike* human children. It is the work he performs as a man that makes him worthy of our worship. Mary's sorrowful expression, meanwhile, indicates that she is contemplating her son's fate, anticipating his sacrifice. Mary and Jesus don't look like a "real" mother and infant because, the icon reminds us, they were *not* a typical mother and son.

By the time that Berlinghiero painted his *Madonna and Child* in the early thirteenth century, additional ways of representing Mary were gaining popularity in the Western church. Through the plagues, wars, natural disasters, and church upheavals that afflicted Europe throughout the twelfth and thirteenth centuries, Jesus seemed more like a stern, distant judge. Longing for stability, anxious Christians sought comfort in the person of the Virgin Mary, Christ's mother. Theologians and popular preachers in Western Europe expanded further upon Mary's life and her role in human salvation. Mary, some believed, was born without sin herself, and her body ascended to heaven when she died. Other teachings insisted that Mary remained a virgin for her entire life, wholly consecrated to God. The virgin was venerated as the bride of Christ, the personification of the church, queen of heaven, and intercessor for the salvation of humankind.[2] She sat on glittering thrones in church mosaics, crowned in glory beside Christ himself.

Furthermore, Mary's devotion and commitment to her son offered both a model for Christians to follow and the hope that her compassion would extend to common sinners. The mother of God could be a mother to us all. One especially literal variation of this was the "Madonna of mercy," a type of image in which Mary towers over clusters of tiny worshipers, spreading her blue, star-studded cloak over them like a tent. Still, as in the stiff Berlinghiero painting, these Marys were so *unlike* other women that she could hardly be a model for actual mothers to follow. A medieval mother might long to receive Mary's tender care, but she would hardly aspire to be like Mary herself. Where, then, did the Mother story we know today come from?

The Impossible Mother

After long, roller-coaster months, anxious waits under buzzing fluorescent lights in a fertility specialist's office, and many prayers, my husband and I see a flickering heartbeat on a grainy, black-and-white screen. I'm pregnant. We're ecstatic and grateful and terrified as we try to imagine a new life as a family of three. As I begin researching pregnancy health recommendations, I also start to pay attention to public expressions of motherhood in a way I hadn't previously.

I learn from an issue of *Vogue* magazine that Oscar-winning actress Gwyneth Paltrow quit Hollywood and spent the first year of her daughter's life caring for her full-time while touring with her husband's band. Now a mother of two, she has researched the ingredients in every snack for health risks, developed a set of easy go-to meals to cook, determined a stylish "mom uniform," and maintained her body thanks to two-hour-a-day workouts. When she chose to return to acting, she was somehow even better and more focused than before, able to get her work done and return home, where she can "follow [her kids] around" and "do what they want to do."[3] Paltrow's approach to motherhood seems to echo some of the expert books on child development and attachment theory that I've begun reading. I half imagine a reality in which I quit graduate school to devote myself entirely to power-walking miles with a stroller and researching what baby toys will be maximally safe and educational.

Unbidden, an image of another celebrity mom—once glimpsed on the cover of a fashion magazine—comes to mind (see fig. 4.3). The slender supermodel wears a glamorous, silvery gown, framed against a summery blue sky and green meadow. One hand reaches down to gather the folds of her dress, and her body curves into an elegant pose. And there, on her hip, she holds her naked, chubby son. Mother's and child's heads press together gently, and their shared bright-blue eyes, creamy skin, and rosebud lips further unify their bodies. She is both effortlessly beautiful and effortlessly maternal, perfectly in tune with her child, who seems utterly content. Instead of recalling a *medieval* image of the virgin and child, however, this contemporary image—and dozens of others like it—follows a model begun in the Italian Renaissance.

In the early fifteenth century, artists in Italy grew increasingly interested in emphasizing Christ's *humanity* as an infant. Scholars continue to debate the reasons for this shift, but the illusionism that developed meant that mischievous, sleepy, or tender, roly-poly toddlers became the preferred way to represent Jesus. The gold backgrounds were replaced with believable landscapes or detailed, domestic interiors. In one of the numerous images of the Madonna and child produced by Sandro Botticelli's workshop, a chubby toddler Christ with chestnut curls perches on his mother's lap and nuzzles against her cheek (see fig. 4.3). Mary presses her son against her while gazing dreamily into the distance. She seems to be entirely focused on soaking in her son's closeness. Like earlier

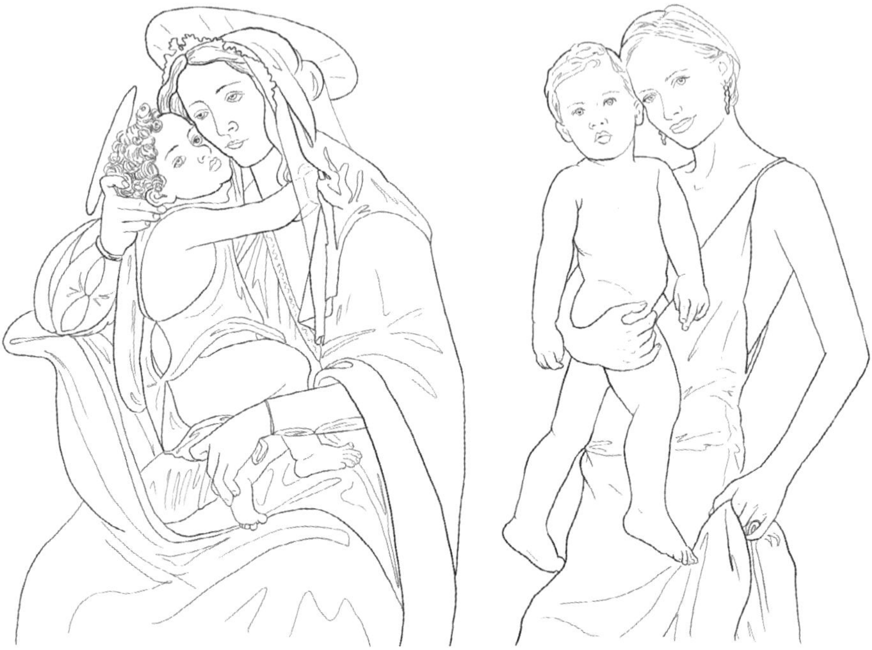

Figure 4.3. Supermoms, drawn from Botticelli's workshop, *Madonna and Child*, ca. 1490s, and *Vogue*, July 2002 cover, shot by Annie Leibovitz

Madonna and child paintings, their bodies still form a familiar, stable, triangular composition, and Mary still wears blue. But Christ's body seems to have weight and energy, and his pudgy hand reaches toward his mother with sweet contentment. Even with the delicate, gold halos that still hover around his and Mary's heads, he looks like a far more believable, squirming baby than his medieval predecessors.

Yet as Western European artists like Botticelli took greater pains to emphasize Christ's humanity, the same cannot be said for Mary. Certainly, on the surface, the proportions and modeling of her face and body are more believable than Berlinghiero's flat, pinched-face Mary. Relieved of her theological duty to call attention to Christ's incarnation and impending sacrifice, she ostensibly becomes a relatable woman, a mother cuddling her adorable baby. But this new Mary is also reliably, perpetually calm, perfectly attired, and utterly removed from the lived experience of motherhood. Renaissance-era Madonnas never have dark bags beneath their eyes. They never sweat, and they certainly never appear to be on the verge of swearing in frustration. The parts of early motherhood that include clogged milk ducts, dirty diapers, endless laundry, picky eaters, public meltdowns, medical bills, and sleepless nights go unremarked upon.

The Renaissance Madonna is a believable confection of motherhood, just close enough to reality that she functions as an aspirational guide. She is the template for my postage stamp Madonnas and for the supermodel and Hollywood moms whose images appear on the covers of magazines and in my Pinterest feed. To be clear, the glamorous celebrity moms are not dressing up as Mary or trying to make a religious statement. They do, however, present themselves as *good*, not just beautiful.

During my first pregnancy, the overlap between a Renaissance religious painting and a contemporary celebrity photograph does not seem particularly strange to me. If anything, it reaffirms that the singular Mother story they tell is natural and true. Likewise, the approaches to motherhood promoted by both secular and evangelical culture reiterate the same script: A mother's virtue is measured through her utter devotion to her child.

In their 2004 book *The Mommy Myth*, sociologists Susan Douglas and Meredith Michaels chart the extraordinary pressures applied to mothers in the late 1980s and into the 1990s. At precisely the same moment that more women than ever were entering the workforce—due to desire, economic necessity, and a host of other reasons—the expectations of motherhood were also rapidly increasing.[4] Douglas and Michael's book considers how changes in parenting advice, the twenty-four-hour news cycle, advertisements, and the emergence of celebrity moms all played a role in this steady transformation into all-consuming mothering. There were more reasons than ever to be afraid of what could befall your child *and* more examples than ever of perfectly manicured women with rich, attractive, committed husbands and children who had consistent sleep schedules, ate all their vegetables without complaining, and loved to sit quietly while neatly completing elaborate craft projects. Celebrity profiles suggested that the physical, emotional, and intellectual well-being of both women and children was entirely under a mother's control. As mommy blogs and social media continued to grow, the message was everywhere.[5]

If you just prayed—or meditated—enough, woke up early, read the right books, cooked the right food, chose the right discipline philosophy, and had a good planner, you, too, could experience the utter contentment described by Hollywood moms. There was another, unspoken implication. If your kid had a meltdown over a missing pacifier or you couldn't fit back into your prepregnancy jeans, then *you* were the only one to blame.

The demands of all-in mothering seemed fairly in line with the books on "biblical womanhood" that I had read in high school. In *Let Me Be a Woman*, for example, Elisabeth Elliot writes, "Motherhood requires self-giving, sacrifice, suffering. It is a going down into death in order to give life."[6] Certainly, because of the fall, self-denial needs to be part of any flourishing human relationship, including motherhood. But I understood Elliot to be saying that motherhood demands self-annihilation in a way that other relationships, including fatherhood, do not. She also asserts that this position is countercultural, resisting what she sees as the devaluing of motherhood in the so-called secular world, especially among feminists. Yet again, with the spiritual language stripped away, the argument that motherhood is both a woman's most fulfilling task and something that requires total commitment is perfectly consonant with what *The Mommy Myth* authors called the "new momism" of the early 2000s.[7]

It is easy to extend Mary's virtuous devotion not just to the supermodel mom on the magazine cover but to the solemn Central African women in photographs used to solicit humanitarian aid. Thin and silent, they hold their frail children in their lap while gazing steadily back at the camera.[8] I assume that they, too, are noble, worthy mothers, beset by tragedy but caring only for their children. Indeed, it is *because* I see these women as blameless, self-sacrificial mothers that I am compelled to donate to the organization's cause. Living into the Mother story and being a good woman seem virtually interchangeable.

But does a woman have to be a mother to be a good woman at all? If a woman—particularly a married woman of a certain age—does not look like the Madonna, she is often the object of questions and scrutiny. Contemporary politicians, religious leaders, and online commentators have publicly slandered women without biological children as selfish, soulless, and incapable of caring for others. The absence of motherhood is interpreted as an absence of virtue.

Reforming Motherhood

Yet the equation of motherhood with moral superiority was not always the case. Throughout the medieval era and into the Renaissance, virginity and celibacy were a woman's highest expressions of piety. Unmarried women without children—women like the sisters of St. Katharinenthal convent and Hildegard of Bingen—were celebrated for their devotion to Christ and the church. By joining a religious order, women demonstrated their commitment to God by denying themselves the bodily pleasure of marriage and family.[9]

Following the Protestant Reformation, this attitude underwent a dramatic shift in significant parts of Western Europe. Martin Luther, the leading German Reformer, ushered in a new emphasis on marriage in the church.[10] This developed in part from his belief that salvation was a gift, not earned, and that all believers had access to God, without the hierarchy of the Catholic Church. The celibate life, Luther declared, had no greater merit than other vocations. Marriage was part of God's divinely ordained plan to "fill the earth, and subdue it" (Gen. 1:28). As wives, women could be a companion to men, bear them children, and help satisfy and control men's sexual appetites. While the relationship was to be based in love and mutual care—not a means of abuse or political and financial gain—wives were expected to follow what Luther saw as a creational structure and obey their husbands. Sermons, books, and printed pamphlets by other Protestant preachers took up this position. A well-ordered household—where wives submitted to their husbands while bearing and caring for children—could be a foretaste of heaven.[11]

In Western art history, we see evidence of this shift in seventeenth-century paintings from the newly formed, primarily Protestant Dutch Republic. The rejection of Catholic practices and beliefs resulted in images largely being banned from churches. Instead, the burgeoning middle class—fueled by Dutch exploration and colonization—began to fill their homes with new kinds of images: landscapes, still lifes, portraits, and genre scenes. Paintings of the Virgin Mary virtually disappeared, but the image of a devoted Mother did not. In everyday scenes of spinning wool, sewing, cooking, nursing, writing, reading, and even picking lice out of their children's hair, Dutch mothers became a fixture in Protestant art.

Pieter de Hooch's *Mother Nursing Her Child* is one example of the Madonna-fication of Dutch Protestant women (see fig. 4.4). As the title suggests, the oil painting depicts a woman seated on a stool in her bedroom, breastfeeding her swaddled baby. De Hooch anchors the composition on the stable form of the woman. Her wide skirt, the rocking bassinet to the right, and the seated dog to the left join together to create a sturdy triangle. The woman, dressed in red and blue with a white cap, seems to glow against the darkened background. Light also pours in through a window near the stairs, visible through a door on the left-hand side of the painting.

In many ways, the painting is very similar to paintings of the annunciation—or Gabriel's announcement to Mary in Luke 1—that were made for the Catholic Church in preceding centuries. In those images, Mary is often shown kneeling or sitting in her bedchamber, dressed in red or blue, with a window allowing a beam of light—or the Holy Spirit—into the space. De Hooch keeps many of these elements, but instead of representing the Virgin Mary or painting a particular Dutch woman, he paints an everywoman, someone his buyers would associate with Dutch women in *general*. A woman literally nurturing her child, accompanied by a familiar symbol of marital fidelity—a dog—indicates a rightly ordered, virtuous household and, by extension, a well-ordered republic.

Or does it? There remains some debate among scholars over how we should understand these paintings. Are they patriarchal constructions, meant to subordinate women?[12] Or are they evidence of the value placed on women and the home, especially at a time when so many husbands were gone to war or at sea?[13] Did the women who viewed these paintings see them as stifling or as affirming their place in the new republic?[14]

Protestant theology certainly elevated the roles of wife and mother for women, a change that affected women across social classes. The emphasis on reading the Bible for oneself, rather than depending on the interpretation of a priest, also created new educational opportunities for middle- and

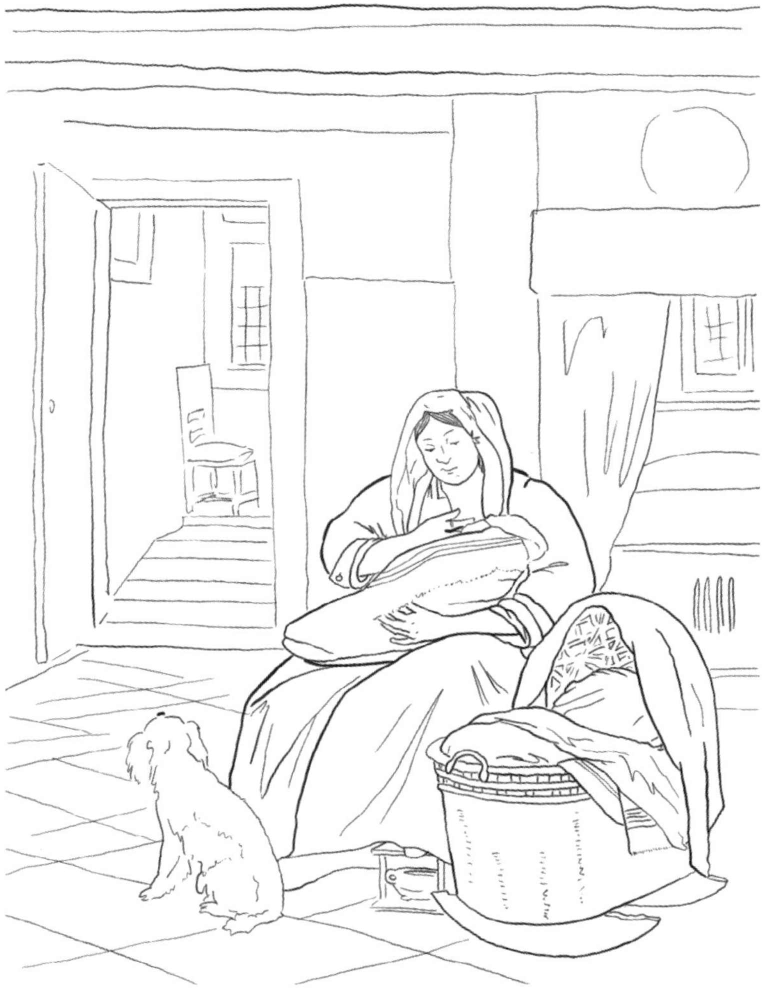

Figure 4.4. Drawn from Pieter de Hooch, *Mother Nursing Her Child*, ca. 1674–76

upper-class girls. At the same time, some earlier options that existed for wealthy women—such as joining a convent to pursue a life of service and teaching—largely disappeared. Women's divine purpose would be found by embracing their sexuality and fertility within the bounds of marriage rather than denying their desires in a religious order. Motherhood, not celibacy, would be the highest virtue.

Ironically, even as Protestants demoted Mary from her unique position within Catholic thought, they imbued motherhood itself with a kind of mysterious holiness. Mary was no longer distinctively virtuous as the mother of God; rather, all women were offered the opportunity to distinguish themselves as devoted mothers. Eventually, as we've already seen, a supermodel could be as good as the Madonna.

A Natural Fit?

Well into my final trimester of pregnancy, I stand in Target's infant bedding aisle, trying to figure out what swaddling blankets should go on our baby gift registry. Are they supposed to be a specific size? Is a polyester blend okay, or am I supposed to get only 100 percent cotton? As I sift through options, a gray-haired woman pushes her cart by and says in passing, "Don't worry. It will all come naturally once Baby is here."

I feel a panicky pressure in my chest. She's well-meaning, but she has also managed to hit upon a particular fear that goes far beyond baby blankets. What if "it"—what if motherhood—*doesn't* come easily to me? What if I can't immediately identify and satisfy my child's needs? What if I make a choice that ends up endangering or damaging them? Does that mean something is fundamentally broken in me as a woman?

Of course, motherhood has a physical component, and some of this anxiety can be blamed on pregnancy hormones. But my fears also point to another part of the Mother story: the assertion that total maternal devotion is not just desirable but *natural*. The stranger's attempt at encouragement echoes beliefs in certain conservative evangelical circles. An essay in the popular book *Recovering Biblical Manhood and Womanhood* argues not just that men and women are biologically different from each other but that those physiological differences determine "a divinely ordained . . . division of gifts between the sexes."[15] That is, generalized differences between male and female biological systems—like how quickly we digest food or how we respond physically to stress—are the root cause of different social roles for men and women. In this view, women are formed on an essential level to be nurturers and thus the primary caregivers and teachers of children.

A similar logic—just without theological language—seems to underpin much of the online advice I am finding for expectant mothers. Practices like breastfeeding, co-sleeping, and babywearing are extolled as "natural" choices. For some women, these approaches offer a means of resisting what they see as the medical establishment's disregard for mothers' intuitive knowledge. For others, scientific studies on the virtues of breastmilk or disciplinary approaches offer authoritative proof that "natural mothering" secures the best outcomes. In either case, biology plays a key role in defining good mothers.

The notion that motherhood is innate and instinctual developed amid emerging Enlightenment ideals in the eighteenth century. While Protestant Reformers celebrated motherhood as a spiritual calling, Enlightenment thinkers offered a secular rationale. New beliefs about natural law and individual liberty reshaped expectations for family life, especially for women.

Despite the title, we have to search for *The Well-Beloved Mother* in Jean-Baptiste Greuze's immensely popular sketch that depicts a father's return home to his joyful, content family (see fig. 4.5). We can almost hear the man on the left-hand side of the painting—standing with feet planted wide, arms outstretched—announcing, "Honey, I'm home!" We follow his gaze and the line of his arm across the composition. The leaning bodies of his dogs merge with the kneeling form of an elderly grandmother until we finally arrive at a pile of enthusiastic, plump bodies. As a visual counterbalance to the father's erect, open form, we find no less than six children pressing into, clamoring onto, and snuggling with their seated mother. Her oldest son stands behind her, gently kissing her forehead, while her youngest child curls onto her breast. A toddler squeezes between her legs and lays his head on her stomach while grasping at her hand. Despite the crumpled coat on the floor and the overturned basket of food near her feet, she appears ecstatic, her head lolling back in almost orgasmic pleasure as she receives the love of her children.

Greuze's sketch was distributed as an engraving, with hundreds of copies sold to French families. A wealthy French banker even commissioned Greuze to rework the composition as a family portrait![16] For contemporary viewers, Greuze's drawing was a new visual story of the good life. In response to seeing the drawing in an exhibition, philosopher Denis Diderot remarked, "This is excellent both for the talent it demonstrates and for its moral content; it preaches population, and paints a sympathetic picture of the happiness and advantages deriving from domesticity; it announces to any man with soul and feelings: Maintain your family comfortably, make children with your wife, as many as you can, but only with her, and you can be sure of a happy home."[17]

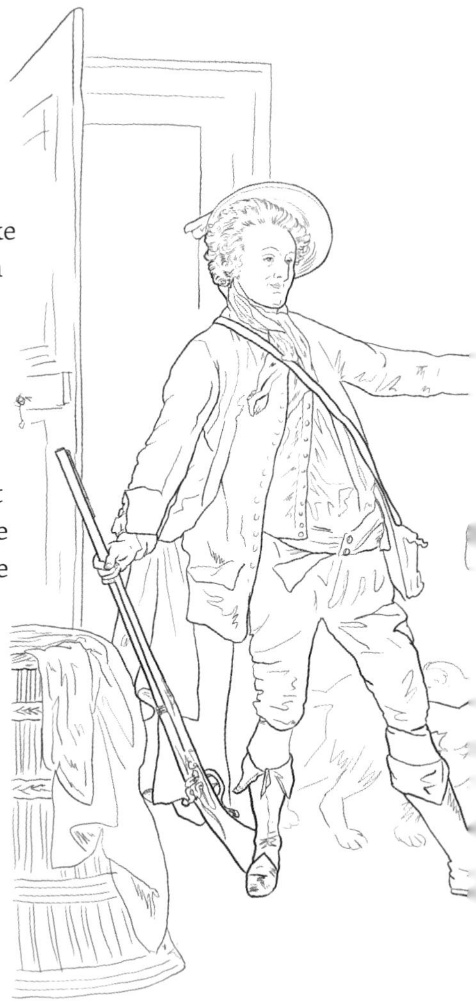

Figure 4.5. Drawn from Jean-Baptiste Greuze, *The Well-Beloved Mother*, ca. 1770

But Greuze's drawing—and others like it—depicts a relatively new phenomenon in the mid-eighteenth century.[18] In medieval and early modern Europe, marriage was primarily a legal contract meant to establish a line of inheritance, and households included unmarried relatives, apprentices, and servants, not just the nuclear family we assume as the norm today. Servants or an older relative who could no longer perform physical labor took care of the children. Adultery on the part of the husband was expected, and once a wealthy wife had given birth to "an heir and a spare," she was also given leave to pursue her own sexual pleasure.

In eighteenth-century France, new attitudes toward the sexes and family life developed from several converging forces. First, as discussed in chapter 2, the two-sex model of sexual difference began to replace the older, classical belief that women were stunted

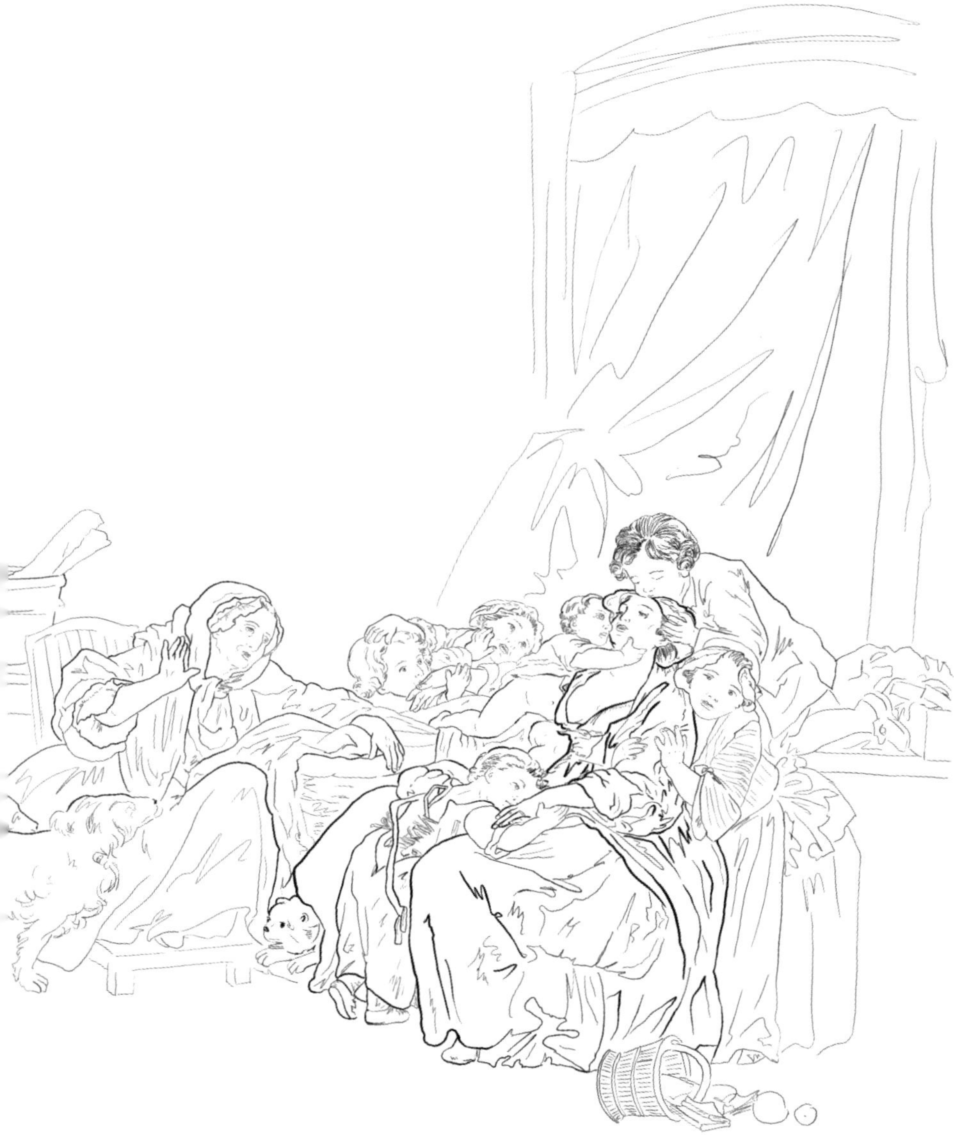

or botched men. The characteristics that made female bodies distinct from male bodies dictated their different purpose according to natural law.

Second, the growing emphasis on individual liberty impacted expectations of marriage. Thinkers like Jean-Jacques Rousseau promoted marriage as an institution that could provide stability while satisfying social and individual needs. The father's role was not to be authoritarian and greedy. The mother's job was not simply to produce a biological heir. Despite his own actions to the contrary, Rousseau passionately argued that it was *parents'* responsibility to protect children and cultivate them into moral adults through education and care.[19] While a wealthy French woman of the seventeenth century could expect to have a wet nurse care for her child, enabling her to regain her figure and resume her social commitments, Rousseau chastised women who did not breastfeed their own children, calling them animals.[20]

Another development in the Enlightenment, also touched on in chapter 2, was the boundary line drawn between public life and private life. The home and family provided a needed haven from the pressures and stresses of public life. Women, according to Rousseau, should be educated precisely to find personal fulfillment in creating such an environment in the home. In Rousseau's novel *La Nouvelle Heloïse*, the protagonist Julie does not marry for love but does find fulfillment in pleasing her husband and caring for her children. "I am a woman and a mother and I know how to keep my proper sphere," she says.[21]

Rousseau and most other Enlightenment thinkers were not offering a return to "biblical family values." Historians have shown how they were instead responding to fears over population decline and the public's increased resistance to rule by the monarchy and aristocracy.[22] Enlightenment thinkers were seeking a reordering of social relationships altogether. Biological sex—not social class—would determine a person's abilities and work. In *Emile*, his treatise on education, Rousseau outlines two models of education that would allow men and women to play their respective parts "in the physical and moral order."[23] This, in turn, would have social and political consequences. Rousseau lays this out as a direct chain of events: "But when mothers deign to nurse their own children, there will be a reform in morals; natural feeling will revive in every heart; there will be no lack of citizens for the state; this first step by itself will restore mutual affection."[24]

As with Reformation-era depictions of motherhood, scholars have questioned and re-questioned how we should understand Rousseau's approach and the approaches of other, similar Enlightenment thinkers to women's role in society. Was Rousseau a woman hater who wanted to withhold important skills and education from women and virtually enslave them in their homes? Was he a duplicitous hypocrite who preached the joys of domestic life but abandoned his five children to an orphanage? Did he begin with an idealistic belief in men's and women's equality but then abandon it for practical reasons? Was his emphasis on the home the result of recognizing that cultural change could not be achieved by purely political means? Did he empower women to play an influential role that was previously demeaned in French society?[25] It's impossible to completely reconstruct the motivations behind Rousseau's beliefs, but we *can* pay attention to how women in that same context chose to navigate this new story, that motherhood was the best, most natural state for all women.

Working Mom

In 1787, French artist Élisabeth Louise Vigée Le Brun (1755–1842) had three paintings included in the Salon, the biggest public exhibition of art in Paris. Every other year, members of the Royal Academy of Painting and Sculpture in France combed through thousands of submissions and displayed the chosen artworks in the Louvre. Of her selected paintings, Vigée Le Brun's most prominent work was a large portrait of Marie Antoinette and her three children (see fig. 4.6).

The queen sits in the center of the composition, gazing steadily back at us. She wears a voluminous red velvet dress and a matching turban adorned with fluffy white feathers. Her daughter, also in red, nestles beside her. The girl leans against the queen, pressing her cheek into her mother's shoulder and looking up at her adoringly. A wriggling baby, dressed in white lace, sits on Marie Antoinette's lap. One hand grasps at his mother's dress, while the other reaches out to his older brother. The young prince stands on the right-hand side of the composition, separated slightly from his mother and siblings by a large bassinet draped in blue. The prince gestures at the empty bed while also looking out at the painting's viewers.

Vigée Le Brun cleverly uses light, shape, and color to present us with a stable, unified royal family. Soft, white light falls on the faces of the children, glinting in their eyes and catching on the gilt trim of their garments. Marie Antoinette's own face and décolletage seem to emanate light, attracting our

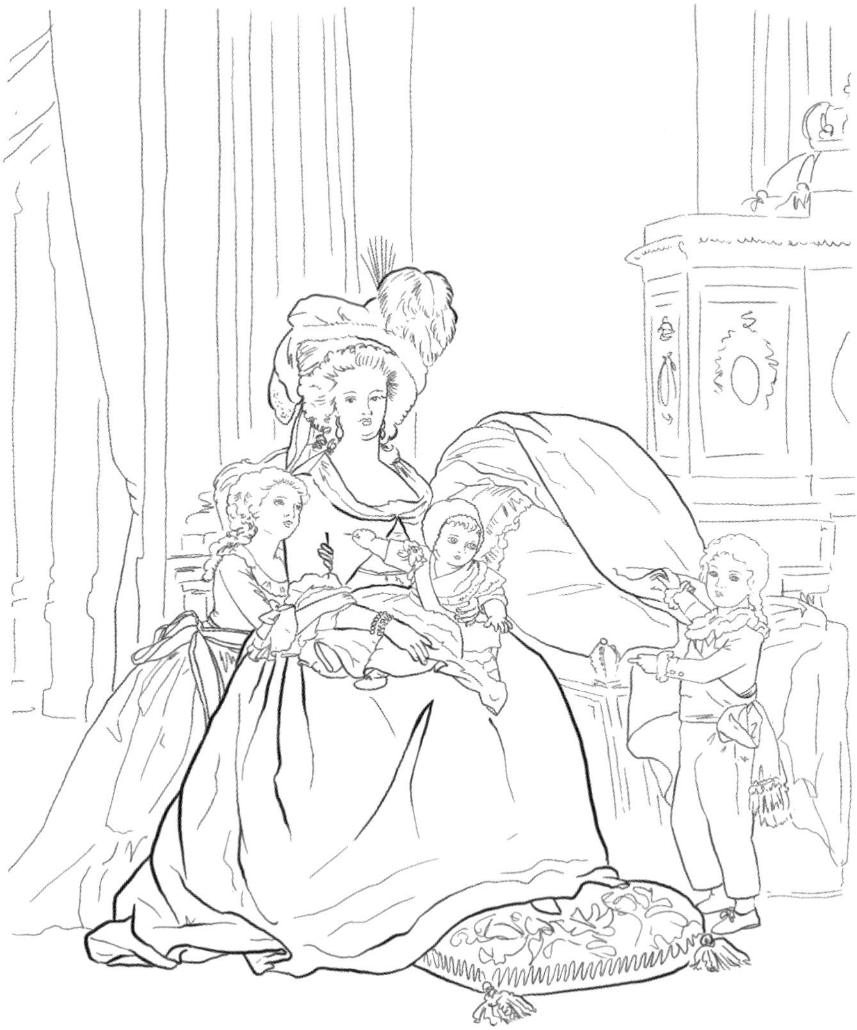

attention like a moth. The full skirt of the seated queen and her daughter's leaning body anchor the composition as an equilateral triangle. Their bodies literally press together to form the left edge of the triangle, while her son's gesture completes the right. Vigée Le Brun also unifies the individual family members using color. The queen and princess wear matching red dresses that even have similar necklines and trim on the sleeves. It's like an eighteenth-century "Match the Fam" promotion before the existence of Old Navy. The three children also have blue sashes that link them together and connect them to the bassinet. Visually, Vigée Le Brun asserts that these are *all* Marie Antoinette's babies, birthed from her own body.

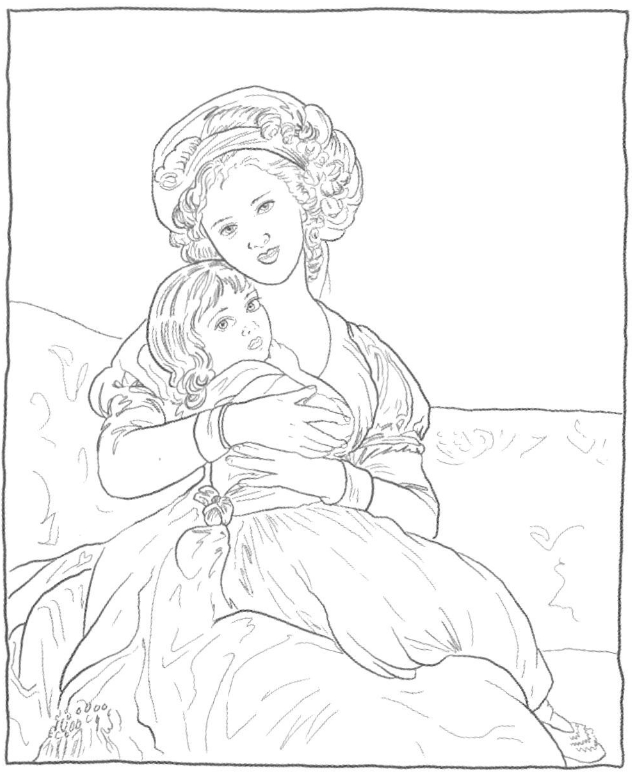

Figure 4.6. Drawn from Élisabeth Vigée Le Brun, *Marie Antoinette and Her Children*, 1787 (on the left), and *Self-Portrait with Her Daughter, Julie*, 1786 (above)

The same year that Vigée Le Brun was commissioned to paint the queen, she also submitted a self-portrait to the Salon exhibition. But rather than depicting herself alone or with her paint palette and brushes, as she had done in earlier self-portraits, she painted herself embracing her six-year-old daughter, Julie (see fig. 4.6).

Vigée Le Brun sits on a dark-green chair, her arms wrapped around a wide-eyed, brunette girl dressed in white. The artist wears a mustard skirt and a pearl-gray jacket, with her curly hair bound up in a simple but fashionable white turban. Both sitters look back at us, Julie with apparent shy curiosity and her mother with a slightly open-mouthed smile.

As with her portrait of Marie Antoinette, Vigée Le Brun uses a triangular composition, with Julie's body melting into her own to form a single shape. Likewise, Julie's white dress is almost indistinguishable from Vigée Le Brun's white underdress, and the pale, rosy peach of Julie's face matches her mother's complexion. Visually they are a single unit. Their physical closeness suggests their emotional intimacy as well. Julie is an extension of her mother, and Vigée Le Brun holds her daughter tightly, with apparent, singular delight.

Vigée Le Brun's third painting in the Salon that year was yet another maternal portrait, a depiction of two aristocratic women and their sons. What was with all the moms? Vigée Le Brun did not specialize in motherhood as a subject. She had positioned herself as an ambitious portrait painter whose clients had already included the queen as well as political dignitaries and male and female aristocrats. But in 1787, Marie Antoinette found herself facing some public relations issues. A recent portrait of the queen by the Swedish artist Adolf Ulrik Wertmüller—depicting her walking in the palace garden with two of her children—had received harsh criticism. Even more recently, gossip was swirling thick and fast, accusing her of infidelity and of using public funds to buy an extravagant diamond necklace. To counter this slander, the queen hired Vigée Le Brun to present a positive image of a dignified and virtuous woman.[26]

Vigée Le Brun's new portrait ticked all the requirements. Marie Antoinette appears Madonna-like, surrounded by her children in a glow of light. The tall jewel case in the background and the queen's relatively simple attire allude to the legend of Cornelia, an important Roman matron whose sons played a pivotal role in the ancient republic.[27] When a wealthy neighbor asked to see her friend's jewelry collection, Cornelia responded by pointing at her children and announcing, "These are my jewels." In eighteenth-century France, the legend had become popular among artists and writers as a moral tale for women. By referencing this story in her portrait of Marie Antoinette, Vigée Le Brun asserts that the queen is just as virtuous as the honored mother of the Gracchi brothers. Furthermore, by drawing viewers' attention to the empty bassinet, Vigée Le Brun also reminds the public that the queen has suffered the loss of a child, the one-year-old princess Sophie-Béatrice, who died from tuberculosis while the painting was being made.

In addition to these symbolic gestures, Vigée Le Brun throws the weight of her own identity as a mother behind the queen. You might question Marie Antoinette's maternal sensibilities, but with her enthusiastic embrace of Julie, Vigée Le Brun seems to say, "You cannot doubt *mine*." In her three 1787 Salon portraits, Vigée Le Brun presents motherhood as a shared experience that transcends class.[28]

It's clear how Vigée Le Brun's efforts served the queen. But emphasizing her own motherhood also served her professional aspirations.

While Vigée Le Brun was certainly not the only successful woman artist in late eighteenth-century France, she was still something of an anomaly. Shifting cultural expectations of how a virtuous woman should act put Vigée Le Brun and other women artists in a difficult position. According to Rousseau, a woman who tries to be in the public realm "always makes herself ridiculous."[29] She engages in "trickery" and is "pretentious."[30] A truly decent woman, on the other hand, is content to let her honor be unknown.[31] This created a conundrum for female painters. If virtuous women were supposed to stay in the domestic sphere, how could they also have a career as an artist? The profession demanded visibility in order to be successful.

Ironically, Vigée Le Brun could remain in the public eye if she did so as a mother. Or, to be more precise, she could do so if she told the new Mother story, painting herself as a paragon of virtuous femininity—entirely devoted to her home and child—even as she negotiated with clients, responded to critics, and navigated murky political waters. Indeed, at least one reviewer of the 1787 Salon exhibition praised her paintings for teaching the "most tender and delicious of affections," motherhood, "better than the lessons of the moralist."[32]

On the surface, at least, Vigée Le Brun appears to be a triumphant, eighteenth-century model of a middle-class, working mom. Her self-portraits with Julie depict her deep maternal devotion, *and* she remains at the top of her field professionally. Yet the story is a fiction. There's a gap between the world Vigée Le Brun concocts in these paintings and her actual, lived experience.

First, representing Marie Antoinette as the embodiment of Enlightenment ideals did not stop the rising discontent with the monarchy. Within two years, Vigée Le Brun and her daughter would flee France altogether, unwelcome as royalists in the midst of the Revolution. The Mother story could not, in the end, save her, or the queen.

Second, Vigée Le Brun's relationship to motherhood in general and to her daughter, Julie, in particular was far more fraught than what her paintings suggest. In her autobiography—written in her seventies and distanced from the pressures of early revolutionary France—Vigée Le Brun narrates a different story. Against the advice of her friends, Vigée Le Brun marries her husband in a bid to escape her exploitative stepfather. But Jean-Baptiste-Pierre's gambling habit and adulterous affairs do not provide her with the security she craves. After two years of marriage, she is overjoyed to realize she is pregnant. Notably, however, Vigée Le Brun immediately goes on to use her pregnancy to prove her deep commitment not to virtuous womanhood but to painting. "My devotion to art," she writes, "made me careless in the day-to-day details of life; for happy as I was at the idea of becoming a mother, after nine months of pregnancy, I was not in the least prepared for the birth of my baby."[33] In what we might now call a "humble brag," she continues: "The day my daughter was born, I was still in the studio, trying to work . . . between labor pains."[34] In her old age, Vigée Le Brun wants to be known for her passionate dedication not—as we might think from her earlier paintings—to motherhood but to her profession.

When I first learn of these frictions between Élisabeth Vigée Le Brun's depictions of motherhood and her actual experience, I'm frustrated. She seems like a sellout, trying to keep people in power happy by pretending to be a devoted mother, even though she disliked her husband and preferred her studio to the nursery. Yet as I begin my own negotiation of motherhood and higher education, my attitude toward Vigée Le Brun softens. Her tensions, frustrations, and contradictions grow increasingly relatable. What should I do with them all?

Hidden Mothers

While pregnant with my first child, I enroll in a feminist theory course as part of my doctoral program. I begin the semester with a slightly bloated abdomen, and I end it with my taut belly grazing the attached desk of the classroom chair. Although I am the only one who is pregnant in the class, I find unexpected comradery in the writings of continental philosophers who offer me a new, unfamiliar language of motherhood.

I read Julia Kristeva's 1981 essay "Woman's Time" and lead a class discussion while my unborn son pushes his heel firmly against my lowest rib with remarkable strength. "Pregnancy seems to be experienced as the radical ordeal of the splitting of the subject," Kristeva writes, "redoubling up of the body, separation and coexistence of the self and of an other, of nature and consciousness, of physiology and speech."[35] This could be seen as a threat to the woman's sense of self, a breach of her boundaries of identity. But when the child is born, the mother can enter "into the labyrinths of an experience that, without the child, she would only rarely encounter: love for an other."[36] Kristeva argues that this love is unique. It is not a self-love, nor love for one's double, nor a romantic, sexual love. Instead, motherhood is "the slow, difficult, and delightful apprenticeship in attentiveness, gentleness, forgetting oneself."[37] She concludes, however, with a seeming contradiction: "The ability to succeed in this path without masochism and without annihilating one's affective, intellectual, and professional personality—such would seem to be the stakes to be won through guiltless maternity. . . . It then becomes a creation in the strong sense of the term."[38]

I'm fascinated by how Kristeva describes this paradox of motherhood. The language of "forgetting" oneself without also "annihilating" oneself loops constantly through my mind. Reframed within my own understanding of the imago Dei and the Christian life, Kristeva's words strike me as a potent, common grace. This is not the entirely self-effacing, total devotion of Renaissance Madonnas and celebrity super moms. As a Christian, I am called to love others as I would myself and to willingly give of myself on behalf of another (John 15:13). But to sacrifice myself on the altar of my child is nothing more than idolatry. I presume that my intensely researched discipline methods and carefully prepared, organic meals will ensure my child's wholeness and safety. I disregard the care of my own body and the development of my own interests and skills as if they are not worthy gifts from almighty God. Perhaps the intensity of the Mother story is simply a means of maintaining my own sense of control, dressed up in the language of care for another. Perhaps the Mother story can be yet another strange, twisted means of self-fulfillment.

I laugh ruefully as I recall the strange phenomenon of "hidden mothers" in Victorian photography (see fig. 4.7). Hundreds of studio portraits of young children—photographs taken through the nineteenth century in the United States and Britain—share a peculiar similarity. While the ostensible focus of the photograph is a somber-faced child, another figure is also present. Shrouded in black, draped in a patterned tapestry, crouched behind a piece of furniture, or occasionally scratched out on the photographic negative itself, the child's caregiver—often the mother—partially conceals her presence while also firmly holding the little one still. Art historian Geoffrey Batchen observes that the mothers are never truly invisible; it's just that we're not supposed to *see* them.[39] The very act of annihilation is understood as part and parcel of being a mother.

But Kristeva asserts that a mother's self-giving can be generative, not simply a deletion. And my theology compels me to believe her. Self-forgetfulness is not the same as self-annihilation. After all, I am a purposefully formed creature with good, God-ordained limits and talents. I am responsible for stewarding those gifts as well.

I look again at descriptions of mothers in the Bible. Now, I see mothers teaching (Prov. 31:1), writing poetry (Luke 1:46–55), running businesses (Prov. 31:16, 18), and extending hospitality (Acts 16:15). Instead of expecting my own erasure, I begin to anticipate how motherhood will reshape

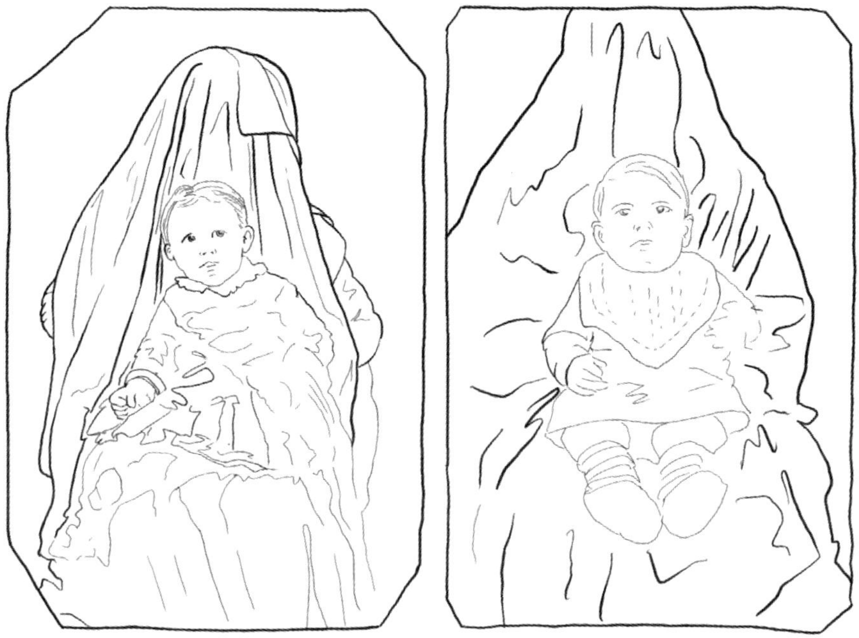

Figure 4.7. Drawn from anonymous nineteenth-century photographs of "hidden mothers," collected by Linda Fregni Nagler

the way that I see and work in the world. I wonder how my child will make me attentive to new things or prompt me to ask new questions. I prepare myself to welcome paradox.

Within three years, and while still completing my doctorate, I become the mother of two sons. Each time, I am transformed. My body stretches to nurture and accommodate a new life. My heart rends open to accommodate a new love I could not previously fathom. And, despite all my earlier fears, I *love* motherhood. I even love toddlerhood. My boys are energetic and curious, and their enthusiastic celebration of excavators, trains, dinosaurs, the color red, crispy sheets of nori, and the music of A Tribe Called Quest fills me with an exuberance that stretches my own capacity for joy. At the same time, no other human beings test the limits of my patience or physical endurance the way my children do.

I try to hold it all gently.

Often, that's easier said than done.

#Momfluencer

I feel the tendrils of self-loathing curling up the back of my neck like greedy, grasping vines. Nothing compares to the way I doubly despise myself when I look at other moms on social media. I hate that I'm not like the beautiful, good moms on the internet, *and* I hate that I am so quick to dismiss and despise them.

In a culture that supposedly celebrates "authenticity," social media moms are easy targets. Plentiful websites and accounts devote themselves to making fun of the matching outfits, organic linen swaddling blankets, charming pet goats, homemade pretzel chips, and sun-drenched laundry that cannot possibly be true, at least not all the time. In fact, other mom influencers have built their personal brands around supposedly showing the reality of motherhood, blow-out diapers and all. But I wonder if our demand for "authenticity" is less a reflection of our love for truth and more evidence of our inability to hold contradiction.

Cultural critics and sociologists have rightly begun to analyze the complex web of pressures and systems that have made this latest iteration of the Mother story possible.[40] Political anxieties and social inequalities shaped expectations of motherhood in the Reformation and Enlightenment eras, and of course they continue to do so today. But as scholars begin to construct the history of the #momfluencer, I hope that they reach back to the nineteenth century and look at the art and life of Lilly Martin Spencer.

I think Lilly Martin Spencer (1822–1902) would have been big on nineteenth-century Instagram. Born to educated, progressive French parents in England but raised in Ohio, Spencer became one of the most popular painters of American life—known as "genre scenes"—in the United States. Her 1849 canvas, *Domestic Happiness*, is one such work (see fig. 4.8). The painting depicts a smiling father and mother standing next to a bed, gazing down lovingly at their two sleeping children, who are tangled together in a tender embrace. It is the kind of sweet, even saccharine, image that we might imagine as a concluding scene in a Hallmark Christmas movie. But while Spencer paints both parents, she primarily emphasizes the mother and her connection to the children.

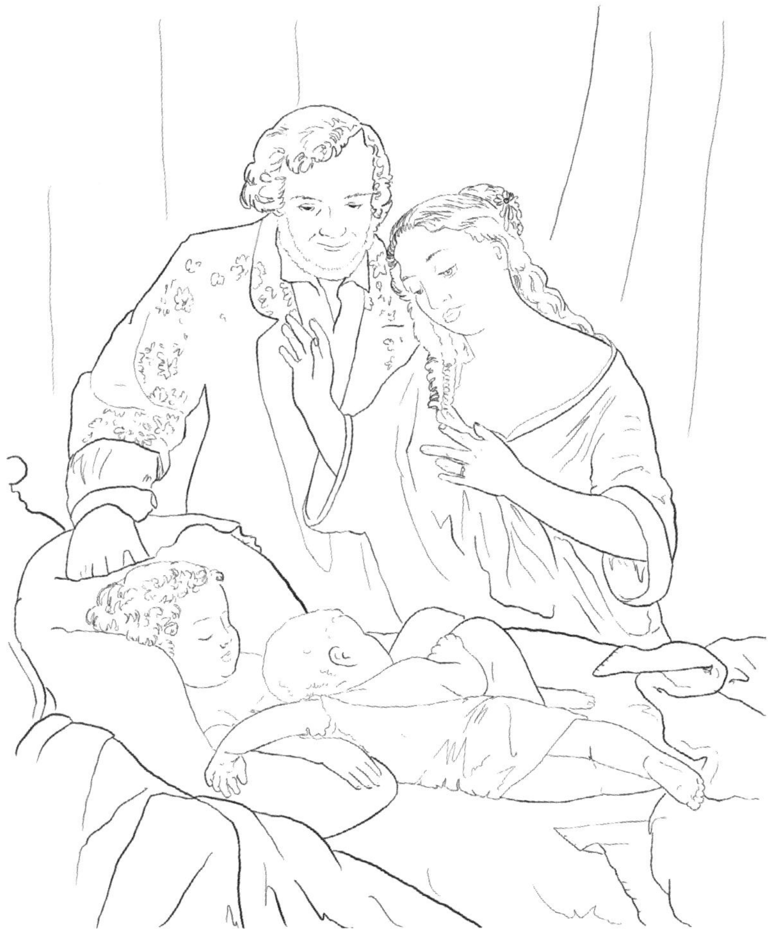

Figure 4.8. Drawn from Lilly Martin Spencer, *Domestic Happiness*, 1849

The father is present and integrated, but he is not a *necessary* part of the whole.

Spencer achieves this in a few ways. First, she uses the mother to connect the contrasting dark, upper portion of the painting and the much lighter bottom third. The bed in the foreground is covered in soft white sheets, and the children's barely peach skin and sheer sleeping clothes blend into pale warmth. Above them, however, their father's brown hair and deep-blue, floral-patterned jacket seem to emerge from the darkened background. Tucked against his side, the mother creates a visual bridge between the light and dark. Her skin and dark-blond hair catch the same light as her children. The creamy expanse of her shoulder and décolletage echoes the bare back of her sleeping babe. Likewise, her rose-colored gown picks up the pink undertones of the children's flushed cheeks, lips, and fingertips. Although the father's jacket has splashes of pink in its pattern, it's the mother's body that primarily links the children's space to that of the adults.

There's more. Together, the family forms a stable triangle, the favored composition of nativity scenes and images of the Madonna and child. But while the father's head is the triangle's apex, he could also be excised from the scene and the balanced shape would remain with just the mother and children. Finally, even though the implied lines of the couple's gazes unify them with their sleeping offspring, the mother's gesture creates a sense of separation. She lifts her right hand and presses it against her husband's chest, as if keeping him from drawing any closer and possibly waking the children. In her use of light, color, shape, and space, Spencer visually asserts the *mother's* importance in the family unit.

Genre paintings like this one shaped mid-nineteenth-century American ideas of social relationships and the good life.[41] Even as the threat of Civil War hung over the nation and immigration and industrialization were challenging older social norms, genre paintings—of cheerful laborers, peaceful race relations, and calm domesticity—offered stability. While most Americans could not afford original artworks for the home, mechanical printing offered new ways to see and own these images. Many of Spencer's paintings, including *Domestic Happiness*, were owned by art unions that authorized printed copies. Black-and-white engravings, sometimes hand-tinted with color, sold briskly to the public. But the images were not intended just to decorate homes. They also served an educational role, offering a refining influence on viewers' hearts and minds.[42] Spencer understood her paintings in this way. In a letter to her mother, she wrote, "I want to try and make all my painting have a tendency toward moral improvement as far as it is in the power of painting."[43]

What "moral improvement" was *Domestic Happiness* seeking to provide? The painting, in agreement with evangelical Protestant thinking of the time, preached that women's reign in the home was for the good not only of the woman but also of her children and husband. If the Reformation elevated motherhood to a worthy role and the Enlightenment argued for women's natural affinity for the task, the Industrial Revolution created the conditions for middle- and upper-class white women to ostensibly save humanity.

The booming economic possibilities of mechanization, mass production, long-distance communication, and efficient transportation moved the workplace firmly outside the home. But the joining of the public sphere with capitalism and the lure of profit also meant that the private sphere needed to become a refining haven. As we saw earlier in chapter 3, a dramatic switch occurred after the Middle Ages. Instead of being seen as more susceptible to sin, women were deemed morally superior to men. This apparently innate piety made them the perfect "angels of the household," responsible for not only their own behavior but also that of others.[44] In Spencer's *Domestic Happiness*, the mother visually links her children and husband together while also keeping her husband from doing something wrong—in this case, waking the babies. The gesture would easily be understood as a metaphor for the mother's ultimate role as the keeper of the home and the family's guiding light.

Women were elevated from their previous status, but they found themselves on a tiny, precarious pedestal. Sermons, books, women's magazines, and images like Spencer's preached the universal value of this arrangement, but it remained firmly out of reach for many women. Certainly, enslaved women—sexually vulnerable and forced to labor for another's gain—could not achieve this role. Likewise, for immigrant and working-class women, the Industrial Revolution created demand and opportunity to work outside the home, often in unsafe factories and for very little pay. The ideal of domestic bliss dangled like a lure perpetually out of reach.

But, of course, the painting is telling us the Mother *story*; it does not—and cannot—show us the parts of Spencer's own life that did not fit the script.

Lilly Martin married the tailor Benjamin Rush Spencer in 1844. Remarkably, especially for that time, Benjamin soon stopped working outside the home as a tailor and began overseeing household affairs and helping

Lilly with business demands while she focused on painting.[45] The couple went on to have thirteen children, seven of whom lived to adulthood. Benjamin served as the primary caregiver for the children, and Lilly was the breadwinner. This certainly wasn't the ideal financial situation. In an 1848 letter to her parents, Lilly writes, "Still we hope on and struggle on and help each other harmoniously . . . and though poor, we are happy with each other."[46] Although money was tight throughout their forty-nine-year marriage, the arrangement remained and the couple seems to have had enduring, mutual love for each other.

When I first see Spencer's paintings, I want to scoff at their obvious, indulgent sentimentality. No one's life looks like that. Later, I read scholars who argue over how we should understand the tension between Spencer's personal experience and the images of motherhood she produced for consumption.[47] Is she a sellout, complicit in the oppression of women? Or, if we look at the painting just so, can we find some subversive message of gender equality hidden in the details?

Now, over ten years into my career as a professor and a mother of teenaged children, I wonder if Spencer felt like her years of promoting the Mother story were worth it. Even though she made work intended to appeal to a broad audience, she never achieved financial security. After the Civil War, American tastes shifted toward European-style Neoclassicism, and Spencer's charming, buoyant scenes were dismissed as out of date. Yet I also wonder if Spencer painted not just for economic reasons but because doing so brought her some degree of personal satisfaction.

Certainly, that is worth something too.

My own experience of motherhood has been full of such frictions. I'm kneeling on my sons' bedroom floor, a hastily grabbed apron covering my trousers and blouse as I blot at a patch of dried vomit on the rug. Multiple damp paper towels and a few bleach wipes later, I throw soiled sheets and pajamas into the washing machine, strip off my latex gloves, and dispense Gatorade to a child who, while at a family gathering the night before, ate four-too-many cookies and a bag of chips. I kiss my husband—who has been cleaning the kitchen and overseeing breakfast for our other son—and head out the door to give a lecture on representations of poverty at a local economic development conference. I'm admittedly flustered when

I arrive, wondering if a "good" mom would have stayed home. But once I start my talk, I feel a deep contentment welling up inside me as I begin describing the photograph on the screen and drawing together different scholarly threads. It is a sense of forgetting myself and being myself at the same time. I experience the fullness of faithfulness.

I still struggle to explain the utter joy I find in snuggling on the couch with my sons *and* the unique aliveness that comes when I lead a rousing classroom discussion with college students. The well of joyful tears that comes when I watch my sons participate in a theatrical performance exists alongside the profound wonder of seeing my book in other people's hands. The triumphs of my children's first steps, first words, and first solo bike rides mingle with my victories of tracking down an obscure source or taming an unruly first draft. I have missed my son's track meets due to teaching commitments, and I have missed academic conferences because of familial needs. God has said no to my prayers for more children and yes to my prayers for more students. There has never been a perfect life-work balance. I do not have it "all," whatever that might mean. But I have learned that my delight in one sphere need not negate my pleasure in another. I can make room for complexity, remembering the both-and of my very human life. But to do so, I need a different story of what it means for a woman to be fruitful.

COUNTERSTORY:

Cultivating

More Than Madonna

As we've already seen, many women artists used the Mother story in their own work without overtly challenging its contours. Representing motherhood in a culturally acceptable fashion eased the way for Élisabeth Vigée Le Brun, Lilly Martin Spencer, and others to pursue their unusual paths as professional artists. But there have also been artists who questioned, rejected, or expanded the singular focus of the dominant Mother story.

Käthe Kollwitz focused on the experiences of poor and working-class women, especially mothers. A recurring theme in her work, beginning in the early 1900s, was mothers huddling over their children, offering protection or expressing sorrow. In a haunting, gestural drawing from 1903, an almost skeletal mother sits cross-legged on the ground, clutching her lifeless child to her chest. In 1919, Kollwitz began a series called *Krieg* (War), responding to the tragedies experienced by women and children during the Great War. In one stark, black-and-white woodcut, a naked mother holds her infant aloft, offering, as the title suggests, *The Sacrifice* (1922). These gut-wrenching prints expressed some of Kollwitz's own pain. Her younger son, Peter, was killed in 1914 while fighting in the Great War. In Kollwitz's work, motherhood is never rose-colored. It is suffused with both deep love and deep pain.

Another, more critical view of motherhood comes from Remedios Varo, a Spanish-Mexican surrealist painter. In *Celestial Pablum* (1958), Varo depicts a woman trapped in a small, cylindrical tower, feeding a caged crescent moon while endlessly grinding stars into baby food. Varo never had children herself, and the painting perhaps suggests why. The expectations of the institution of motherhood seem like too great a cost.

Indeed, numerous white, mid-century women artists chose not to have children, believing that doing so would destroy their careers. Still, the politically radical Black artist Elizabeth Catlett embraced motherhood as both experience and subject. While still in graduate school in the 1930s, and before she had children herself, she began making sculptures of mothers holding their children close. Many of her sculptures reference African art, such as masks from Gabon and Dogon statues. Catlett spent much of her career in Mexico, where she married a fellow artist and had three children. Throughout her long career, she remained committed to representing working-class mothers.

Later, second wave feminist artists explored motherhood as a subject. Some, like Judy Chicago in her *Birth Project* (1980–85), celebrated the act of giving birth as a form of divine creation. Others, like Mary Kelly in her *Post-Partum Document* (1973–79), recorded their experiences of motherhood with almost scientific precision. Since then, a growing roster of artists have offered intimate, visceral images of birthing, postpartum bodies, nursing, and child-rearing.[48]

Some artists have offered completely new ways of imaging motherhood without representing the human figure at all. Janine Antoni's *Hearth* (2014), part of her ceramic Pelvic Vessels series, considers the mutual transformation that a mother's and child's bodies undergo during the process of labor and delivery. Antoni was fascinated by how a woman's sacrum—the triangular bone at the base of the spine—shifts back to allow a baby to pass through the birth canal. But even with this adjustment, the child's soft head is still shaped by the mother's pelvis. Antoni began the work by throwing three small pots, but while the clay was still wet and on the wheel, she scraped the inner edge of a model sacrum around the edge of each vessel, creating new indentations. Likewise, Antoni suggests, mother and child are forever changed by this literal rite of passage.

Another striking reimagining of motherhood comes from the multidisciplinary artist Louise Bourgeois. While in her eighties, Bourgeois began making monumental metal sculptures of spiders. These arachnids symbolized her own mother, whom she saw as "deliberate, clever, patient, soothing, reasonable, dainty, subtle, indispensable, neat, and as useful as a spider."[49] The largest iteration, *Maman* (1999), stands thirty feet tall, allowing visitors to walk under her abdomen, where they'll find an egg sac containing thirty-two marble eggs. Instead of representing her mother's body or referencing the physical reality of biological motherhood, Bourgeois uses a spider to evoke some of her mother's intangible qualities.

All of these reimaginings of motherhood can expand our visual archive of what the embodied, often messy, experience of mothering can look like. But what story do we tell about women who do not bear children?

I think about Bourgeois's *Maman* as I watch my sister-in-law patiently herd my slouching teen son out the door. "I need to go on a walk and you're going with me," she declares firmly. My son casts her a baleful glance but follows her direction. She is unmarried, has no children of her own, and is also recently disabled. But as my family navigates a season of loss and precarity, she chooses to gift us with her resources, putting her energy into the needy, parched soil of our home. Witnessing her do this makes my heart crack open in wonder and gratitude. She fills my sons' bellies with good food, shuttles them to various appointments, makes them do household tasks with little complaint, and surprises them with crocheted squids tucked in incongruous places. While my husband and I stumble through grief, she offers to and coaxes from my children gifts that I simply cannot.

Indeed, long before *Maman*, women were being fruitful—without being mothers. They were telling the story of Cultivating: creating and stewarding new, abundant goodness in and around themselves. And we have the visual stories to prove it.

A Garden of Flowers

I learn about Herrad of Landsberg (1130–95) for the first time when I'm a newly minted professor, preparing to teach my Women, Art, and Culture course. Still fresh from focusing on modern and contemporary art in my doctoral program, I'm unfamiliar with all but the most famous examples of medieval art. But while flipping through my textbook's chapter on art made by women in the Middle Ages, I'm caught by the statement that a twelfth-century manuscript "offers tangible evidence of the transmission of learning between women."[50] Apparently, *Hortus Deliciarum*—Latin for "Garden of Delights"—was itself a kind of textbook, compiled by the abbess Herrad for the women at Hohenburg Abbey near the present-day border of France and Germany. Curious, I scan down the page to find an illumination from the *Hortus*.

What I see makes me chuckle.

Despite being made sometime around 1170, the image bears an uncanny resemblance to a modern yearbook page. Sixty bust-length portraits of women—all dressed in shades of pink, green, and blue—form six neat, horizontal rows (see fig. 4.9). The women sit in a three-quarter pose, much like a school photo, facing toward the left. Their faces are drawn with simple, stylized features: wide eyes, rosy cheeks, and a small, rosebud smile. The repeated shape of their bodies, the limited color palette, and the similarities of their features create a steady visual rhythm that marches down the page. The visual unity suggests a unified identity as well; we assume they are a team, community, or family of some sort. Still, the artist also asserts each woman's individual identity, writing a name in a small, neat script above each figure: Margareta, Gerdrut, Anna, and so on.

On the far right, near the bottom of the page, the rhythm breaks and we find the only full-length portrait: a depiction of Herrad of Landsberg, the convent's leader. Herrad's face and attire echo those of the other women on the page, and she too faces to the left. However, her standing figure spans the two bottom rows of portraits, and she holds a dangling scroll in her hand. Herrad's feet skim the top of a green hill, decorated with simplified leaf forms, that curves up to meet the left-hand edge of the page.

The bottom row of women's portraits seems to be emerging from the plant-filled landscape, inviting comparison between the women and the rows of flowers. This is a fitting connection since the scroll that Herrad holds proclaims, "O snow-white flowers giving forth the scent of virtue / Always resting in divine contemplation / Hasten to heaven, after despising earthly dust / That you may be able to see the Bridegroom, who is now hidden."[51]

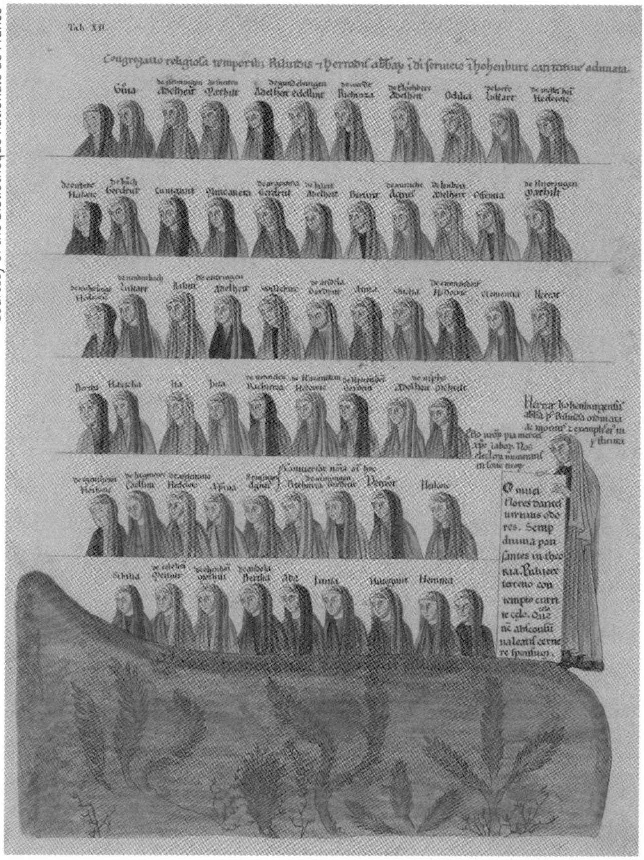

Figure 4.9. The women of Hohenburg Abbey as depicted in *Hortus Deliciarum*, fol. 323r, ca. 1167–85, from a facsimile made by Christian Moritz Engelhardt in 1818. A full-color image of this array of figures is included in the color insert section.

The image is sweet, if also quaint. Yet the more I learn about the *Hortus*, the more I realize that Herrad is pointing me toward a counterstory of Cultivating, a story that women can inhabit regardless of their maternal status.

A Sweet Honeycomb

Begun sometime before 1175 and completed in 1185, Herrad of Landsberg's *Hortus Deliciarum* has been described as an illuminated encyclopedia consisting of theological, philosophical, poetic, and scientific texts with accompanying, colorful illustrations. In her introduction, Herrad dedicates the book to the women under her care at Hohenburg Abbey on Mont Sainte-Odile in present-day France. She writes:

> Herrad, by the grace of God, abbess, although unworthy, of the church of Hohenburg, to the sweetest virgins of Christ faithfully working at Hohenburg as though in the vineyard of the Lord Christ, be grace and glory, that the Lord will give. . . . Like a little bee inspired by God, I collected from the various flowers of sacred Scripture and philosophic writings this book, which is called the Garden of Delights, and I brought it together to the praise and honor of Christ and the church and for the sake of your love as if into a single sweet honeycomb.[52]

Sadly, the original manuscript was destroyed by a fire in 1870.[53] Nineteenth-century scholars who had studied the book described it as a resplendent work full of colorful illuminations. But it was also one obviously compiled and revised over time and well-used by its readers. Most of the pages were a larger size, making it possible for multiple women to read it at once. But numerous additional leaves in varying sizes—ranging from half pages to stubs—were inserted at different dates, providing additional texts or commentary. The pages were never bound into a final, singular book, suggesting that Herrad expected her garden to literally grow.[54] While the main text was written in a neat and regular hand, pages were also crowded with notes added by different readers in the margins or between lines. Thanks to the work of these earlier scholars, a partial facsimile of the *Hortus* was carefully compiled. Although only half of the original 346 illuminations were copied and some key texts are missing as well, the facsimile serves as a rich, if incomplete, resource.

By examining what remains of the *Hortus* within its twelfth-century religious and social context, we can get a sense of who Herrad's readers were, how she understood her relationship to them, and what she considered crucial to their intellectual and spiritual development. And importantly, we can learn how Herrad understood her story of Cultivating.

Hohenburg Abbey, where Herrad lived and worked, was founded in the late seventh century by the daughter of a local duke. At first the abbey was home to nuns—women who had taken vows to fully separate themselves from the world and live a cloistered life of contemplation. By the eleventh century, however, the abbey housed "canonesses," women who took vows of chastity and obedience but also saw the education of others as one of their duties. In the twelfth century, when Herrad joined the abbey under the guidance of the abbess Relinde, the women lived according to the Rule of St. Augustine. This "rule of life" had grown in popularity across Europe over the last century as a wave of reform rippled through monastic communities. Unlike the Rule of St. Benedict—which called for a retreat from the world—the Rule of St. Augustine emphasized *teaching* through word and deed.[55]

The women at Hohenburg who received Herrad's "sweet honeycomb" were likely daughters of noblemen in the region who expected to both receive an education and offer knowledge and care to others. Some came to the abbey as young girls; others arrived when they were older or even widowed. Their virginity—their abstinence from sex—is repeatedly praised throughout *Hortus Deliciarum*. But remember, in the medieval conception of the world, women were not seen as pure vessels that needed to be preserved; instead, they were believed to be animalistic and uncontrolled in their sexuality. It was precisely by denying those carnal urges in order to focus on studying and serving Christ that women could pursue holiness. Their vow of virginity was ultimately a vow of attention, a promise to resist distraction and focus on only Christ and the church.

As the abbess of the convent, Herrad provided oversight and guidance for the women under her care. The *Hortus* was part and parcel of her efforts. Herrad opens and closes the manuscript with her own words, with poem and prose dedications and exhortations to her readers. Here, we find evidence of her deep affection for the women at Hohenburg and how she imagines her relationship to them.

In her opening poem, she describes herself as "Herrad / Your most devoted and faithful / Mother and little handmaid."[56] Perhaps on one level Herrad is simply reiterating her official title; as abbess she would be referred to as "Mother." But the term was not simply an honorific. There were specific ways that an abbess was expected to "mother" the girls and women at her convent, acting in many respects as a biological parent. Herrad would have been responsible for providing for physical needs such as food and shelter. She might not literally be cooking meals or building walls, but ultimately the responsibility to oversee or delegate that care began and ended with her. Likewise, she needed to make sure that sick canonesses were tended to, that disputes were handled justly, and that all the women were equipped with necessary skills.

But her primary task, and one that Herrad clearly took seriously, was to care for the women's intellectual and spiritual development. And from the language of gardening that runs through *Hortus Deliciarum*, it's also evident that Herrad wanted to cultivate not just knowledge but delight. She wanted the women in her abbey to grow in both knowledge and love. She was, as we might say today, interested in "whole-person formation."

The overall framework of *Hortus Deliciarum* is the narrative of salvation, from the creation of the world to Christ's return. Within this overarching story, Herrad selects and organizes texts by a variety of medieval theologians. Herrad also includes illuminations that celebrate philosophy and the liberal arts as flowing from the Holy Spirit. Thus, she claims, even the wisdom of Socrates and Plato—seated below the allegorical Queen of Philosophy—comes from God. Following other theologians of the time, Herrad believed that the "memory" of God is what guides humans to salvation. The fall has corrupted that memory, but it could be restored through study.[57] Humans might misuse knowledge, as they did in the garden of Eden, but Herrad's *Garden of Delights* is intended to encourage the opposite movement. Seeking knowledge rightly is a way of seeking God.

Little Bees

Some early twentieth-century scholars dismissed Herrad as being "merely" a copyist or curator, not the real *author* of the *Hortus*. However, even the partial facsimile that exists provides ample evidence of Herrad's purposeful shaping of the text's meaning. She chooses specific sections from scholars' works and disregards others. She offers her own German glosses—or loose translations—for some Latin phrases that reveal the connections she wants her canonesses to see.[58] She organizes texts from different sources in order to suit the overarching salvation narrative she seeks to convey.

Indeed, when Herrad compares herself to a little bee in the prologue, she is making a serious claim about her own work. Beehives were frequently cited as an ideal metaphor for monasteries because of the industry and organization of communal living.[59] Medieval theologians also used bees as a symbol of chastity, because bees seemed to procreate without coupling.[60]

In addition to these theological connections, Herrad seems to have been familiar with the ancient philosopher Seneca. Seneca declares that the bee is an appropriate metaphor for a writer's act of composition. Just as honeybees gather pollen from numerous flowers, scholars should read widely, then turn "all the various nectars we have tasted . . . into a single sweet substance."[61] In doing so, authors generate something new that did not previously exist, something that utterly transforms its sources and becomes more than the sum of its parts. Thus, when Herrad calls herself "a little bee inspired by God," she is not trying to be modest or cute. Instead, she asserts that she is a diligent, chaste, and generative worker who has produced something entirely new and sweet for her spiritual daughters.

The comparison to a bee suggests Herrad's own fruitfulness. Her vow of chastity does not bar her from being fertile in a real and valuable fashion. The future of a convent depended on the abbess cultivating younger women who could continue the work. It's significant, then, that a poem written about the women of Hohenburg and included in the *Hortus* describes all the canonesses—not just Herrad—as "little bees."[62] All of them are called to do cultivating work, gathering the nourishing nectar of doctrine and Scripture to sustain the work of the abbey. Not having biological children did not keep them from being generative.

There's another striking detail in the group portrait of the Hohenburg canonesses. The first and final portraits remain unlabeled. While every other woman is named, they are bookended by two anonymous figures. Perhaps these nameless women represent the ladies of Hohenburg before and after Herrad's tenure. Herrad implies that the community of Hohenburg will be perpetuated; women are seeking Christ through knowledge now and will continue to do so in the years and decades to come.[63] It is an assertion of her own fecundity. The *Hortus* is not just a textbook. It is a familial inheritance.

From Me to Thee

The story of Cultivating is hardly limited to medieval convents. As I look at the group portrait of the Hohenburg women—their faces turned like spring flowers toward the sun—I'm reminded of another imagined garden made by and for cultivating women.

Around 1833, Philadelphia schoolteacher and abolitionist Sarah Mapps Douglass (1806–82) painted a black swallowtail butterfly for her friend Amy Matilda Cassey (see fig. 4.10). The insect sits perched on a slender branch tipped with simple four-petal blossoms. Douglass unifies flora and fauna in several ways. The curve of the stem and leaves echoes the swell of the butterfly's wings. Meanwhile, the delicate patterns that fan across the wings contain the same pinks and greens as the foliage. But Douglass also creates a striking contrast. The whisper-thin magenta lines and rows of crisp green blocks contrast with the wings' opaque jet-black ink. The geometric shapes are also markedly different from the curling organic forms of leaves and flowers. Just below the vignette, written in elegant, swirling script, are the words "A token of love from me, to thee," followed by Douglass's signature.

The painting and its accompanying inscription were part of a "friendship album." These leather-bound books, full of tributes, poems, and artworks, were popular among young middle-class women in early nineteenth-century America. While most friendship albums were kept by white women, Amy Matilda Cassey and Sarah Mapps Douglass were both part of a small circle of well-educated, free Black women in Philadelphia. Both were also active in the Philadelphia Female Anti-Slavery Society and the Female Literary Association. Douglass's flower and butterfly paintings—in Cassey's album and several others—are considered to be the earliest signed artworks by an African American woman.

Historians have only recently begun to explore the functions and implications of Black women's friendship albums. While obviously different from Herrad's *Hortus Deliciarum*, some notable similarities emerge. Like the *Hortus*, friendship albums helped create and maintain a community of shared knowledge and morality. Albums circulating between friends and displayed in parlors allowed women to build networks as well as dispense advice. Cassey's album includes original and transcribed poems and essays that cover topics ranging from feminine beauty to friendship, motherhood, and even death. In addition, Black women's friendship albums often contain pleas for political action. Paintings by Douglass in other albums, for example, have inscriptions that explicitly support the abolitionist cause.[64]

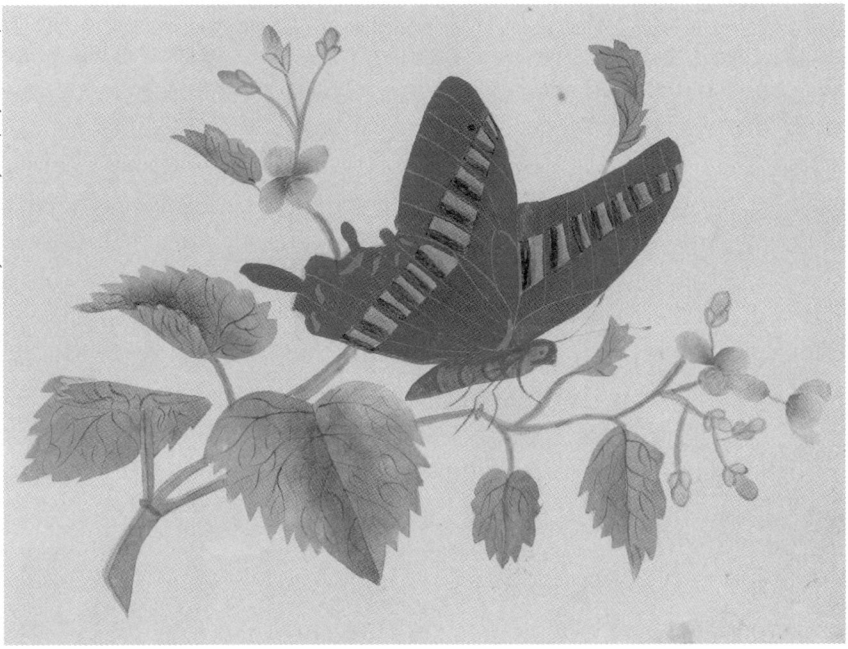

Figure 4.10. Sarah Mapps Douglass, *A Token of Love from Me, to Thee*, ca. 1833, watercolor and gouache. A full-color image of this watercolor is included in the color insert section.

Like Herrad, Douglass was a well-educated woman who never gave birth to children. Born in 1806 to a prominent Black Quaker family, she taught science, literature, and arts to African American girls in Philadelphia. She loved natural history and kept a personal cabinet full of shell mineral specimens in her classrooms.[65] After taking classes from the Female Medical College of Pennsylvania and the Pennsylvania Medical University, she also began lecturing on health and hygiene to working-class Black women. She was active in multiple political and literary women's organizations and advocated throughout her life not just for the abolition of slavery but for racial equality. Later in life, at age forty-nine, she married a widower with numerous children. Her husband passed away from illness within a few years, however, and Douglass returned both to living with her brothers and to leading the primary department at the school she helped found.

Also like Herrad, Douglass used her ranging education to be generative. Historian Katherine Isabel Bondy has demonstrated that Douglass's paintings of butterflies and flowers reflect her careful study of both botanical illustrations and Christian moral texts.[66] Bondy argues that Douglass's deliberate selections and alterations of her source material offer her readers a new vision of Black femininity, using flowers as a stand-in for African American women's bodies. Douglass could thus, for example, encourage her mentees to be both outwardly modest and internally driven—like a fuchsia plant.[67] At a time when African American women's bodies were being publicly scrutinized and mocked, Douglass encourages her friend Amy Matilda Cassey with a black swallowtail butterfly instead of the more common yellow variety. Perched on the sprig of flowers, ebony wings depicted mid-flap, the butterfly is beautiful and lively, ready to continue its pollinating work. Douglass celebrates Black women symbolically while protecting their bodies from objectification.

In the face of discrimination on account of both her race and her gender, Sarah Mapps Douglass still cultivated a garden of gifts to share. She was fruitful, indeed.

Fruitful Women

I'm humbled to realize how much the modern Mother story—shaped by the effects of the Protestant Reformation, Industrial Revolution, and contemporary culture war politics—directed my reading of the Bible. In my seasons of infertility, the only women in the Bible I could think of were mothers: Mary, of course, but also Naomi and Ruth, and even Bathsheba and Tamar. Sarah, Rebekah, Rachel, Hannah, and Elizabeth were once barren, like me. But God heard their cries and undid their curse. Was becoming a mother the *only* way that God blessed women?

Learning Herrad's story of cultivating and seeing resounding echoes elsewhere in history pushed me to reread my Bible. In both Old and New Testaments, we find examples of women who are never identified as mothers but who use their positions and abilities to cultivate shared justice, security, and delight. Deborah is called "a mother in Israel" (Judg. 5:7), but it is the Israelite military captain Barak whom we find under her care. She nurtures a nation. Jael pounds a peg through the head of an enemy captain, preserving the lives of others' children during a time of war (4:16–24). And Esther, who was motherless herself, saves her people through her God-ordained, courageous intervention—not by bearing an heir or a prophet. In the New Testament, Mary and Martha of Bethany, Mary Magdalene, Priscilla, Phoebe, and many others are given to us as examples of Christian faithfulness, participating fully in the family of Christ without special regard given to their maternal status. I missed so much evidence of abundance when I thought being barren was the same as being lifeless.

In her poignant personal reflection on being childless, Elizabeth Felicetti describes driving into the high desert of her home state of Arizona, marveling at the saguaro cacti, wildflowers, and hummingbirds of a supposed wasteland. "If all this desert life meant being barren," she writes, "then perhaps I wanted to be barren too."[68] Felicetti looks to women in the Bible, childless but cultivating life, as a model for reimagining her own generative potential. Maternity, she points out, is not the only path for fruitfulness.

I see what she means when I look at my friends who are not mothers but who are multiplying goodness around them. They plant their various gifts like seeds, writing books to meet people in their suffering, singing songs of welcome, teaching theology through bread and politics and history, surrounding the struggling with care and connection, analyzing data to improve public health, building systems for sustainability, fighting for justice in labyrinthian court systems and sharing stories in order to house the most vulnerable. That is not to say that they never grieve the absence of motherhood, but like the pilgrims of Psalm 84:6, they make springs in the valley.

My Flowers

"I bet you wish you had daughters."

"Aren't you going to keep trying for a girl?"

As long as I have been a mother of sons, people have asked me if I wouldn't prefer to be a mother of daughters. Sometimes I find myself slipping into a spiral of shame, wondering if I should have said yes to another round of fertility treatments. The ache still lingers, and sometimes it prickles intensely.

But Herrad's yearbook page in the *Hortus* lets me tell a different story. I will never see my own, round cheeks in a daughter's face, but I do know the pleasure of seeing my way of asking questions show up in another woman's scholarship. There are other ways to give an inheritance.

I think of so many of my students, women and men who have sat in my classroom but also cried in my office, drunk my tea, eaten in my home, washed my dishes, edited my manuscript drafts, and laughed at my jokes. They've confided their fears, shared their hopes, asked for prayer, received correction, and sometimes even borrowed my clothes. I would not call myself a mother to them, but I marvel at the strange intimacy of pressing into another human's life with persistence and care. I am reminded that I can be fruitful in my giving and my receiving. I am living the story of Cultivating.

I reimagine the tiny, handwritten names hovering above the rows of canonesses in *Hortus Deliciarum*. Instead of Agnes and Berta and Junta, I see the names of students who have clustered together in my Monday night classroom to study artworks made by, for, and about women. And I want for them what Herrad desired for her spiritual children: a life abundant and a delight that persists through struggle and grief.

5

Monster

Mirror, Mirror, on the Wall

I spread my fingers apart on my phone screen, zooming in on the photograph. My worst fears are confirmed, and a bitterness begins to collect in the back of my mouth. I know I'm supposed to be okay with growing older; I'm supposed to do it gracefully, resisting patriarchal norms that fetishize youth and offer only a narrow definition of beauty. Still, all I can think of as I peer at the digital image—and see the crepe paper folds of skin on my neck—is that I am well on my way to becoming a hag. Everything smooth is wrinkling. Everything firm and round is softening and shriveling. Soon, I'll be a monster.

The Venus, Vessel, Maiden, and Mother stories are all scripts that Western visual culture has told and retold as acceptable, pleasing versions of womanhood. There are more paths, however, to becoming a monster. While each popular story offers a kind of outline for women to fill, those who fail to conform—through either excess or absence—become a threat.

The desirable Venus can be monstrous if she uses her beauty to ensnare and control men. But a woman without any beauty is also vilified. The Vessel is a blank slate, a carrier of others' meaning. Thus, a woman with her own ambition is necessarily selfish, cold, and unrelatable. The helpless, reclining Maiden becomes a hideous hag by trying to take a man's place in the world or growing old and withered. The devoted Mother is a monster when she abandons her children or smothers them with attention. And of course, a woman without children at all is certainly grotesque. Sometimes the monsters have names: witch, harpy, siren, Medusa, or Jezebel. Sometimes their fearsome appearance announces their depravity and danger. At other times, we fear their duplicity, their ability to conceal their ugliness until it is too late for us to escape.

Folklore scholar Jeffery Jerome Cohen observes that monsters are always projections of a culture's fears and anxieties. Every monster is "a double narrative, two living stories: one that describes how the monster came to be and another . . . detailing what cultural use the monster serves."[1] Indeed, even the term "monster" comes from the Latin verb *moneo*, meaning "to warn, remind, or instruct."

Historians and literary critics can point to numerous examples of this.[2] The monster in Mary Shelley's *Frankenstein* is widely understood as a caution against unchecked technological progress. Godzilla embodies a post–World War II fear of nuclear weapons' effects. There are also examples of monsters being used to control a society's attitudes and actions. In medieval Europe, dragons were cast as demons in disguise or agents of Satan himself. The belief that saints could kill or tame dragons encouraged medieval listeners to likewise pursue piety. Dragons could also represent foreign, pagan powers that needed to be defeated in literal battle. It is unsurprising, then, that the story of Saint George slaying a dragon was often invoked during the European crusades to retake Jerusalem from the Muslim Seljuk Empire.

Monster stories have certainly been effective in policing *my* actions. As a young girl, I worried regularly about both imagined creatures under the bed and the criminals profiled on *America's Most Wanted*. To avoid such threats, I obeyed rules scrupulously. I stayed in bed when I was told, and I refused to talk to strangers.

But now, I'm trying to avoid becoming a monster myself.

I find the histories of monstrous women in high art and popular culture. I hear echoes in everything from contemporary advertisements to evangelical theology. The story underneath it all is this: To be a good woman, I must refrain from being a threat. In order to keep others—and myself—safe, the monstrous woman must be domesticated or destroyed.

A Temptress

Not all monsters are ugly.

I find my first female monster in my childhood Bible. *The Picture Bible* offers a comic book–style retelling of biblical narratives, with figures rendered like 1980s superheroes. After handing Adam the fruit from the Tree of the Knowledge of Good and Evil, Eve stands in profile in the shadows, her hand raised in a beckoning gesture. I didn't know it at the time, but years later I recognized an echo of that dangerously sensual silhouette while watching black-and-white movies with my high school friends. The femme fatale, the deadly woman, is also one of the oldest monsters in history. The Mesopotamian deity Inanna, for example, was the beautiful but violent goddess of both love and war. The ancient Greeks told stories about the enchantress Circe, who controlled men with her powers, and mythical sirens, who lured sailors to their death.

I'm far too much of a Goody Two-shoes to consider a purposeful embrace of this story. And as a freshman in college with cropped, dark hair, a straight figure, and a preference for pants over dresses, I find myself struggling to present a version of femininity that is acceptable—much less desirable—in the American South. So when an older woman pats my hand at church and tells me, "You're very pretty," I start to swell with gratefulness. Then she finishes, "So you must be very careful not to tempt young men. We are all daughters of Eve."

While the story of Eve and the fall can be found in Genesis 3, this other story of a monstrous Eve—the darkly glamorous bad girl and conniving temptress—has little to do with the Bible. We find its origins, instead, in the medieval church.

The so-called Portal of the Virgin may seem like a strange place for a temptress, but I find her carved into the exterior of Notre Dame Cathedral in Paris (see fig. 5.1). The thirteenth-century relief carvings around the massive wooden doors mostly depict the Virgin Mary's death, assumption into heaven, and coronation as the queen of heaven by Christ himself. But the central pillar that separates the doors also contains a sculpture depicting the temptation in the garden of Eden. Adam and Eve flank the Tree of the Knowledge of Good and Evil. Rendered nearly the same size, with smooth, sturdy bodies, the first man and woman are also unified by actual and implied lines. As Eve lifts the forbidden fruit to her mouth to take a bite, she looks across the tree's branches and meets Adam's gaze. As Adam reaches his right arm toward his wife, she places another fruit

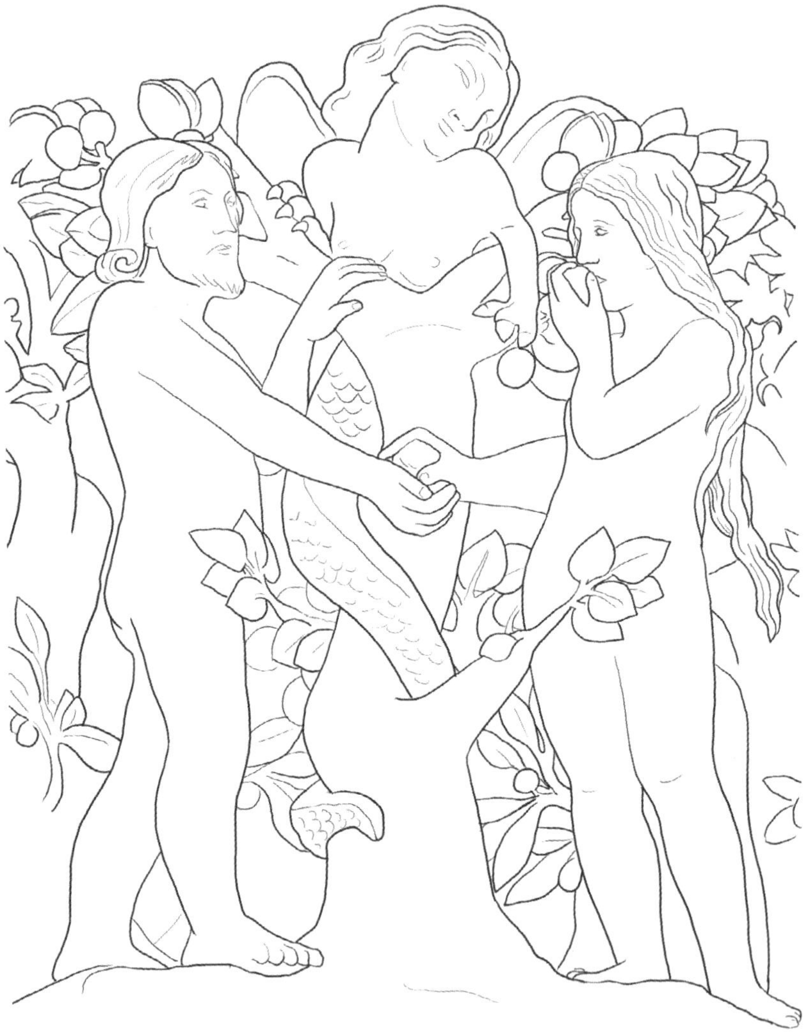

Figure 5.1. Drawn from *The Temptation of Adam and Eve* in the Portal of the Virgin, Notre Dame Cathedral, Paris, France, ca. 1210–20

into his open palm. But there's one other figure in the scene who also links the composition together.

A winged serpent twines around the tree and emerges between the topmost branches, forming the apex of a triangle between Adam and Eve. But where we might expect to see the pointed head of a snake, we instead find the head, shoulders, and breasts of a woman. She is beautiful, with soft features, wavy hair, and a knowing smile. But she also arcs back, like a cobra preparing to strike, twisting toward Eve. It is an eerie twinning. The woman-serpent and Eve mirror each other, linked together visually as securely as the serpent is wrapped around the tree.

The sculpture may be one of the oldest public depictions of the serpent with a woman's head, but it was not the last. The visual story of Eve, the first woman, colluding with Satan-as-woman became increasingly popular during the Middle Ages. Centuries later, even Michelangelo rendered Eve's twin emerging from a snake's body on the ceiling of the Sistine Chapel.

Certainly, the association of snakes with women predates Christian art by millennia, and literary scholars have shown how the story of Eve in the garden plays with and against ancient Near Eastern myths.[3] But the Western *visual* history of linking the woman with the serpent—and thus with the devil—has also had far-reaching implications.

In Genesis 3:1–5, Eve is tempted by a creature referred to as "he" and described simply as a serpent. In the Latin translation that would have been most familiar to medieval scholars, the word *serpens* is gendered masculine. Yet in the influential *Historia scholastica* (ca. 1173)—a paraphrase of the Bible sometimes called the Medieval Popular Bible—the French theologian Peter Comestor makes a new claim. According to Comestor, Lucifer, the angel cast out of heaven, decides to inhabit the body of a serpent with a woman's face because "like praises like."[4] The snake with the pretty face, possessed by Lucifer, convinces Eve to distrust her Creator. She, in turn, convinces Adam, and humanity's fellowship with God is broken. Even before the serpent speaks a lie, its *appearance* is a lie. In Comestor's tale, Eve—who already shares the serpent's beautiful appearance—goes on to share the serpent's duplicity. Later theologians like William of Auvergne, who oversaw part of the construction of Notre Dame in Paris, further elaborated on and solidified the belief that women were, by their very nature, both more easily deceived and more successful at perpetuating deceit.[5]

The woman-headed serpent in the Notre Dame sculpture also had another name: Lilith. The story of Lilith gained popularity in medieval Europe through *The Alphabet of Ben Sira*, a supposedly Jewish text that was likely a work of satire.[6] In the *Ben Sira* retelling of the creation narrative, Lilith is Adam's first wife, made from the dust of the earth like her husband, not formed from his rib. Lilith refuses to submit to Adam and flees. When angels try to bring her back, she defies them and announces that she will henceforth be responsible for the illness and deaths of infants. When describing later medieval depictions of the temptation—like the one in the Notre Dame portal—commentators sometimes identified the serpent as Lilith, coming back to wreak further havoc on Adam and his new wife, Eve.

While the practice of depicting the serpent with a woman's head eventually disappeared in Western art, the visual story took on a new form again in the late nineteenth and early twentieth centuries. Artists could use the character of Eve or Lilith as a kind of shorthand for temptation and as an excuse for painting dangerously beautiful women. In his painting *Lady Lilith*, Dante Gabriel Rossetti depicts a European woman but invokes the idea of a conniving, sexually powerful temptress with the title (see fig. 5.2). The porcelain-skinned beauty pouts in the corner of the composition, her dress slipping from her shoulder as she dreamily brushes her long, strawberry-blond hair. The woman's mane of hair is both evidence of her beauty and a sign of her dangerous hypersexuality that could entrap an unwitting man.

When the church lady patted my hand and warned me against being a temptation to men, she was telling a version of this Monster story. My body and my beauty were a threat. This same story can often be found lurking beneath the so-called Billy Graham rule, a popular code of conduct in evangelical circles that prohibits men from being alone with a woman who is not their wife or daughter. The rule, along with other guiding principles for running his growing ministry, was adopted by evangelist Billy Graham in 1948. Over time, it gained popularity among other evangelical men as a rule of life. In 2017, the practice was dubbed the "Mike Pence Rule" when

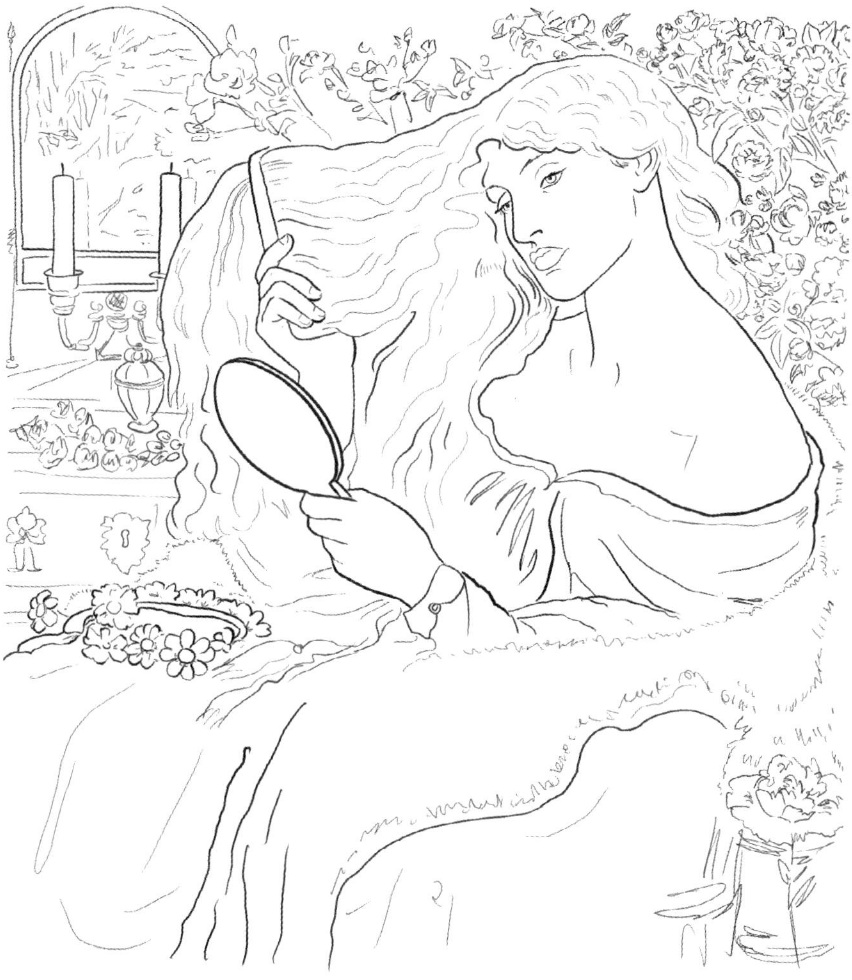

Figure 5.2. Drawn from Dante Gabriel Rossetti, *Lady Lilith*, 1866–68

the vice president acknowledged that he, too, declined to dine alone with women other than his wife.[7]

Many who abide by the Billy Graham rule see it as practical wisdom, keeping them from even the appearance of impropriety. Yet it can also have other consequences. For example, a strict, legalistic application can exclude women from opportunities for mentorship and networking that then remain available only to men.[8] Even more troubling is how some men use the rule to reinforce a Monster story, insisting that a woman, by her very nature, might use any opportunity to seduce and trap them in sexual sin. After all, women are daughters of Eve.

Notably, though, a 2017 *New York Times* poll found that a majority of *women*—more so than men—believed that it was inappropriate to have dinner or drinks with a man who was not their spouse.[9] A few months later, as accusations of sexual assault tumbled into public view as part of the #MeToo movement, some of the reasons for women's hesitancy to be alone with men in those contexts became more apparent. Who is a threat to whom?

In every case, the Monster story of the temptress leverages fear to turn the complexities of particular relationships, personal responsibility, power dynamics, and cultural expectations into a blunt weapon.

A Monstrous Venus

While an excess of feminine sexuality and desirability can be dangerous, so too can the *absence* of acceptable feminine beauty. While particular standards can and have shifted over time, the Western ideal has long demanded a young and lithe body, smooth and fair. Women's bodies with wrinkles or pubic hair, menstruating or in menopause, round, disabled, or scarred all become deviant bodies. As we have already seen, these narrowly drawn boundaries of acceptable feminine desirability also deliberately excluded Black women.

The life of Sara Baartman (1789–1815) shows us with excruciating clarity how Monster stories don't remain abstracted tales or moral fables. They can have a real impact on real bodies. Sara Baartman was a nineteenth-century Khoisan woman from South Africa exhibited as a freak show attraction in England, Ireland, and France as the "Hottentot Venus."[10] The facts of her early life remain unclear, but historians agree that Baartman arrived in England in 1810 with her former employer, Hendrik Cesars, and a Scottish surgeon, Alexander Dunlop. Dunlop believed that British scientists—and the public more generally—would be fascinated by Baartman's body, especially her large buttocks. Once in London, Dunlop printed up posters, charging one shilling for visitors to see what he called "that most wonderful phenomenon of nature."[11]

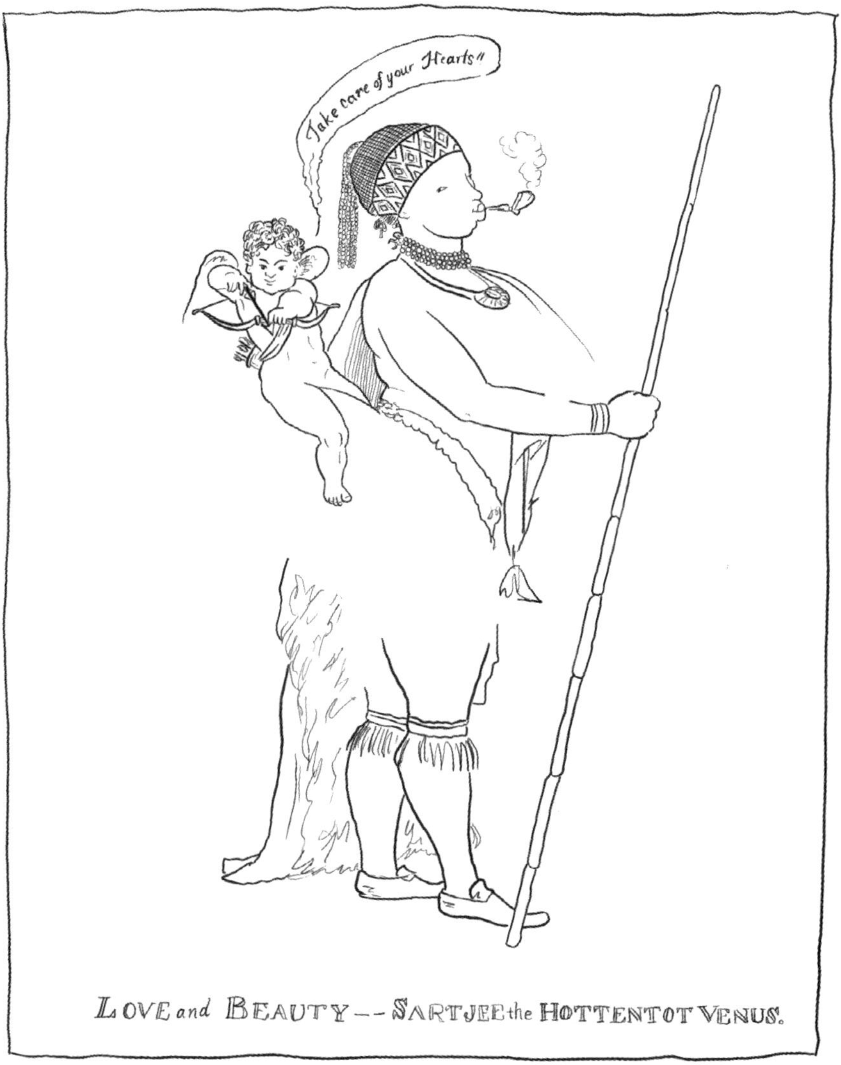

Figure 5.3. Drawn from a caricature published in 1811 by Christopher Crupper Rumford, England

An anonymous but highly circulated cartoon from around that time depicts Baartman standing in profile, smoking a short pipe and holding a long pole in her right hand (see fig. 5.3). While adorned with jewelry, a patterned cap, and European-style shoes, she is naked save a pink, sheepskin-lined cloak that highlights rather than covers her expanse of bare skin. A winged cupid—all rosy skin and blond locks—sits astride Baartman's exaggerated buttocks, aiming an arrow at the viewer. "Take care of your hearts!!" he warns in a speech bubble that floats above Baartman's head. Below her, we read, "LOVE and BEAUTY: SARTJEE the HOTTENTOT VENUS."

By billing Baartman as a "Venus," her handlers accomplished two seemingly contradictory goals. First, the moniker "Venus" announced her availability to a sexualized, desiring gaze. At the same time, however, the modifier "Hottentot"—a Dutch colonist term for Baartman's ethnic group—suggests that this is not a universal ideal of beauty and love. She is the *Hottentot's* Venus. So, a European viewer is not expected to find her attractive. As the argument goes, her ugliness proves that the Khoisans' sense of beauty—and by extension their morality, intellect, and worth—is inferior, if not completely broken.

The satirical print is hardly an accurate representation of Baartman's actual body. Indeed, contemporary accounts insist that she was always clothed, albeit in snug garments that showed the contours of her form. By definition, a caricature is an exaggeration of reality intended to make a critical or humorous point. But the more I learn about Sara Baartman, the more I realize that the excesses of this cartoon actually serve to conceal some of the lived horror.

Baartman's large buttocks and genitalia were considered typical of women of African descent but also visual evidence of an oversized, animalistic sexuality.[12] Thus, Baartman's actual display and the advertisements that represented her both reflected and furthered European assumptions about Black women's sexual availability. When Baartman left England to tour France, she endured even more invasive inspections under the guise of "science."

Baartman died in France in 1815 at the age of twenty-six. The French naturalist George Cuvier dissected her body, looking for evidence that Baartman possessed ape-like traits and hoping to prove an emerging theory of racial difference and European superiority.[13] Horrifyingly, Baartman's skeleton, genitals, and a cast of her body were displayed at two French museums until 1976. Her remains were not returned to South Africa until 2002.

While such dehumanization was the norm, there were other responses too. The Africa Association—a British abolitionist society—sued Baartman's white companions, alleging that she was participating in the display under duress and subject to inhumane conditions. But Dunlop produced a signed contract and sworn affidavit from Baartman, seemingly proving her willing participation in the scheme.[14] While scholars continue to question if Baartman was coerced, the existence and circulation of the Hottentot Venus cartoon tell us that putting a Black woman's body on display as an example of monstrosity was widely accepted.

There is also an echo here of the so-called exotic Venuses we discussed in chapter 1. The submissive Asian women and Middle Eastern odalisques, the spicy Latina bombshell, and the Black Jezebel can also be seen as variations of this Monster story. If the smooth, pale, available body of the classical Venus is the assumed norm, then anything other than that is seen as abnormal or perverse.

Isn't it an unholy, ugly knot? If you're not desirable, you're a freak. If you're too desirable, you're a temptress. And if you're desirable for the "wrong reasons," then you probably deserve whatever humiliation you have coming.

An Ambitious Woman

I press my lips together, swallowing the excited swell of words that wants to spill out. My theology professor eyes me, silently inviting me to continue speaking if I want to, but I give a small shake of my head and tuck my hands beneath the table. I want to keep talking, to keep tugging at this theological thread. But an unbidden image of a woman with wild hair and a gaping mouth, limbs akimbo as she gestures wildly, fleetingly passes through my mind. I can't quite identify the picture, but I'm afraid that if I continue my public, passionate theological wrestling match in front of the class, I'll become some kind of monster, taking up space and demanding attention.

Years later, I can better name that Monster. She's ambitious, opinionated, and forceful, and we call her a harridan, a shrew, or, more crassly, a female dog. I find her in visual form, raging in the centerfold image of a 1913 satirical American magazine called *Puck* (see fig. 5.4). The illustration depicts a fair-skinned woman holding aloft a yellow flag that reads "Woman Suffrage." But another woman—this one older and bug-eyed, with a hooked nose and wrinkled, olive skin—seems to emerge from her body and is running directly toward the viewer. Concerningly, she carries a

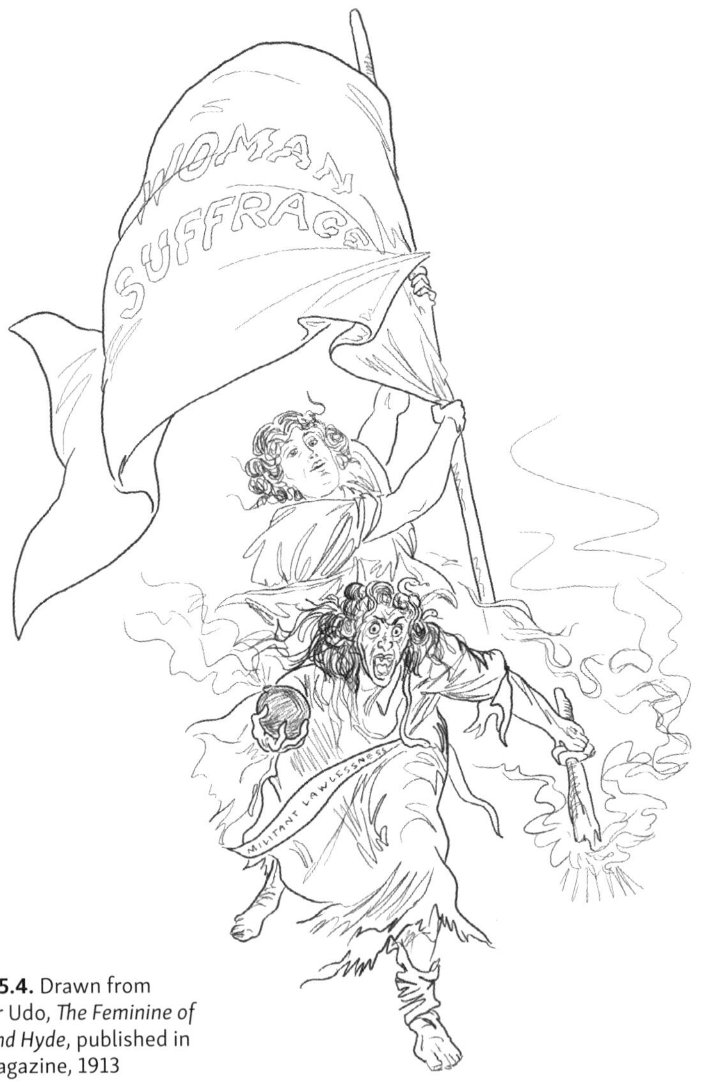

Figure 5.4. Drawn from Keppler Udo, *The Feminine of Jekyll and Hyde*, published in *Puck* magazine, 1913

lit bomb in one hand and a flaming torch in the other. The overall composition echoes the central figures of Eugène Delacroix's iconic *Liberty Leading the People*. But instead of Liberty summoning virtuous foot soldiers, a militant harridan terrorizes the world, threatening violence if she doesn't get her way. She's monstrous not just in appearance but in her rejection of the emptiness and constraint that mark the Vessel and Maiden stories.

The image in *Puck* was just one example of imagery in the United States and Britain that depicted activists for women's suffrage as ugly, aggressive, and dangerous. Certainly, some images, including this one, were responding to particular acts of arson or violence carried out by suffragist activists. But many anti-suffrage cartoons applied the same visual Monster story to suffragists in general. A British postcard from 1909, for example, depicts a woman—in a purple dress and a floral headpiece—announcing, "We want the vote." But the suffragist is a hideous shrew, with pointed teeth, wrinkled and wart-pocked skin, and stringy hair. Chillingly, this particular card was mailed to British activist Christabel Pankhurst with the message "Don't you think you had better sew a button on my shirt?" and signed "Joe."[15] Other cartoons represented suffragists as bespectacled, bitter, older women or as square-jawed women with buck teeth and unflattering buns. The message was clear: By demanding the right to vote, white women were betraying the feminine ideal. Stepping into the public sphere of politics made them unattractive, unwomanly, and even inhuman. Conversely, the images suggested that perhaps only monstrous women were the ones advocating for suffrage at all.

There's a particular irony to *Puck* magazine depicting a suffragist as Liberty gone rogue. That same year, a new weekly newspaper actually called *The Suffragist* featured an image of Columbia—the female personification of the United States—standing on the bow of an open boat, arms stretched in welcome as she floats toward the Capitol building.[16] Advocates *for* women's right to vote used Columbia—the woman-shaped container for the idea of the nation—to suggest that suffrage was a natural culmination of women's long-standing presence as a symbol. Now, Columbia, Liberty, and Justice would *do*, not just *be*. Instead of women representing democracy, they would participate in it. The visual argument was clever and effective.

But the *Puck* illustration of Liberty as an irrational, dangerous harridan argued that the opposite was true. Women who wanted to participate in politics were essentially giving up their womanhood altogether. By exceeding the contours of the Vessel story—by acting to create meaning and change rather than just holding meaning like a container—a woman would inevitably become a Monster. Such imagery also suggested that suffragists were rebelling against an eternal, fixed norm of womanhood instead of rejecting the relatively new Enlightenment notion of separate spheres that we discussed in chapters 2 and 4.

An ambitious woman is an ugly sight, or so the anti-suffragist propaganda would have us believe. And an ugly woman is often an *old* woman as well.

A Crone

As I stand in front of my bathroom mirror, chin lifted yet again to examine the creases in my neck, an image from my first art history textbook flashes into my mind. *Drunken Old Woman* is a Roman copy of a life-sized Hellenistic Greek sculpture from the late third century BCE (see fig. 5.5). An old woman squats on the ground, ankles crossed, clutching a large wine flask in her lap. Her draped garment falls off her shoulder, revealing a skeletal collarbone and breastbone jutting through papery thin flesh. She tilts her head upward, and her sagging cheeks fall in deep wrinkles as she opens her mouth in a toothless grin.

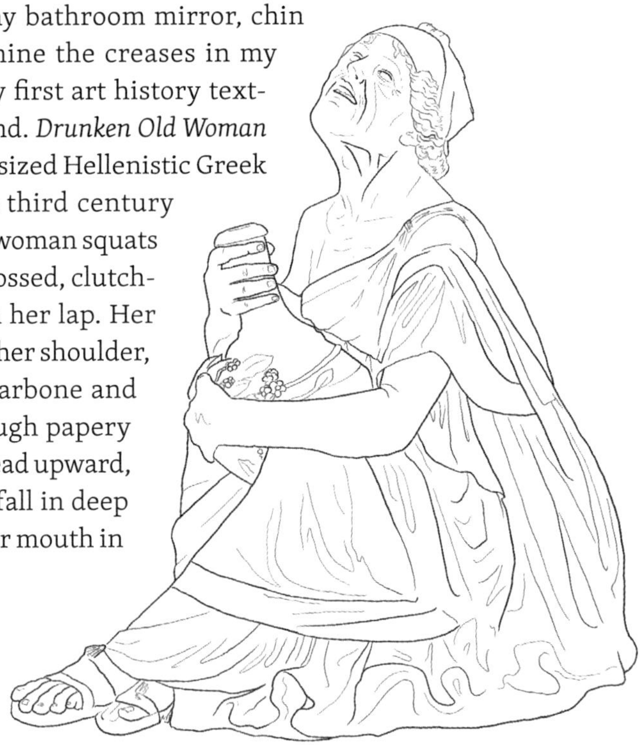

Figure 5.5. Drawn from *Drunken Old Woman*, copy of a third-century BCE statue

My classmates and I laughed at her. Indeed, viewers have been laughing at her for centuries. Our visual archive teaches us not only whom we should admire but also whom we should despise. Her slipping robe is not seductive; it is silly. She's not a fun, carefree girl; she's an absurd crone. She may not be exactly frightening, but she's a monster nonetheless, a threat that we disarm with derision.

"What now?" I wonder, as lines begin to appear on my own skin. What happens when the maiden matures?

Compared to the Venus and the Maiden stories, crones appear far less frequently in Western art history. Still, historian Patricia Simons has demonstrated that Italian Renaissance artists borrowed both desirable, idealized bodies and ugly, old women from the classical past.[17] Importantly, these women were not just aesthetically displeasing. They were also morally suspect. Throughout the fifteenth century, magistrates in Italy, Switzerland, and France aggressively identified, pursued, and executed people they suspected of being witches. Three-quarters of those killed were women, and many of them were elderly.[18] Simons's research traces how—through the reproduction of popular prints—the grotesquely aged female body became virtually synonymous with "evil."

For example, in his dense, dynamic engraving *Battle of the Sea Gods*, Andrea Mantegna depicts an imagined epic encounter between Neptune and other sea deities. Muscled, male figures confront each other, while a gaunt, older woman—with drooping, gourd-like breasts, a wrinkled face, and windswept hair—screams over the entire scene (see fig. 5.6). She holds a small tablet in her hand that identifies her as the personification of envy. Mantegna's composition suggests that she is ultimately responsible for the ensuing chaos. While she represents the vice of envy in this print, the crone also looks very much like the stereotypical witch of contemporary pop culture; she's just missing the pointy, black hat.

Why make this association between evil and old women? Or, to put it another way, if monsters are made from our cultural anxieties, what made older women so threatening to the status quo of the Renaissance era?

Many believed that the experience and wisdom of an aged woman could make her dangerous.[19] Unlike an innocent maiden, a crone could have sexual knowledge. If she was widowed, she would also have more

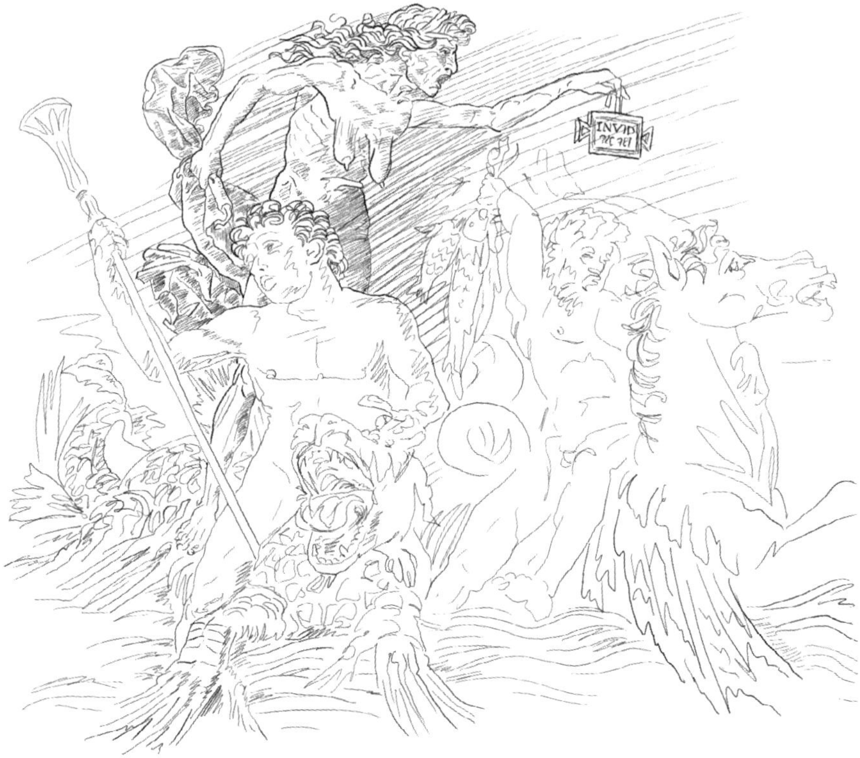

Figure 5.6. Detail drawn from Andrea Mantegna, *Battle of the Sea Gods*, ca. 1481

social freedom and capital, without the constraining hand of a husband. Older women assisted in childbirth and attended to the sick and dying. But their work as healers could also mean that they knew how to harm. No longer soft and fertile, the body of an older woman seemed more like a man's. It was thus more independent, less open to being contained and captured like the maiden's.

The reality, however, was that the thousands of women who were burned as witches in fifteenth-century Europe were not in cahoots with the devil or plotting to overthrow the social order. Most were vulnerable, living in poverty and socially marginalized. Lacking legal or cultural protection, older women served as readily available scapegoats in a time of rapid social change.[20] The monster was imagined, but the consequences were real.

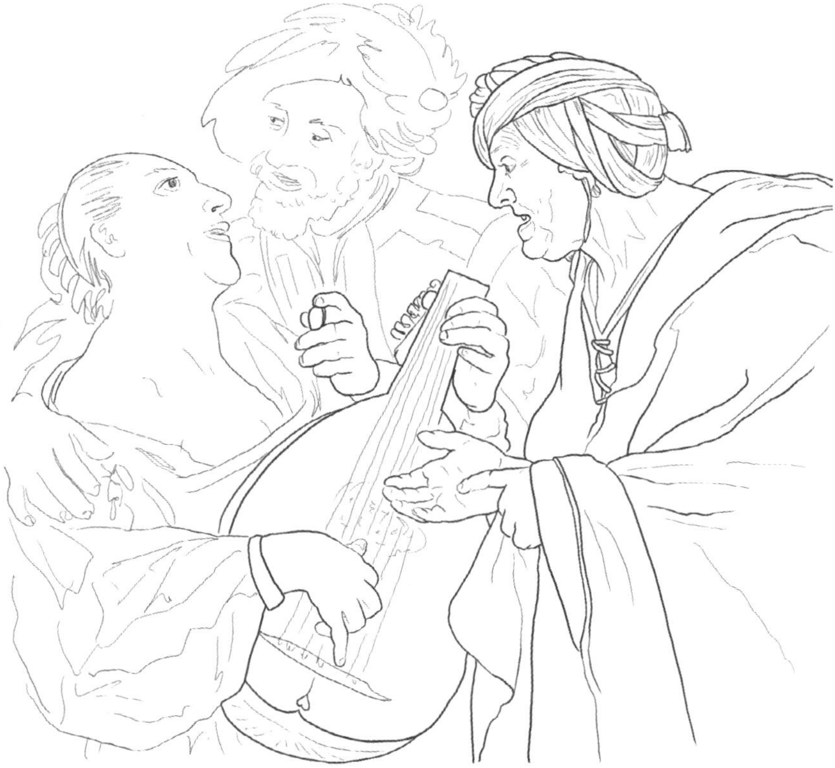

Figure 5.7. Drawn from Dirck van Baburen, *The Procuress*, 1622

A similar disjunction between visual stories and reality occurs again in seventeenth-century Holland. Some seventeenth-century Dutch artworks feature positive, even tender depictions of older women. Often, they are shown as wise and pious matrons, contrasted with foolish maidens. Still, the vicious story of the crone also makes regular appearances. *The Procuress* by Dirck van Baburen, made around 1622, is one such example (see fig. 5.7). Within the closely cropped, almost square frame, we see three figures: a young woman in a low-cut dress playing a lute, a bearded man with his arm draped over her shoulder, and an old woman with a hooked nose impatiently pointing at her empty hand. To Golden Age Dutch viewers, the implied narrative would be clear. We are in a brothel, and the crone is the "procuress" of the title, negotiating the price that the client will pay.

Van Baburen and his contemporaries made multiple variations on this same theme. The brothel keeper was always a woman with a lined face, hooked nose, and fleshy chin, her hair covered by a turban. Her weathered body contrasted with the glowing, smiling faces and voluptuous figures of the young women cavorting and flirting with well-dressed, jovial male clients.

It may seem almost unbelievable that these paintings were bought by middle-class patrons and hung in their homes. In the seventeenth-century Dutch Republic, sex outside the marriage bed was both a sin and a criminal offense; brothel keepers were prosecuted as well. How do we make sense of Dutch Protestants' criminalization of prostitution *and* their choice of painted subjects?

Given how detailed and naturalistic these paintings are, we might assume that they accurately represent what sex work looked like in seventeenth-century Holland. But after looking at seventeenth-century court records and letters, scholars have determined that brothel paintings by van Baburen and others actually offer us *fictional* scenes.[21] While van Baburen paints well-dressed women playing musical instruments, most prostitutes in the Dutch Republic were immigrants living in poverty. Most brothel keepers were—as the paintings suggest—women, not men, but many were also younger than thirty.

This mismatch between van Baburen's painted world and Dutch people's actual lives helps us understand the artworks' possible appeal. Because older women were associated with evil, the crone's presence alerts viewers to the fact that the young people's gaiety and beauty are not all they seem to be. Physical pleasure and beauty are fleeting; vice may be attractive in the moment, but its ugliness will appear eventually. The procuress's monstrous body serves as this reminder.

Back at my bathroom mirror, I shift my face again, watching the light catch on the lines fanning out from the corners of my eyes. The Monster story wants to tell me that my aging body is inherently ugly, useless, and dangerous. But when I look at my mother, I see her silvery hair as a crown and her wrinkled knuckles as hard-won, jeweled rings. I recall the pillowy soft arms of my grandmother with nothing but fondness. I cherish the memory of the sparkling eyes of my hundred-year-old "*obaaban*" and how she would flash me a gummy smile before slipping her dentures back into her mouth. I imagine all of these women as full—not depleted—overflowing with stories and wisdom.

I recognize the irony, even as I reach for a retinol cream. Are women's bodies ever acceptable? The story of the Monster teaches me that I am responsible for stopping the inevitable, natural decline of my body. Yet not too long ago, I feared that I was monstrous for *failing* to exhibit a supposedly natural urge.

An Unnatural Obsession

During my junior year of college, many of my friends earned extra money by babysitting. One of them once offered me a job she couldn't take. I declined. I did have a scheduling conflict, but I felt like I was also carrying a secret: *I would rather study than babysit.* It's not just that I disliked the parts of childcare that dealt with snot and slime and dirty diapers. I didn't like the supposedly sweet parts either. I would much rather have been reading a philosophy book than bouncing an infant or playing pretend kitchen with a toddler. I was pretty sure that this frame of mind meant that I was neither marriage nor maternal material. What kind of woman doesn't want to play with babies? Only a monster.

I can't remember when I first saw the cartoon from *Les Bas-Bleus*, but years later, Honoré Daumier's print floated at the periphery of my consciousness as a new professor and mother of young children. Somehow, the nineteenth-century artist and satirist had rummaged about in my head and drawn one of my secret fears.

The black-and-white 1844 lithograph depicts a room cluttered with overturned furniture, scattered clothing, and abandoned cleaning supplies (see fig. 5.8). Our eyes land immediately on the lower left corner, where we find a toddler head down, partially submerged in a large white tub. His bare bottom is exposed, and his skinny legs kick vainly as he tries to free himself. Those same legs direct us across the room to the child's mother. Instead of recognizing her son's distress and rushing to save him, the seated woman is turned resolutely away, hunched over a table and writing furiously with her quill. On the wall above her we see a pinboard full of historical art reproductions, perhaps giving us insight into the subject of her writing.

Her desire to write and to study results in the rejection of the Mother story of total devotion. Although we can't see her face clearly, her severe bun and hawkish nose suggest that we would not find her to be beautiful. In fact, Daumier anticipates that his viewers will understand the woman's disordered home and displeasing appearance as a reflection of her ugly,

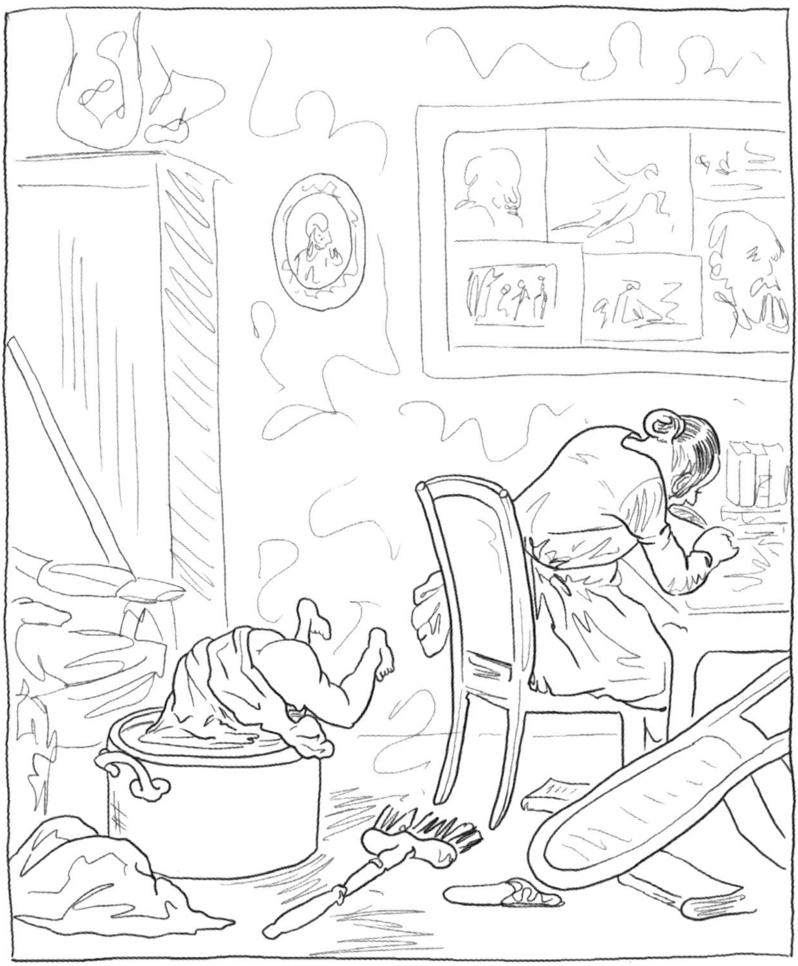

Figure 5.8. Drawn from Honoré Daumier, *Les Bas-Bleus*, 1844

distorted womanhood. Because she has ignored her true and natural calling as a mother and keeper of the home, her household has fallen apart and her child is in danger. But Daumier and his viewers are less concerned by the toddler and more troubled by the monstrous woman.

This print is part of a series of almost seventy that Daumier made skewering the *bas-bleus*, or "bluestockings," a derogatory term used in the nineteenth century to describe intellectual women who "sp[oke] a little too loudly, a little too much, a little too much for the whole world."[22] The notion that such a woman was not just poorly mannered but dangerously unnatural was made explicit. In a book titled *Les bas-bleus*, published a bit later in the nineteenth century, another French author exclaims, "A woman-man! That's almost monstrous!"[23]

While Daumier prided himself on being politically progressive, his views on women and family life remained conservative, more in line with Napoleon I's civil code of 1804: "Woman is given to man so that she can have children. She is thus his property as the fruit tree is that of the garden."[24] Daumier uses biting humor to trivialize the intellectual woman, depicting her as "deviant, a creature who disrupts households, neglects children, and uses her fame to satisfy unnatural sexual appetites."[25] Daumier wasn't alone in his anxious critique. Theatrical plays and popular satirical booklets depicted intellectual women as old, unattractive, and disruptive. The lesson was clear: Women who pursue the life of the mind are not really women at all.[26]

While much of my earlier concern over my maternal fitness has been soothed by the deep delight I find in my children, Daumier's cartoon still sometimes looms like a threat. I can hear the voices of conservative evangelical pastors in my head, telling me to give all my attention to my children's needs and to turn my family into ministry.[27] Even my relatively flexible schedule as a professor still takes me away from my children, and a not insignificant portion of my creativity is directed toward developing lesson plans and teaching college classes, not directing childhood enrichment activities. Are the dusty shelves and dirty stairs at home the first step in my inevitable descent into monstrosity? In writing this book, am I ignoring and endangering my children—in mind and spirit if not in body?

The fact that a nineteenth-century cultural critic and a twenty-first-century pastor have overlapping concerns about a woman's rightful place seems to suggest, at least initially, that an eternal, "natural" order has been disrupted. But historian Janis Bergman-Carton points out that Daumier and his contemporaries—like the twentieth-century artists who depicted monstrous suffragists and the Renaissance artists who rendered conniving witches—were actually responding to particular social anxieties of their own moment.[28] Recent political shifts in France prompted the reemergence of a women's emancipation movement. In the 1830s, middle- and working-class women increasingly participated in the dynamic and profitable French literary industry as writers, editors, and journalists. Around the same time, new censorship laws prohibited newspapers from directly criticizing the government. Illustrated magazines like *Le Charivari*, which had built their reputation on political caricature, now directed their attention to social critique. Bergman-Carton argues that male journalists, unable to express their anger at the monarchy, turned their wrath "toward a figure they saw as the female usurper of the male place, the newly professionalized [female writer]."[29] Daumier's ugly, cold-hearted woman is a monster born of her moment.

Remembering that Monster stories are, in fact, *stories*, allows me to release a long breath. I believe, still, in a God who created a world with a glorious design and purposeful potential. I believe, too, that the fall has broken our relationship to that world, to each other, and to our God. I believe that Jesus is making all the sad things untrue. And I believe, more and more, that I will be surprised by what that looks like. God asks me to be faithful and fruitful. I don't need to name monsters, and I don't need to fear them. The more I study history, the more I am humbled and convinced of my own limited ability to imagine all that a good God might have in store not just for me, not just for women, but for all his children.

Perhaps the threat comes not from the Monsters but from what we do to them.

The Monster Defeated

How do most Monster stories end?

Two archways down from Giambologna's *Rape of a Sabine Woman*—that virtuosic marble sculpture that tells the story of the captured, helpless maiden—we find one more Monster story. Beneath the leftmost arch of the Loggia dei Lanzi, that grand, elevated stage in one of Florence's most important piazzas, stands a triumphant hero. Benevuto Cellini's ten-foot-tall bronze *Perseus with the Head of Medusa* is perched on a seven-foot-tall, square base (see fig. 5.9). Perseus steps forward, planting one foot on the writhing body of his decapitated foe. He is nude except for his winged helmet and sandals, and his muscular body and curly hair echo the sculptures of classical antiquity. In his right hand, Perseus holds his wide, curving sword. With his left, he holds the head of his foe aloft: Medusa. The monster is defeated.

In Greek mythology, Medusa was a Gorgon, a hideous creature with snakes for hair and eyes so terrifying that anyone who looked at her would immediately be turned to stone.[30] The hero Perseus executes a clever plan to kill Medusa without directly looking at her, thus slaying the Gorgon and avoiding his own death.

I see this sculpture on my first visit to Florence. I enter the piazza from the north, heading toward the covered porch of the Loggia dei Lanzi. Even from a distance, Perseus arrests my attention. The dark-green patina of the bronze contrasts with the surrounding stone architecture and nearby marble sculptures. Initially, it's hard to see what he's holding, so his raised arm serves almost as a gesture of greeting. As I get closer, Perseus's elevated position on the stone and bronze

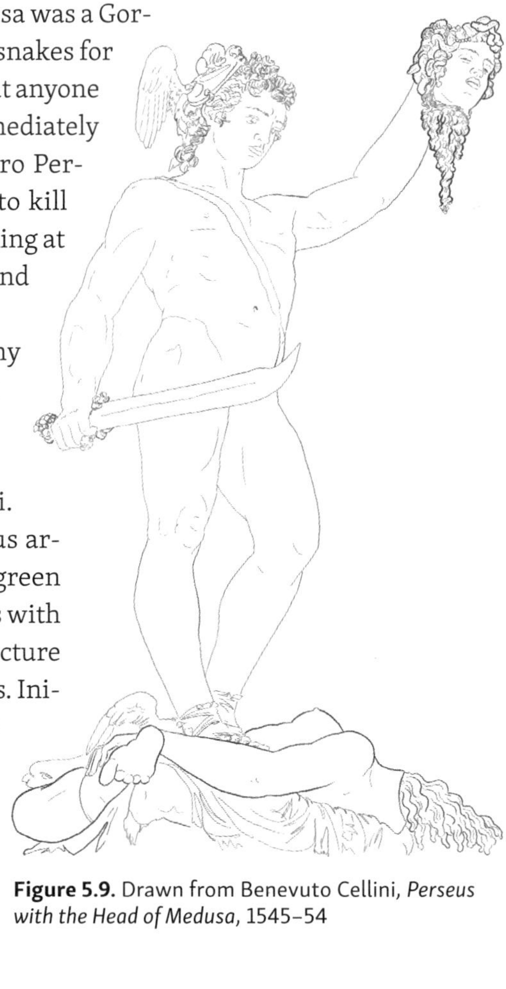

Figure 5.9. Drawn from Benevuto Cellini, *Perseus with the Head of Medusa*, 1545–54

pedestal becomes more obvious. I have to tip my chin up to gaze at the hero's face, and then I can finally see Medusa's head in his grasp. Strangely, perhaps, she does not immediately strike me as grotesque. The twisting snakes are almost indistinguishable from Perseus's own curly hair as well as the blood that rigidly extends from her neck. I know she's a monster because I've been told she's a monster, not because she particularly looks like one.

Now my eyes follow that vertical line of gore from Medusa's head down to what I slowly realize is her awkwardly twisted, naked body. As I walk around the pedestal, I try to make sense of what I see. Medusa's firm, round breasts defy gravity, even as Perseus steps on her ribcage. From the front of the sculpture, it seems as if Medusa's right arm is hanging limply, but when I move to the side, I can see that her elbow is slightly bent and her fingers are tensed. Then when I climb up onto the loggia so I can see the sculpture from behind, I realize that Medusa's hips are rolled over her body to the left. Her legs bend sharply, concealing her genitalia and fitting her more neatly on the square pedestal.

My stomach twists.

This is not the body of the scaly, tusk-toothed monster described in Greek myths. This is a smooth, sensual body, writhing in the throes of sexual pleasure, not death. Cellini represents not just physical defeat but sexual conquest.[31]

It's strange how we can miss all of this, however, and simply notice the general, heroic contours of the artwork. It's easy to accept that Perseus has slain a monster without looking too closely at what or who the supposed monster actually is. But of course, Cellini and his patron, Duke Cosimo I de' Medici, were not simply telling a story for purely aesthetic reasons. They knew the power of visual scripts in public spaces. Here, it turns out, there was another story they deliberately hoped to silence.

As we saw in chapter 3, the Loggia dei Lanzi was developed as a kind of political stage. In 1545, Cosimo I governed the city from the Palazzo Vecchio, a medieval-era palace adjacent to the loggia. Outside the building stood Michelangelo's famed sculpture, the seventeen-foot-tall marble *David*, which was used as a symbol of Florence. If Milan—the large, powerful city to the north—was Goliath, then Florence was God's appointed underdog.

When Cosimo I commissioned Cellini to make a sculpture for the nearby loggia, he intended it to likewise be politically charged.

Cellini's *Perseus with the Head of Medusa* evoked the kind of strongman rule that Cosimo I favored.[32] The Duke of Florence subscribed to the political theory of Niccolò Machiavelli, who—in his influential treatise *The Prince*—argued that a ruler's primary goal must be to maintain power even if he must use deception or violence to do so. But when Cellini completed *Perseus* in 1554 and unveiled it in the Loggia dei Lanzi, it wasn't the only bronze sculpture of a beheading in the square. Donatello's seven-foot-tall sculpture *Judith and Holofernes* (1457–64) also sat on the covered porch.

Donatello's bronze depicts the climax of a popular apocryphal tale. Judith, a pious Hebrew widow, stands with a raised sword, ready to bring the blade down on the neck of the slumped, sleeping Assyrian captain. Unlike the dramatic violence of Artemisia Gentileschi's later rendering of the tale, Donatello's Judith is quietly poised and modestly covered.

Originally, the bronze sculpture was made for the palace garden of the Medici family. However, in 1506, *Judith and Holofernes* was moved to the Loggia dei Lanzi with a new inscription that celebrated the citizens of the Florentine republic.[33] Like the biblical figure of David, Judith—another underdog whose courageous faith earned God's favor—was likewise cast as a symbol of Florence.

For a long time, historians assumed that Cellini's newer *Perseus* was a complement to Donatello's older *Judith*; they were, after all, two sculptures with heroes beheading monstrous threats. But as more recent scholarship has pointed out, if Cellini had wanted to create visual unity with Donatello's work, he should have made his Medusa kneel or sit like Donatello's Holofernes.[34] Instead, Perseus completely dominates Medusa while also humiliating and objectifying her. In this, Cellini's sculpture more accurately represents Cosimo I's political beliefs. A prince is not merely the "head" of a republic; his rule is more like a man taking possession of a woman.[35] Indeed, less than thirty years after Cellini's *Perseus* was installed in the Loggia dei Lanzi, Donatello's *Judith and Holofernes* was moved to the back of the public stage. In its place, the next Medici ruler installed Giambologna's *Rape of a Sabine Woman*, another sculpture that—as we learned in chapter 3—echoed Machiavellian politics.

I think about the thousands of people who have walked through this piazza in Florence over the last 450 years. Governments have come and gone, cultural expectations for men and women have changed, and pigeons have made themselves at home in the Loggia dei Lanzi, despite multiple efforts to stymie them. Through it all, Cellini's *Perseus with the Head of Medusa* has remained constant, an aesthetically beautiful reminder that a monster's inevitable and desired end is death at the hands of a singular hero. I find myself wondering: Why does it seem easier to slay a dragon than to engage with the complexities and contradictions of other human beings?

COUNTERSTORY:

Partnering

Claim It, Name It, Reframe It

One way to respond to the Monster story is to embrace it. Monsters are, after all, powerful creatures who tend to get their way. Indeed, in the 1960s and '70s, second wave feminist artists and activists recast figures like Lilith and Medusa as icons of women's empowerment and pleasure. Evoking older images of Lilith, Carolee Schneemann photographed herself nude, lounging sensually as snakes slither up her body. Mary Beth Edelson used photo collage to reimagine herself as a Minoan snake goddess, the Gorgon Medusa, and other ancient goddesses and trickster figures. Lilith's defiance and Medusa's stony glare could serve as models of feminine strength, not cautionary tales. Cuban American artist Ana Mendieta invoked goddesses of Santeria, asserting her resistance against not just misogyny but colonial erasure. Other artworks, like Judy Chicago's *Menstruation Bathroom* (1972) and Mary Kelley's *Post-Partum Document* (1973–79), pushed aspects of women's bodily experiences into public view. "Who's afraid," they seemed to ask, "of menstrual blood and breastmilk?" According to their telling, the patriarchy has been correct to live in fear of women unleashing their knowledge and creativity.[36]

Staking a claim on a monster remains both a lucrative and a dangerous business in contemporary pop culture. Insults hurled from the mouths of politicians and cultural commentators can be quickly defused and inverted, making their way onto T-shirts, pins, and trucker hats. You can be a "Nasty Woman," a "Childless Cat Lady," or "the granddaughter of the witches you tried to burn" for $24.99 via your preferred online storefront. Infamous magazine covers and viral music videos have also revealed some of the strategy's limitations. Can we always differentiate between reclamation, appropriation, and uncritical repetition? Who reaps financial rewards, and who pays a cultural cost?

Another response has been to unmask the monster. Artists have asked viewers to confront the monster as a *fiction*, like pulling back the curtain on the Wizard of Oz. In her 1980 *Self-Portrait*, completed at age eighty, artist Alice Neel painted her aging body with frank honesty. She is seated in front of a canvas, paintbrush in hand, gazing steadily at the viewer through her yellow-rimmed glasses. She is also naked. Her stomach folds over her thighs, and her breasts hang low on either side of her chest. Neel outlines her body—including these fleshy ripples—with a sinuous, bright-blue line. Flashes of lime green and hot pink peek out beneath layers of softer, pastel tones. Her body is unidealized but also full of life. She isn't the young, available Venus, but that doesn't make her the dangerous crone.

This strategy of unmasking has been especially fruitful for Black artists negotiating the stereotypes of the Jezebel and the mammy. In her black-and-white photograph *Hottentot Venus* (1994), Renee Cox poses like the satirical cartoon of Sara Baartman, using obvious prosthetics to enlarge her breasts and buttocks. And instead of remaining in profile, Cox turns her face toward the viewer, demanding that we account for our gaze and our response. Meanwhile, in her *Liberation of Aunt Jemima* (1972), Betye Saar pulls together various iterations of the mammy stereotype, gathered from antique malls and pancake mix boxes, into a small, wooden shadow box. But Saar also arms the vintage, ceramic mammy with miniature weapons and collages a Black Power fist—with a painted red fingernail—on top of a vintage mammy postcard. Saar shows us how the story of the mammy has been constructed through seemingly endless repetitions before literally weaponizing her.

If monsters feed on our most shameful fears, then it is perhaps unsurprising that Kara Walker's 2014 monumental installation, *A Subtlety, or the Marvelous Sugar Baby*, revealed something ugly in its viewers too. The site-specific exhibition filled a Domino Sugar refining plant slated for demolition in Brooklyn, New York, and the central work was a seventy-five-foot-long, thirty-five-foot-high white sugar sculpture of a woman crouching on the ground like a sphinx, but with the broad nose, full lips, and kerchief-covered hair typical of the mammy. Walker, who is African American, has built her career on confronting and repurposing ugly racial stereotypes while using the genteel visual language of nineteenth-century paper silhouettes and porcelain figurines. The long subtitle for *A Subtlety, or the Marvelous Sugar Baby* suggests something of Walker's intent with this sculpture: *Homage to the unpaid and overworked Artisans who have refined our Sweet tastes from the cane fields to the Kitchens of the New World on the Occasion of the demolition of the Domino Sugar Refining Plant*. Walker sought to unmask the exploitation of Black labor that made the sugar industry so profitable.

Reactions to Walker's sculpture ranged from penitence to confusion to outrage. But perhaps most telling were the responses that were quietly filmed over the course of the exhibition and then released as an additional artwork titled *An Audience*. While many visitors shuffled by solemnly, others posed for selfies with the sculpture, some even pretending to cup her breasts, slap her buttocks, or lick her exposed vulva. Walker was unsurprised. "Human behavior is so mucky and violent and messed-up and inappropriate," she said later. "And I think my work draws on that. . . . It pulls it out of an audience."[37] Walker made a monster, but she anticipated that her viewers would become monsters too.

Part of the horror of the Monster story is that we can begin to imagine everyone—even ourselves—as a threat. That belief is so pervasive, in fact, that bestselling books present even romantic relationships as a battle between opposing forces. And now we're back again in the garden of Eden, where Adam and Eve believe the lie that God has not given them "enough." The shattering effects of the fall so often blind us to the abundance that flows to us from Jesus, the second Adam, born of a woman.

It's no wonder that the apostle Paul prays fervently that the Ephesian church—men and women of different social classes and from different backgrounds—would know "the length and width, height and depth of God's love" (Eph. 3:18), a love that could do all that they could ask or even think. That perfect Love has conquered death itself.

Though the monster has been defeated, we still look for its shadows. We still adopt a defensive posture, worried that even now God has not given us "enough." What story could the church tell if we rested in the reality of God's full and expansive love?

The women—and men—in the early medieval mosaics of Santa Prassede offer me a story that is woven through Scripture but often ignored, even by the church. Instead of anticipating scarcity, they are Partnering in abundance.

Sisters in Arms

The doors to the ninth-century church of Santa Prassede in Rome are tucked away on a narrow street, just two blocks away from the double domes and impressive bell tower of the larger, more famous church of Santa Maria Maggiore. I walk there for the first time with a dear friend, who has visited the church before and can't wait to see my reaction. When we enter the cool, quiet space, we find ourselves at the front of the nave, and the bright frescoes on the upper walls catch my initial attention. But once we're fully in the sunlit sanctuary, we turn to the right and see a curving, half-dome mosaic nested inside two mosaic-encrusted arches and set behind a large granite and marble altar.

The centuries-old mosaic depicts a triumphant Christ against a brilliant blue sky, flanked by sunset-hued clouds and two mirrored sets of three figures (see fig. 5.10). Beginning in the center and moving outward on each side are a bearded male saint, a dark-haired female saint, and another beardless male. Below their feet, a long, wavy strip of light blue—labeled the Jordan River—ripples across pale-green grass. Below that are a row of thirteen standing sheep and a band of Latin text. Composed of bits of colored and gold-leafed glass, the mosaic glimmers in the shadowed apse, then glows luminously once someone sticks a euro in a nearby machine to switch on the electric lights.

While the overall effect is dazzling, the mosaic has a clear organization. Every visual element points us back to Christ. He is larger than all the other figures, and he hovers above the ground. His companions' heads reach only his waist. Because the mosaic follows the architecture of the apse, Jesus quite literally moves toward us in space. And at the central apex of the composition,

Author photo

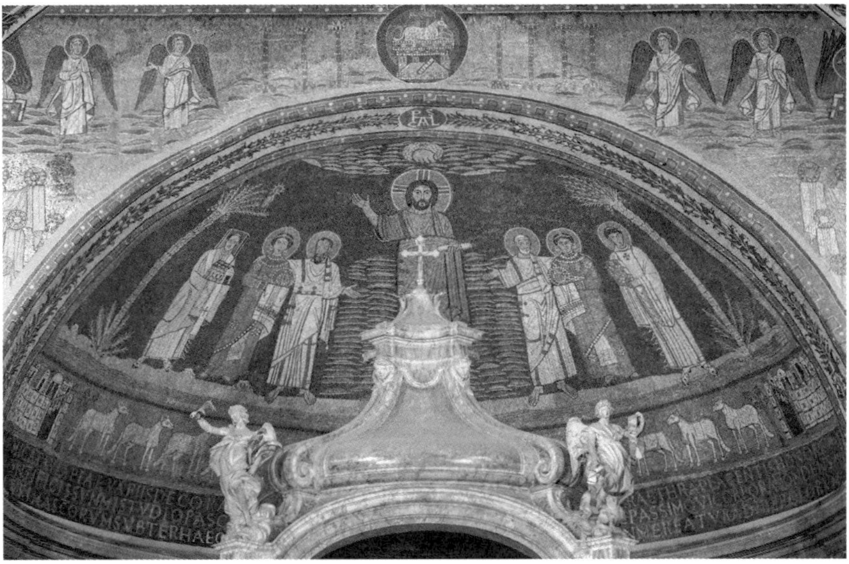

Figure 5.10. Apse mosaic of Santa Prassede, Rome, Italy, ca. 822. A full-color image of this mosaic is included in the color insert section.

a hand—belonging to God the Father—pushes through stylized white clouds and reaches down to crown his Son.

At first glance, the mosaic is symmetrical. But the longer I look, the more differences I find between the two halves. A red-orange bird with a small halo perches on the left-hand tree. The male figure farthest to the left is the only one wearing a yellow drape. He also appears to be carrying a small building and has a square, turquoise halo, distinct from the circular, golden halos of his companions. The bearded man immediately to the left of Christ has dark hair and the letter *P* emblazoned on his robe, while the bearded man on the right side has white hair. The tonsured man on the far right of the mosaic is holding a large book with a bejeweled cover. The women, however, are virtually mirror images of each other.

"Look at the women!" my friend says softly in my ear. And I do. While Jesus is clearly the headlining feature, the two female saints serve an important visual role in balancing and unifying the composition. There's a rhythmic color pattern across the apse: white, gold, white, gold, white, gold. The men wear white robes, while the women wear golden dresses with elaborate, jeweled collars. Although the women are not standing closest to Christ, their gold robes link the three of them together visually.

The women are also connected—quite literally—to the bearded men on Christ's immediate right and left. The pairs stand immediately next to each other, shoulders touching. I squint and blink. Actually, each man has one arm wrapped around the woman's shoulder, while his other hand gestures toward Christ as if introducing one dear friend to another.

Standing in the quiet church with my friend, seeing this mosaic for the first time, I am undone. I have never seen women—besides the Virgin Mary—represented so prominently in Christian church art. Question after question bubbles up. Who are these women, and what are they doing here? Are they allegorical figures, like the vessel discussed in chapter 2? Maybe they're symbols of wisdom and prudence or some other virtues. I presume that, given their proximity to Christ, the two bearded men are apostles. But then why do they have their arms around these women? Are the dark-haired ladies their wives, inexplicably dressed to attend a much fancier party than their partners? My experience in the twenty-first-century evangelical church colors my confusion. If some contemporary pastors advise men against being alone with—much less having any physical contact with—women who are not their own wives, I assume the ninth-century church was even more strict.

All these initial impulses are, it turns out, wrong. But my line of questioning reveals a lot about the ways I have been shaped by other stories about women, especially the Monster narrative. If women are constantly threatening a natural social order and men's sexual self-control, then it seems impossible that the apostles would embrace actual women who are not their spouses. Yet the mosaic in front of me tells a different story altogether.

The second time I visit Santa Prassede I'm shepherding a group of undergraduate students. We cluster in the nave of the church as I stage whisper some basic facts to them. A house church associated with the name Prassede was located near the current church from around 112. Part of the current building's foundations date from the eighth century, and the general floor plan and mosaic decorations were established around 822. They were commissioned by Pope Paschal I (r. 817–24), who included his name as a monogram in the mosaic-covered double arches. As with much medieval art from Western Europe, the names of the artists who designed the mosaic and installed its thousands of tiny pieces of glass and stone are lost to history. It is likely, however, that they were monks who had fled Byzantium due to the emperor's recent policy of iconoclasm, or the banning of images in churches.[38] The church has seen a number of additions and varying restorations in the intervening centuries, including the installation of an elevated stone canopy that partially obscures our view of the apse mosaic. Thus, the church we're standing in today is a hodgepodge of multiple eras and their varying—and sometimes opposing—aesthetic and theological goals.

But even focusing on just the apse mosaic is akin to pulling a slice out from a multilayer cake. Histories stack one on top of the other. Our understanding of the work's power deepens as we give attention to the represented figures, the theological symbolism, and its social context. When we do so, we find a church just as complicated and contradictory as the ones we attend today, where glimpses of wholeness emerge insistently between the weeds of hypocrisy and politicking. Still, it's a history that also helps me live more hopefully—a counterstory of men and women Partnering together, welcoming Christ side by side as good and faithful servants.

An Eternal Family

So first, who is represented in the mosaic? The apse dramatically compresses past, present, and future, depicting figures from different moments in church history hailing Christ at his second coming. The mosaic follows a template already well established in earlier Christian art. Paul, dark-haired and balding, stands to the left of Christ, while Peter, with short, white hair, stands to the right. In other artworks that follow this format, the figures standing beside Paul and Peter would be saints associated with that particular church. Thus, most scholars identify the black-haired women as Prassede and Pudenziana (also known as Praxedes and Pudentiana), second-century Roman women who cared for Christian martyrs during a period of persecution. The figure on the far right has been identified variously as Saint Zeno—who also has a chapel dedicated to him in the same church—or possibly Stephen, one of the first deacons of the church and the first martyr. Finally, on the far left, we find Pope Paschal I, the one responsible for rebuilding the church and commissioning the mosaic!

Two clues suggest that this is a portrait of Paschal. First, the rectangular, turquoise "nimbus" behind his head indicates that this person was alive when the mosaic was made.[39] And second, the man holds a small church building in his hands, offering it like a gift to Christ. Portraits of clergy who sponsored a church were common by this point. Thus, the mosaic depicts first-century apostles, second-century saints, and a then-living, ninth-century pope bearing witness to Christ's future, triumphant return.

But the names Prassede and Pudenziana are unfamiliar to many twenty-first-century American viewers. Who were these sisters? Their hagiography—or idealized life story—was first told in the late fifth or early sixth century, then expanded in the eighth century.[40] According to that tradition, the women were the daughters or granddaughters of the Roman senator Pudens, whom Paul mentions in 2 Timothy 4:21. After the death of their father, they dedicated their lives to the church. Instead of marrying, they used their wealth to help the poor and offered their family home as a place of worship during imperial persecution. Pudenziana died after years of service. Though grieved, Prassede continued to labor on behalf of the church, hiding Christians and tending to those who were tortured until her own death in her eighties.

Is any of this story verifiable? Scholars have debated for centuries over whether there is archaeological or genealogical evidence for the lives and work of these sisters. Trying to sift out fact from fiction in a saint's hagiography is largely beside the point. What we *do* know is that the story of the sisters was well-known and celebrated in the Roman Church even before Pope Hadrian built a church at the current site of Santa Prassede in 780. In fact, seventh-century travel guides directed Christian pilgrims to tombs with the sisters' names in the Catacombs of Priscilla![41] When Pope Paschal I expanded the church in the ninth century, he also transferred the bones of twenty-three hundred martyrs to Santa Prassede, including what he believed to be the remains of Prassede and Pudenziana. Their sarcophagi now lie in the crypt below the altar.

Instead of asking, "Were the sisters real?" we might ask instead, "What does the popularity and persistence of their story teach us about the church then and now?"

Simply naming individuals in the mosaic is just the start of unfolding the story of Partnering that we find here. We also need to understand the work's iconography. "Iconography" is a system of symbols that a culture uses to make meaning. While it sounds like an old-fashioned term, we still have our own contemporary sets of symbols. For example, we use a sideways triangle to indicate the act of starting a music track or video. It seems intuitive to us because it is so familiar. Likewise, a medieval Christian viewer wouldn't think twice about identifying a peacock as a symbol of eternal life.

One of my favorite things about older Christian art globally is how early Christians identified potent symbols in their own cultural contexts and appropriated them for Christianity. Images of a shepherd in the Christian catacombs, for example, mimic common Greek and Roman depictions of young boys bringing rams to temples for sacrifice. But in their new theological context, the ram bearers now point to the Good Shepherd, Christ. Even halos, so strongly associated with Christianity, were borrowed from Roman depictions of deities. The symbols in Santa Prassede's apse blink like beacons, orienting viewers, locating them on a theological map.

The mosaic is telling a story not just about Prassede and Pudenziana or Peter and Paul or Paschal and Zeno but about the church across time and history. The date palms on the far ends of the composition symbolize resurrection and eternal life, connotations that early Christians borrowed from ancient Greek and Egyptian cultures. The bird perched on the left-hand tree is a phoenix, a mythological creature that bursts into flames and is reborn from its own ashes. The scroll that Christ holds in his left hand represents the Law, now fulfilled.

In the green strip below the figures' feet, we see a symbolic representation of the church. The twelve sheep signify not just the twelve apostles but all Christians shepherded by Christ. They stream out of two stylized cities on the far ends of the mosaic. The building on the left represents Bethlehem, where the first gentiles—the Magi—worshiped Christ; the building on the right represents Jerusalem. Together, believers from the old and new covenants join together in adoration of the central Lamb.

Iconography also gives us more information about the people represented in the mosaic. Christ's larger size, the scroll of the Law, and the blue cross set inside his halo are what art historians call his "attributes."

These are the consistent, visual distinctives that function like a name tag, allowing us to recognize different biblical or historical figures. The mosaicists were not suggesting that the historical Jesus was actually taller than everyone else, that he had a shimmering, golden plate behind his head, or even that he was brown-haired and bearded. Instead, they used imagery that would have been familiar to original viewers, a visual language that pointed to *who* these figures were rather than recording their physical appearance.

Likewise, the mosaic represents Prassede's and Pudenziana's "symbolic selves." The sisters wear robes, jeweled collars and diadems, and red slippers like Byzantine aristocracy. Their rich garments suggest the eternal value of their service to the church, not their actual clothing or social status as historical figures. They also carry elaborate crowns, though the hands that hold them are covered by white veils. The crowns are a symbol of martyrdom (Rev. 2:10), while the cloths that put a barrier between the women and the precious objects they bear suggest their humility. But because of Revelation 4:10, we can anticipate that the sisters are not planning to wear the crowns themselves. Instead, like the twenty-four elders in John's vision, they will cast them at Christ's feet in worship. Additional imagery from Revelation 22 adorns the arches that frame the apse.

Altogether, the mosaic depicts a triumphant, jubilant church that has endured suffering but did so for the sake of Christ, who is King, Shepherd, *and* sacrificial Lamb. Prassede's and Pudenziana's beautiful robes and crowns as well as their proximity to the apostles and Christ himself encourage viewers to persevere in their own lives of service to the church, believing that they will participate in this same heavenly abundance.

Much of this mosaic follows the general script for early medieval images of the second coming of Christ. The symbolism and overall organization of the mosaic seem familiar to me from other, better-known examples of Christian art. But my eyes keep going back to Paul and Peter pulling these women close as they point toward Christ. How did ninth-century viewers understand the mosaic and its meaning? How does it compare to other artworks from the same time and place? And how does it relate to women's lived experiences in ninth-century Rome?

Church Ladies

Looking up at the curved conch of the apse, I am struck by the visual equality that Prassede and Pudenziana share with Paul and Peter (see fig. 5.11). While the artists use size to announce a clear difference of power between Christ and the human figures, no such hierarchy exists between the sisters and the apostles or the sisters and the other men, including Pope Paschal. In

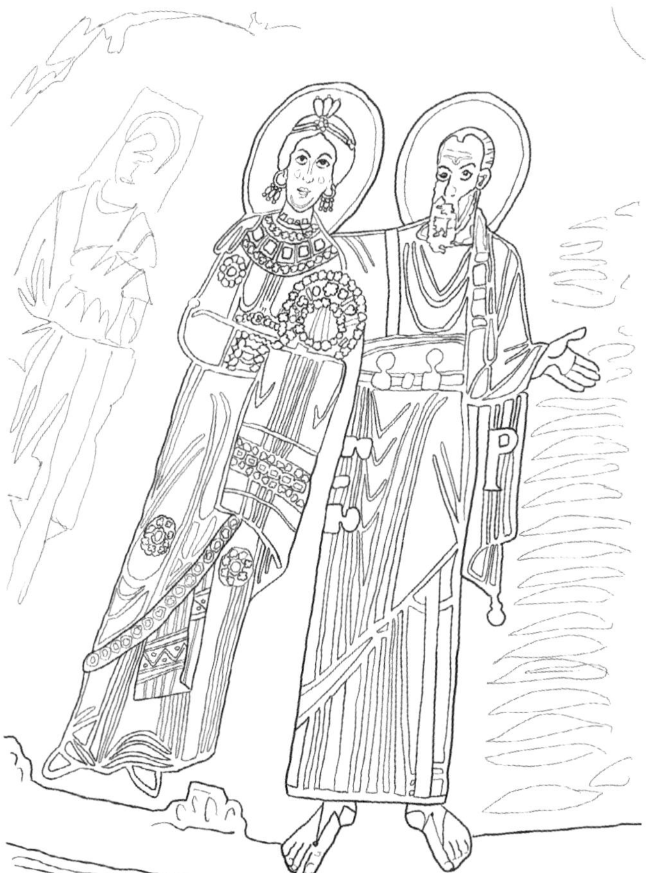

Figure 5.11. Detail of Prassede and Peter drawn from the apse mosaic of Santa Prassede

fact, as we noted earlier, the artists encourage us to see the sisters and the apostles as a visual unit, and they also underscore the women's connection to Christ through the shared use of gold. Their presence contributes to the formal balance and coherence of the mosaic as a whole.

Does this visual equality of first-century male apostles and female saints reflect men's and women's *actual* equality in the ninth century, when the mosaic was made? At that time, the city of Rome was part of the Carolingian Empire. Amid other complex political machinations, Pope Leo III (r. 795–816) had crowned the Frankish King Charlemagne "Emperor of the Romans" in 800. When Paschal I became pope in 817, Charlemagne's son, Louis the Pious, was the new emperor. Reconstructing attitudes toward and experiences of women in Rome during this period is tricky work. Scholars acknowledge that the historical record is fragmentary, that most of what we do know concerns wealthy women, and that class—not gender—primarily shaped individuals' experiences.[42] Generally, though, we know that aristocratic women had some legal rights, such as the ability to own property, and that they played an important social role in maintaining familial legacies.[43] We also know that women took vows and participated in emerging religious orders.

In the context of church art, the depiction of women in the Santa Prassede apse is somewhat unusual. Other church mosaics depicting Christ's return—including that of the well-known, sixth-century church of Saints Cosma and Damiano—feature *male* saints alongside the apostles Paul and Peter. Later Roman apses depict the Virgin Mary with Christ in heaven, but not Christ with other female saints. Helpfully, we can compare the mosaic in Santa Prassede to another decorative program commissioned by Pope Paschal I during his seven-year reign.

In the neighborhood of Trastevere, in the church of Santa Cecilia, we find what initially appears to be a smaller copy of the apse decorations in Santa Prassede. There's Christ in the center, flanked by Peter and Paul, two dark-haired women, two beardless men, and two date palms. We might even recognize Paschal himself on the left, again with his square turquoise halo, holding a model of *this* church building as his offering to the triumphant Christ.

There's a small but important difference between the two churches' mosaics, though. Instead of Paul having his arm around the dark-haired female saint and presenting her to Christ, it is the woman—Cecilia—who wraps her arm around Paschal! *She* is the one introducing *him* to their Savior. Her relationship with Paschal is neither one of authority nor one of romance. It is an intimate position but one akin to *familial* closeness. Cecilia is Paschal's big sister or aunty, pulling him into the room to greet Jesus.

Women also appear elsewhere in Santa Prassede. The mosaics of the San Zeno Chapel—a small room off the main church that Paschal commissioned as a mausoleum for his mother—are full of women.[44] Above the chapel's doorway we find depictions of eight unknown women in the company of Mary, Christ, and the twelve apostles. Inside the tiny, jewel box–like room, bust-length images of Prassede, Pudenziana, Mary, and Paschal's mother fill an arched niche. On an upper wall, we find full-length images of the women processing toward an altar, mirroring a depiction of male apostles on the opposite side.

Given the prominence of women in the apse mosaics in Santa Prassede and Santa Cecilia as well as in the San Zeno Chapel, it is tempting to assume that Paschal promoted women's equality with men before God. One prominent historian has drawn from the limited and scattered existing historical, liturgical, and archaeological evidence to argue that Prassede was an ordained church leader, a *presbytera*, in the second century and recognized as such in the ninth century, when the mosaic was made.[45] Other scholars have been more cautious in their interpretation, but the debate will certainly continue.[46]

So much of our contemporary categories and language surrounding church offices, gender identity, gender roles, and individual rights simply did not exist in the ninth century when Paschal commissioned fleeing Greek clergy and artisans to decorate a church dedicated to a second-century saint. Further, we can only speculate about whether Pascal's personal devotion to female saints and his close relationship with his mother impacted how he treated "real" women in the church.[47] Perhaps most importantly, as we've seen, the symbolism in the mosaics represents Christ's second coming, not the present state of affairs in the ninth-century Roman Church.

It *is* clear from existing historical documents that Pascal was concerned with reestablishing Rome's importance to the global church.[48] He built, rebuilt, and decorated numerous churches and chapels, emphasizing sites and martyrs connected to the early church in Rome. While an interest in protecting and growing his own power can't entirely explain Paschal's activities, we also cannot ignore this motivation.

This much is clear: As Paschal built his visual argument, he chose to include women as an integral part of the story. It is through Prassede and Pudenziana that Paschal connects back to the apostles and offers an example of women serving the church. Women's ministry through intense persecution becomes part of the church's public self-narration.

Life Abundant, Life Together

There's another detail that attracts my attention. Prassede's and Pudenziana's feet hover above the strip of green grass (see fig. 5.11). Such disregard for gravity—or illusionistic space—is typical of art from this period. Particularly for artists coming from the Eastern Church in Byzantium, the goal was not to replicate their perceived physical reality but to point to an otherwise invisible spiritual reality. Still, sometimes I indulge myself and imagine that Prassede and Pudenziana, so thrilled to see their Savior, are simply bouncing with joy.

On my most recent visit to Santa Prassede, I am especially struck by the way the mosaics evoke a sense of rich abundance. Some of this stems from their materiality. The irregular glass fragments, some gilt with gold leaf, both encapsulate and reflect light.[49] Light multiplies, dancing off the uneven surfaces of tesserae. Even without the artificial bulbs switched on, and even with far less sunlight than in the building's original plan, the front of the church shimmers like luxurious, rippling silk.

The mosaic also offers us a literal abundance of subject matter. We can't actually look at the apse mosaic without also seeing the two mosaic-encrusted arches that frame it. The arches draw from John's vision in Revelation, inviting worshipers to join in with the processions of saints, surrounded by martyrs holding palms, twenty-four elders with golden crowns, winged angels, and strange, heavenly creatures. Seemingly every square inch is filled with visual reiterations of Christ's kingship. Both arches are outlined with decorative mosaic borders that resemble jeweled chains of emeralds, pearls, and red jasper. And the visual richness doesn't stop there. Even the undersides of the arches are covered with mosaic work! Garlands of flowers, fruit, and vegetation seem to grow up and across the arches. Precious stones, fruiting plants, and the worshipers themselves all seem to multiply before my eyes.

The mosaics are exultant, swimming in abundance. Given Paschal's significant efforts to ensure that the Carolingian king wouldn't mess with Rome, I'm not sure that the pope himself entirely believed in this reality. But I'm grateful for the story that he left behind, a story in which women literally balance the heavenly vision and in which the apostles and clergymen do not shrink away from women and their gifts. Instead, they wrap their arms around women who labored on behalf of the church, pulling them close. This is a vision of the sad things becoming untrue. The fracture of the fall has been reconciled in Christ. The garden has become a flourishing city.

I stand in the cool, airy nave of Santa Prassede with another group of undergraduates. Soon we will make our way back out onto the bright, cacophonous streets of Rome, but for one more moment we listen quietly as a student answers questions about his presentation on the apse mosaic. After he finishes, we pose for a picture together below the glittering figures. I put my arm around his shoulder, and we both point upward. Looking at the photograph later, I laugh at how we inadvertently echo the mosaic. We have folded ourselves into the fellowship of saints above and behind us, the story of Paul and Prassede, Peter and Pudenziana, Paschal, Zeno, and Jesus himself. Surrounded by gold and garlands, by the witness of a spiritual family, we are rooted in the reality of our abundance in Christ.

Even so, come, Lord Jesus.

Acknowledgments

The Basilica of Sant'Apollinare Nuovo in Ravenna, Italy, is a sixth-century church full of sumptuous, glimmering mosaics. High above our heads, two large mosaic bands run down the length of the central nave. On the right, against a golden sky studded with palm trees, we find a row of twenty-six men in white robes, each carrying a crown to indicate their martyrdom. They all face in the same direction, marching toward the front of the church and a mosaic of Christ seated on a throne, surrounded by angels. On the left side of the nave, a row of twenty-two female martyrs, swathed in white and gold and dripping in jewels, also processes forward. They follow the three Magi, bringing their martyr crowns to an infant Christ, seated on Mary's lap.

On my first visit to the church, I stood on the ground below and wept. Mosaics made almost fifteen hundred years earlier offered a poignant, needed reminder: I belong to a family so much older, larger, and more beautiful than I often acknowledge. Folded between these brothers and sisters, united in the same story, I believed my belovedness.

This same sprawling, extended family provided so many of the material, intellectual, spiritual, and emotional resources that made this book possible. Thank you to the administration at Covenant College, especially Collin Messer, Brad Voyles, and Derek Halvorson, who supported the development of this project. I'm especially grateful for Billie Little and her late husband, Norris, whose generosity funded the Little Endowed Scholar program and provided travel, research, and writing support along with a release from my teaching load. Thanks to the team at Brazos Press, especially Bob Hosack, who lets me dream, and Katelyn Beaty and Erin Smith for their curiosity and commitment.

Thank you to Christiana Fitzpatrick for finding the funding for my first visit to Italy. She introduced me to the women of Santa Prassede and cried with me in front of Donatello's *Penitent Magdalene*. This book wouldn't exist without her imagining on my behalf.

Thank you to my colleagues for their varied and persistent support. Kelly Kapic, Jay Green, and Scott Jones offered me their disciplinary knowledge and care, Jeff Morton critiqued my drawings, and I never revised a chapter without thinking, "I wonder what Richard Follett and Jim Wildeman would suggest." Thank you to Ned Bustard and Bill Davis for being my biggest cheerleaders. Amy Bagby, Nesha Evans, Stephanie Formenti, Deb Forteza, and Sarah Huffines always let me whine just enough about how hard writing is and then reminded me that it would be worth it. Thank you to John Holberg, Kimberly Crocker, Michele Pickard, and Rachel Staven for keeping up with all my library requests. Thank you, Stacy Payne, for answering all my frazzled administrative questions.

Thank you to my students—especially those in my Women, Art, and Culture course—for your earnest questions, thoughtful connections, and hopeful gaze. We can be tender toward tension. Rebekah Barbee was invaluable as a first reader, editor, and footnote fixer. Thanks also to Heather Cromartie and Reed Schick for making beautiful images with me for this book's release. Thanks to Anna Mages and Grace Anderson for their enthusiastic, creative marketing efforts.

Friends far and near, our conversations over the years, along with shared frustrations and joys, have helped me tell these stories. Thank you especially to Ila Casselberry, Katie Casselberry, Liz Edrington, Tim Goldsmith, Nola Hecker, Paige Hudson, Tabitha Kapic, Kate Kelly, Rachel Kim, Corinne Mather, Liz Mather, Kim Mather, April Murphree, K.J. Ramsey, Chyela Rowe, Corrin Schlecht, Caroline Sunderland, Hannah Weichbrodt, and Lydia Weichbrodt. Thanks as well to our Thursday happy hour crew and my church aunties. Thank you, Greg Bagby, for Doordash.

Thank you to my mom, June, for keeping me well-fed as I finished my first draft in her backyard and for praying so faithfully for us. Thank you to my dad, Dan, for giving me my first art history books and telling me that of course I could read Augustine as a high school girl. To Josh, Jonjon, and Ian, it means the world to me that you take my work seriously. And to my Weichbrodt family, thank you for your curiosity and love. Thank you in particular to my mom-in-law, Dusty, for your generous, practical support.

Zeke and Miles, this book is for you too. We all flourish when we tell richer, truer stories. Thanks for following me all over Europe to look at art and letting me pause the intro to Columbia Pictures movies to tell you about the Vessel trope. Finally, Noel, thank you for reminding me every day that I am beloved. You help me live into our story.

Notes

Introduction

1. I explain this concept in greater depth in "The Archive," in *Redeeming Vision: A Christian Guide to Looking at and Learning from Art* (Baker Academic, 2023), 45–64.

2. See, for example, Susan Bordo, *Unbearable Weight: Feminism, Western Culture, and the Body* (University of California Press, 1993). For more recent examples in the social sciences, see Alana Papageorgiou, Colleen Fisher, and Donna Cross, "'Why Don't I Look like Her?' How Adolescent Girls View Social Media and Its Connection to Body Image," *BMC Women's Health* 22, no. 1 (2022): https://doi.org/10.1186/s12905-022-01845-4; and Rachel F. Rodgers, Amy Slater, Chloe S. Gordon, Siân A. McLean, Hannah K. Jarman, and Susan J. Paxton, "A Biopsychosocial Model of Social Media Use and Body Image Concerns, Disordered Eating, and Muscle-Building Behaviors among Adolescent Girls and Boys," *Journal of Youth and Adolescence* 49, no. 2 (2020): 399–409.

3. Alicia Stevens and Scott Griffiths, "Body Positivity (#bopo) in Everyday Life: An Ecological Momentary Assessment Study Showing Potential Benefits to Individuals' Body Image and Emotional Wellbeing," *Body Image* 35 (2020): 181–91.

4. In her book *Being God's Image*, Old Testament scholar Carmen Joy Imes explains the significance of man and woman being created *as* the image of God. Being God's image is our fundamental identity as humans, not a role that we perform. Furthermore, she writes, "Together we are God's image. . . . We are not opposites but counterparts. We are neighbors, the closest thing we have to ourselves." Carmen Joy Imes, *Being God's Image: Why Creation Still Matters* (InterVarsity, 2023), 35.

5. My colleagues explore the practical implications of this reality in Brian Fikkert and Kelly Kapic, *Becoming Whole: Why the Opposite of Poverty Isn't the American Dream* (Moody, 2019).

6. I appreciate the thorough, careful discussion of the reality and significance of Jesus's incarnation in Amy Peeler, *Women and the Gender of God* (Eerdmans, 2022).

7. N. T. Wright, *Surprised by Hope: Rethinking Heaven, the Resurrection, and the Mission of the Church* (HarperOne, 2008), 269.

8. Imes, *Being God's Image*, 159.

9. The term "counterstory" has been popularized by Critical Race Theory scholars as writing from marginalized individuals that challenges or casts doubt on accepted majority beliefs. See Richard Delgado and Jean Stefancic, *Critical Race Theory: An Introduction* (New York University Press, 2001), 144. However, the idea and the related term "counternarrative" have been in use far longer. I am using the word "counterstory" to more clearly connect to the popular "stories" we've grown accustomed to.

Chapter 1 Venus

1. Film scholar Laura Mulvey is often credited with introducing and theorizing the term "the male gaze." Her essay "Visual Pleasure and Narrative Cinema" is the most well-known and frequently cited academic essay on the topic. Many subsequent scholars have critiqued Mulvey's assumptions, approach, and conclusions, but it remains a touchstone in gender studies and film studies. Laura Mulvey, "Visual Pleasure and Narrative Cinema," *Screen* 16, no. 3 (Autumn 1975): 6–18.

2. John Berger, *Ways of Seeing* (British Broadcasting Corporation, 1972), 47.

3. Berger, *Ways of Seeing*, 46.

4. This pose is certainly open to interpretation. Christine Mitchell Havelock writes that it is "difficult for [her] to detect either shame or self-consciousness in [the] pose" of the *Capitoline Venus*. Still, she identifies this attitude in other versions of Venus in this pose. Christine Mitchell Havelock, *The Aphrodite of Knidos and Her Successors: A Historical Review of the Female Nude in Greek Art* (University of Michigan Press, 1995), 74, 28. My argument about the friction between a subject's reluctance and the viewer's presumed right to access, however, is based on the function and reception of Praxiteles's original Aphrodite. My interpretation of the *Capitoline Venus*'s pose in particular is shaped by both my own experience and my prior knowledge of its history.

5. Pliny the Elder, *The Natural History*, ed. John Bostock and H. T. Riley, Perseus Digital Library, https://www.perseus.tufts.edu/hopper/text?doc=Perseus:text:1999.02.0137:book=36.

6. For more on the history of this sculpture, see Havelock, *Aphrodite of Knidos and Her Successors*.

7. For a simple overview, see Jean Sorabella, "The Nude in Western Art and Its Beginnings in Antiquity," Heilbrunn Timeline of Art History, January 2008, http://www.metmuseum.org/toah/hd/nuan/hd_nuan.htm.

8. Nanette Salomon, "Making a World of Difference: Gender, Asymmetry, and the Greek Nude," in *Naked Truths: Women, Sexuality, and Gender in Classical Art and Archaeology*, ed. Claire L. Lyons and Ann Olga Koloski-Ostrow (Routledge, 1997), 207.

9. For one summary of how Renaissance artists understood classical nudes, see Thomas Martin, "The Nude Figure in Renaissance Art," in *A Companion to Renaissance and Baroque Art*, ed. Babette Bohn and James M. Saslow (Wiley-Blackwell, 2013), 413–32. For a typical modernist interpretation of Praxiteles and his place in Greek art, see Ernst Gombrich, *The Story of Art* (Phaidon Publishers, 1950), 69–70. The classic defense of the nude as a subject in art comes from Kenneth Clark, *The Nude: A Study in Ideal Form* (Pantheon Books, 1956).

10. Salomon, "Making a World of Difference," and Nigel Spivey, "Revealing Aphrodite," in *Greek Sculpture* (Cambridge University Press, 2013), 194–215. Alternatively, Mireille M. Lee has argued that the sculpture was intended for *female* viewers. However, most scholars have not accepted this claim. Mireille M. Lee, "Other 'Ways of Seeing': Female Viewers of the Knidian Aphrodite," *Helios* 42, no. 1 (Spring 2015): 103–22.

11. Havelock, *Aphrodite of Knidos and Her Successors*, 62.

12. Lucian, *Affairs of the Heart (Amores)*, trans. M. D. MacLeod (Harvard University Press, 1967), 171, https://www.loebclassics.com/view/lucian-affairs_heart_amores/1967/pb_LCL432.171.xml.

13. Lucian, *Affairs of the Heart (Amores)*, 171. Both anecdotes are part of an early Roman dialogue, written in ancient Greek, in which two characters debate the merits of the love of woman versus the love of boys. Rather than being seen as a treatise on sexual identity, however, the dialogue is better understood in the context of ancient Roman rhetorical competition. See James Jope, "Interpretation and Authenticity of the Lucianic Erotes," *Helios* 38, no. 1 (2011): 103–20.

14. Spivey, "Revealing Aphrodite," 202.

15. Spivey, "Revealing Aphrodite," 202.

16. Salomon, "Making a World of Difference," 212.

17. Salomon, "Making a World of Difference," 211–12.

18. Elisabeth Elliot, *Passion and Purity: Learning to Bring Your Love Life Under Christ's Control* (Revell, 1984), 105.

19. Elliot, *Passion and Purity*, 106.

20. Some of the most influential interpretations of the painting, especially its relationship to possible classical sources, include E. H. Gombrich, "Botticelli's Mythologies: A Study in the Neoplatonic Symbolism of His Circle," *Journal of the Warburg and Courtauld Institutes* (1945): 7–60; Umberto Baldini, *Primavera: The Restoration of Botticelli's Masterpiece*, trans. Mary Fitton (Abrams, 1986), 27–28; Charles Dempsey, "Mercurius Ver: The Sources of Botticelli's Primavera," *Journal of the Warburg and Courtauld Institutes* (1968): 251–73; and Paul Barolsky, "Botticelli's 'Primavera' and the Poetic Imagination of Italian Renaissance Art," *Arion: A Journal of Humanities and the Classics* 8, no. 2 (Fall 2000): 5–35. At the time of the writing of this chapter, the newest argument regarding Botticelli's possible sources is Angela Dressen, "Botticelli's Primavera and Contemporary Commentaries," in *Iconology, Neoplatonism, and the Arts in the Renaissance*, ed. Berthold Hub and Sergius Kodera (Routledge, 2020), 137–59.

21. Webster Smith, "On the Original Location of the Primavera," *The Art Bulletin* 57, no. 1 (1975): 31–40.

22. James R. Lindow, "For Use and Display: Selected Furnishings and Domestic Goods in Fifteenth-Century Florentine Interiors," *Renaissance Studies* 19, no. 5 (2005): 634–46.

23. Lilian Zirpolo, "Botticelli's *Primavera*: A Lesson for the Bride," *Women's Art Journal* 12, no. 2 (Autumn 1991): 24–28.

24. Francesco Barbaro, "On Wifely Duties," trans. Benjamin G. Kohl, in *The Early Republic: Italian Humanists on Government and Society*, ed. Benjamin G. Kohl and Ronald G. Witt (University of Pennsylvania Press, 1978), 202.

25. Ovid, *Fasti*, trans. A. S. Kline (2004), https://www.poetryintranslation.com/PITBR/Latin/OvidFastiBkFive.php.

26. Deborah L. Krohn, "Cassone Panels and Chests," in *Art and Love in Renaissance Italy*, ed. Andrea Bayer (Yale University Press and The Metropolitan Museum of Art, 2008), 129–38.

27. Livy, *The History of Rome*, book 1, chapter 13, trans. Benjamin Oliver Foster, Perseus Digital Library, https://www.perseus.tufts.edu/hopper/text?doc=Perseus%3Atext%3A1999.02.0151%3Abook%3D1%3Achapter%3D13.

28. Cristelle Baskins, *Cassone Painting, Humanism, and Gender in Early Modern Italy* (Cambridge University Press, 1998), 103–59.

29. It is beyond the scope of this book to provide a thorough critique of purity culture's damaging misinterpretation of a traditional sexual ethic. For two different responses, see Rachel Joy Welcher, *Talking Back to Purity Culture* (InterVarsity, 2020); and Linda Kay Klein, *Pure: Inside the Evangelical Movement that Shamed a Generation of Young Women and How I Broke Free* (Atria Books, 2018). For a research-based look at the damaging effects of some of these teachings in women's lives, see Sheila Wray Gregoire, Rebecca Gregoire Lindenbach, and Joanna Sawatsky, *The Great Sex Rescue: The Lies You've Been Taught and How to Recover What God Intended* (Baker Books, 2021).

30. A summary of these varied interpretations can be found in Rona Goffen, "Sex, Space, and Social History in Titian's *Venus of Urbino*," in *Titian's "Venus of Urbino,"* ed. Rona Goffen (Cambridge University Press, 1997), 63–90.

31. Mark Twain, "A Tramp Abroad," in *The Writings of Mark Twain* (American Publishing Company, 1899), 268, https://www.google.com/books/edition/The_Writings_of_Mark_Twain/L2xaAAAAMAAJ?hl=en.

32. Goffen, "Sex, Space, and Social History," 67–68.

33. Well-known examples of this include a cassone painted by Paolo Uccello (ca. 1460) in the Yale University Gallery of Art, New Haven, CT, https://artgallery.yale.edu/collections/objects/6082; and a cassone by an unknown artist in the V&A Museum collection, London, England, https://collections.vam.ac.uk/item/O132970/cassone-unknown/.

34. Rebekah Compton, *Venus and the Arts of Love in Renaissance Florence* (Cambridge University Press, 2021), 64.

35. Alberti writes, "Whenever man and wife come together, it is advisable only to hang portraits of men of dignity and handsome appearance; for they say that this may have a great influence on the fertility of the mother and the appearance of future offspring." Leon Battista Alberti, *On the Art of Building in Ten Books*, trans. Joseph Rykwert (MIT Press, 1988), 299.

36. Goffen, "Sex, Space, and Social History," 79.

37. Fred S. Kleiner, Christin J. Mamiya, and Richard G. Tansey, *Gardner's Art Through the Ages*, 11th ed. (Harcourt College Publishers, 2001), 672.

38. Hans Rookmaaker, *Modern Art and the Death of a Culture* (InterVarsity, 1970), 27.

39. Rookmaaker, *Modern Art*, 27.

40. Gotthold Ephraim Lessing, *Laocoon: An Essay Upon the Limits of Painting and Poetry*, trans. Ellen Frothingham (Roberts Brothers, 1887), 10, https://www.gutenberg.org/cache/epub/73078/pg73078-images.html. It's unsurprising that wealthy British families would send their sons—future leaders of their nation—to go see masterpieces of Western civilization that would ostensibly improve their minds and their morals. By the mid-seventeenth century, this Grand Tour of classical antiquity and Renaissance wonders was considered an expected rite of passage.

41. David Batchelor, *Chromophobia* (Reaktion Books, 2000), 17.

42. Batchelor, *Chromophobia*, 29.

43. Amelia Rauser, *The Age of Undress: Art, Fashion, and the Classical Ideal in the 1790s* (Yale University Press, 2020), 15.

44. Rauser, *Age of Undress*, 99–102.

45. Quoted in Rauser, *Age of Undress*, 43.

46. Rauser, *Age of Undress*, 14, 17, 26, 58, to give just a few examples.

47. The engravings of Algonquian women come from Theodor de Bry after John White, "A Young, Genteel Woman, Daughter of Secota," 1590, object G570 in the Harvard Museum of Art, https://harvardartmuseums.org/collections/object/274559. The engravings of West African women come from Johann Theodor de Bry, "Vrouwen van verschillende volkeren," 1602, object RP-P-BI-5265 in the Rijksmuseum collection, https://www.rijksmuseum.nl/en/collection/object/Vrouwen-van-verschillende-volkeren—c99bf6b43d4e1023bdb0646fff13da78.

48. For a collection of primary sources on Enlightenment thought and race, see Emmanuel Chukwudi Eze, ed., *Race and the Enlightenment: A Reader* (Blackwell, 1997). For essays on the development of a racial hierarchy in the Enlightenment, see Nicholas Hudson, ed., *A Cultural History of Race in the Reformation and Enlightenment* (Bloomsbury Academic, 2021).

49. See Paul H. D. Kaplan, "Black Women in Early Modern European Art and Culture," in *The Routledge Companion to Black Women's Cultural Histories* (Routledge, 2021), 44–56.

50. A simple and helpful overview of this concept can be found in Charles Cramer and Kim Grant, "Primitivism and Modern Art," *Smarthistory*, March 7, 2020, https://smarthistory.org/primitivism-and-modern-art/.

51. Kirk Varnedoe, "Gauguin," in *Primitivism in 20th Century Art*, ed. William Rubin (The Museum of Modern Art, 1984), 180.

52. Elizabeth Childs, "Taking Back Teha'amana: Feminist Interventions in Gauguin's Legacy," in *Gauguin's Challenge: New Perspectives After Postmodernism*, ed. Norma Broude (Bloomsbury Visual Arts, 2018), 232.

53. Much of the information on Teha'amana's life comes from archival research and oral histories. See Bengt Danielsson, *Gauguin in the South Seas* (Doubleday, 1965).

54. Answer 1 in The Westminster Shorter Catechism, https://thewestminsterstandard.org/westminster-shorter-catechism/.

55. Jeffrey Hamburger, *The Visual and the Visionary: Art and Female Spirituality in Late Medieval Germany* (MIT Press, 1998), 87.

56. Hamburger, *Visual and the Visionary*, 131.

57. Really, we do not have a single original fourteenth-century manuscript. A number of fourteenth-century German Dominican convents had similar Sister Books, and the texts were copied by and circulated between different communities. For the *Katharinenthal Sister Book*, scholars have pieced together entries from eleven extant manuscripts. The German text most often referenced by scholars is Ruth Meyer, ed., *Das St. Katharinentaler Schwesternbuch* (Niemeyer Verlag, 1995). Excerpts translated into English can be found in Amiri Ayanna, trans., "Selections from the St. Katherinental *Sister Book*," *Asymptote Journal*, January 2016, https://www.asymptotejournal.com/nonfiction/sisters-of-the-convent-selections-from-the-st-katharinental-sister-book/.

58. Adelheid von Spiegelberg, "Selections from the St. Katharinental *Sister Book*," trans. Amiri Ayanna.

59. Adelheid von Holderberg, "Selections from the St. Katharinental *Sister Book*," trans. Amiri Ayanna.

60. Amiri Ayanna, "Bodies of Crystal, Houses of Glass: Observing Reform and Improving Piety in the St. Katharinental Sister Book," *Journal of Medieval Religious Cultures* 43, no. 1 (2017): 24–57; and Frances Lilliston, "'As Clear as Crystal': Transparency in the Katharinenthal Visitation Group and Sister Book," *Lapis* 3 (June 2021): https://wp.nyu.edu/lapis/category/issues/issue-3/.

61. Lilliston, "As Clear as Crystal."

62. Jacqueline E. Jung, "Crystalline Wombs and Pregnant Hearts: The Exuberant Bodies of the Katharinenthal Visitation Group," in *History in Comic Mode: Medieval Communities and the Matter of Person*, ed. Rachel Fulton Brown and Bruce W. Holsinger (Columbia University Press, 2007), 225.

63. Additional helpful ways of understanding this particular choice of material can be found in Jung, "Crystalline Wombs and Pregnant Hearts."

64. William Wixom, "Medieval Sculpture at the Metropolitan 800 to 1400," *The Metropolitan Museum of Art Bulletin* 62, no. 4 (Spring 2005): 47.

65. Jung, "Crystalline Wombs and Pregnant Hearts," 236.

66. Tish Harrison Warren, *Prayer in the Night: For Those Who Work or Watch or Weep* (InterVarsity, 2022), 116.

Chapter 2 Vessel

1. While the personification of Lady Wisdom in the Hebrew Proverbs certainly resonates with similar notions in the West, Old Testament and ancient Near Eastern scholars offer some important cultural distinctions. Michael V. Fox argues that Lady Wisdom is neither modeled on an ancient Near Eastern goddess nor a totally abstract concept. Instead, the pedagogical effectiveness of Lady Wisdom hinges on women's actual role as the initial teacher of their children. See Michael V. Fox, "Ideas of Wisdom in Proverbs 1–9," *Journal of Biblical Literature* 116, no. 4 (1997): 613–33. Christine Roy Yoder also offers a helpful overview of different approaches that scholars have taken to Lady Wisdom in "Personified Wisdom and Feminist Theologies," in *The Oxford Handbook of Wisdom and the Bible*, ed. Will Kynes (Oxford University Press, 2021), 273–85.

2. Ernst Gombrich offers a helpful overview of the history and problems of personification in the visual arts in "Personification," in *Classical Influences in European Culture AD 500–1500*,

ed. R. R. Bolgar (Cambridge University Press,1971), 247–57. See also Marina Warner, *Monuments and Maidens: The Allegory of the Female Form* (University of California Press, 2001).

3. The seven liberal arts consisted of the *trivium*—grammar, logic, and rhetoric—and the *quadrivium*: geometry, arithmetic, astronomy, and music.

4. Historian Marina Warner writes, "Often the recognition of a difference between the symbolic order, inhabited by ideal, allegorical figures, and the actual order of judges, statesmen, soldiers, philosophers, inventors, depends on the unlikelihood of women practicing the concepts they represent." Warner, *Monuments and Maidens*, xx.

5. To read Aristotle's view on the differences between male and female, see Aristotle, *On the Generation of Animals*, http://www.esp.org/books/aristotle/generation-of-animals/index.html.

6. Hildegard of Bingen, *Scivias*, trans. Columba Hart (Paulist Press, 1990), 61, http://archive.org/details/scivias0000hild.

7. Hildegard of Bingen, *The Personal Correspondence of Hildegard of Bingen*, trans. Joseph Baird (Oxford University Press, 2006), 138.

8. See the illuminations at https://www.abtei-st-hildegard.de/die-scivias-miniaturen/nggallery/slideshow.

9. Hildegard of Bingen, *Scivias*, 59.

10. Hildegard of Bingen, *Scivias*, 59.

11. See Barbara Newman, "Hildegard of Bingen: Visions and Validation," *Church History* 54, no. 2 (1985): 163–75.

12. Sabina Flanagan, *Hildegard of Bingen, 1098–1179: A Visionary Life*, 2nd ed. (Routledge, 1998), 6.

13. Hildegard of Bingen, *Personal Correspondence*, 21, 33, 37, 66, and 88, to name just a few.

14. See Kate Bowler, *The Preacher's Wife: The Precarious Power of Evangelical Women Celebrities* (Princeton University Press, 2019).

15. Bowler, *Preacher's Wife*, 154–55.

16. Bowler, *Preacher's Wife*, 175.

17. David Burt, "Do You Hear the People Sing?," track 17 on *Les Misérables*, Original 1985 London Cast Recording.

18. See the engraving at https://www.metmuseum.org/art/collection/search/666288. If you look closely, you can also see some figures turning a human leg on a spit in the background!

19. Joan B. Landes, *Visualizing the Nation: Gender, Representation, and Revolution in Eighteenth-Century France* (Cornell University Press, 2001), 67.

20. Landes, *Visualizing the Nation*, 67–80.

21. Landes, *Visualizing the Nation*, 158.

22. See Landes, *Visualizing the Nation*; Lynn Hunt, *The Family Romance of the French Revolution* (University of California Press, 1992); and Madelyn Gutwirth, *The Twilight of the Goddesses: Women and Representation in the French Revolutionary Era* (Rutgers University Press, 1992).

23. There are numerous examples. Sophie de Condorcet worked with her husband, the Marquis de Condorcet, to argue for full women's suffrage in a July 1790 document titled "Sur l'admission des femmes audroit de cite." The salonnière Germaine de Staël organized gatherings for Enlightenment intellectuals and politicians in the 1780s until being forced to flee France in 1792. Olympe de Gouges was a playwright who advocated for women's suffrage and the abolition of slavery. She was perceived as too radical by the moderates and as a Royalist by the extreme left.

24. T. J. Clark, *The Absolute Bourgeois: Artists and Politics in France, 1848–1851* (Thames & Hudson, 1973), 17–18.

25. Lynn Hunt, "The Political Psychology of Revolutionary Caricatures," in *French Caricature and the French Revolution, 1789–1799*, ed. James Cuno (University of California Press, 1988), 39.

26. Landes, *Visualizing the Nation*, 158.

27. Lynn Abrams, *The Making of Modern Woman* (Routledge, 2016), 24.

28. Annie Smart, *Citoyennes: Women and the Ideal of Citizenship in Eighteenth-Century France* (University of Delaware Press, 2011).

29. "Celebrating Edmonia Lewis," Google Doodles, February 1, 2017, https://doodles.google/doodle/celebrating-edmonia-lewis/.

30. Kirsten Pai Buick, *Child of the Fire: Mary Edmonia Lewis and the Problem of Art History's Black and Indian Subject* (Duke University Press, 2010), 53–54.

31. Lydia Maria Child, "Letter from L. Maria Child," *The Liberator*, February 19, 1864, 3, https://www.loc.gov/resource/sn84031524/1864-02-19/ed-1/.

32. A helpful step-by-step guide to the sculpting process can be found in Karen Lemmey, "From Skeleton to Skin: The Making of the Greek Slave(s)," *Nineteenth-Century Art Worldwide* 15, no. 2 (Summer 2016): http://www.19thc-artworldwide.org/summer16/lemmey-on-from-skeleton-to-skin-the-making-of-the-greek-slave.

33. Charmaine Nelson, *The Color of Stone: Sculpting the Black Female Subject in Nineteenth-Century America* (University of Minneapolis Press, 2007), 55.

34. Charlotte Rubinstein, *American Women Sculptors: A History of Women Working in Three Dimensions* (G. K. Hall, 1990), 53.

35. Nelson, *Color of Stone*, 42.

36. Nelson, *Color of Stone*, 42–43.

37. Buick, *Child of the Fire*, 57.

38. Lydia Maria Child to Sarah Blake Sturgis Shaw, August 1870, Harvard University, Houghton Library, MS Am 1417, 105.

39. Lydia Maria Child to Harriet (Winslow) Sewall, July 10, 1868, Boston Public Library, MS A46 A2, 37.

40. *The Cleveland Gazette*, November 27, 1886, 2, https://chroniclingamerica.loc.gov/lccn/sn83035386/1886-11-27/ed-1/seq-2/.

41. *The Cleveland Gazette*, November 27, 1886, 2.

42. "The Immigrant's Statue," National Park Service, February 26, 2015, https://www.nps.gov/stli/learn/historyculture/the-immigrants-statue.htm.

43. "The Statue of Liberty in Recruitment and War Bonds Posters," National Park Service, August 2, 2023, https://www.nps.gov/articles/statue-of-liberty-and-war-bonds.htm.

44. Quoted in Judith Walker Mann, "Artemisia and Orazio Gentileschi," in *Orazio and Artemisia Gentileschi*, ed. Judith Walker Mann and Keith Christiansen (The Metropolitan Museum of Art, 2001), 253.

45. Quoted in Elizabeth Cropper, "Life on the Edge: Artemisia Gentileschi, Famous Woman Painter," in Mann and Christiansen, *Orazio and Artemisia*, 268.

46. Jesse Locker, *Artemisia Gentileschi: The Language of Painting* (Yale University Press, 2015), 109–10.

47. Locker, *Artemisia Gentileschi*, 111–12.

48. Quoted in Locker, *Artemisia Gentileschi*, 180.

49. Quoted in Mary Garrard, "Appendix B: Testimony of the Rape Trial of 1612," in *Artemisia Gentileschi: The Image of the Female Hero in Italian Baroque Art* (Princeton University Press, 1989), 461.

50. Quoted in Garrard, "Appendix B," 462.

51. For some examples, see Garrard, *Artemisia Gentileschi*; and Richard E. Spear, "Artemisia Gentileschi: Ten Years of Fact and Fiction," *Art Bulletin* 82, no. 3 (September 2000): 568–79.

52. See Joanna Moorhead, "Artemesia Gentileschi: The Baroque #MeToo Heroine Who Avenged Her Rape Through Art," *The Guardian*, February 29, 2020, https://www.theguardian.com/artanddesign/2020/feb/29/artemisia-gentileschi-national-gallery-baroque-heroine-female-caravaggio; and Christopher R. Marshall, "Explainer: Artemesia Gentileschi, a Baroque

Heroine for the #MeToo Era," *The Conversation*, September 12, 2018, https://theconversation.com/explainer-artemisia-gentileschi-a-baroque-heroine-for-the-metoo-era-100676.

53. Cesare Ripa, *Iconologia, ouero Descrittione d'imagini delle virtu', vitij, affetti, passioni humane, corpi celesti, mondo e sue parti* (Pietro Paolo Tozzi, 1611), 429–30, https://archive.org/details/iconologiaouerod00ri.

54. Ripa, *Iconologia*, 429, translation my own.

55. Mary Garrard, "Artemisia Gentileschi's *Self-Portrait as the Allegory of Painting*," *The Art Bulletin* 62, no. 1 (1980): 97–112.

56. Garrard, "Artemisia Gentileschi's *Self-Portrait as the Allegory of Painting*," 101.

57. Garrard, "Artemisia Gentileschi's *Self-Portrait as the Allegory of Painting*," 107.

58. See, for example, the discussion in Herb Bissell, *Artemisia Gentileschi and the Authority of Art: Critical Reading and Catalogue Raisonné* (Pennsylvania State University Press, 1999), 272.

59. Cropper, "Life on the Edge," 278.

60. Patricia Simons, "Artemisia Gentileschi's Susanna and the Elders (1610) in the Context of Counter-Reformation Rome," in *Artemisia Gentileschi in a Changing Light*, ed. Sheila Barker (Harvey Miller, 2017), 52.

61. Simons, "Artemisia Gentileschi's Susanna and the Elders," 52.

Chapter 3 Maiden

1. Patricia Simons, "Women in Frames: The Gaze, the Eye, the Profile in Renaissance Portraiture," *History Workshop* 25 (Spring 1988): 7.

2. Simons, "Women in Frames," 18.

3. Francesco Barbaro, "On Wifely Duties," in *The Early Republic: Italian Humanists on Government and Society*, trans. Benjamin G. Kohl, ed. Benjamin G. Kohl and Ronald G. Witt (University of Pennsylvania Press, 1978), 204.

4. Maria Deprano, *Art Patronage, Family, and Gender in Renaissance Florence: The Tornabuoni* (Cambridge University Press, 2019), 324.

5. Jeffrey L. Myers and Danielle Myers, *Of Knights and Fair Maidens: A Radical New Approach to a Very Old Way of Developing Relationships* (pub. by author, 1996).

6. Elisabeth Elliot, *Passion and Purity: Learning to Bring Your Love Life Under Christ's Control* (Revell, 1984), 97–99.

7. John Eldredge, *Wild at Heart: Discovering the Secret of a Man's Soul*, rev. and exp. ed. (Thomas Nelson, 2011), 9–10.

8. Maureen Dowd, "What's a Modern Girl to Do?," *The New York Times*, October 30, 2005, https://www.nytimes.com/2005/10/30/magazine/whats-a-modern-girl-to-do.html; and Taffy Brodesser-Akner, "Stuff Your 'Rules,'" *The New York Times*, May 14, 2019, https://www.nytimes.com/2019/05/14/style/the-rules-book.html.

9. Ellen Fein and Sherrie Schneider, *The Rules: Time-Tested Secrets for Capturing the Heart of Mr. Right* (Warner Books, 1995), 26.

10. Fred S. Kleiner, Christin J. Mamiya, and Richard G. Tansey, *Gardner's Art Through the Ages*, 11th ed. (Harcourt College Publishers, 2001), 699.

11. Diane Wolfthal, *Images of Rape: The "Heroic" Tradition and Its Alternatives* (Cambridge University Press, 1999), 127.

12. Margaret D. Carroll, "The Erotics of Absolutism: Rubens and the Mystification of Sexual Violence," *Representations* 25 (1989): 5.

13. Carroll, "Erotics of Absolutism," 5.

14. Nicolò Machiavelli, *The Prince*, trans. W. K Marriott (Project Gutenberg, 2006), chap. XXV, https://www.gutenberg.org/cache/epub/1232/pg1232-images.html.

15. Another interesting aspect of Giambologna's sculpture is that he originally made it without a particular narrative in mind. Any mythological abduction scene could both serve his patron's political needs and demonstrate his own artistic knowledge and skill. See Michael Cole, "Giambologna and the Sculpture with No Name," *Oxford Art Journal* 31, no. 3 (2008): 337–59.

16. Gloria Feman Orenstein, "Art History," *Signs* 1, no. 2 (1975): 507–8.

17. For more on this history, see Sheridan Prasso, *The Asian Mystique: Dragon Ladies, Geisha Girls, and Our Fantasies of the Exotic Orient* (PublicAffairs, Perseus Running, 2005).

18. For more on this, see Katharine Moon, *Sex Among Allies: Military Prostitution in U.S.-Korea Relations* (Columbia University Press, 2008); and Sunny Woan, "White Sexual Imperialism: A Theory of Asian Feminist Jurisprudence," *Washington and Lee Journal of Civil Rights and Social Justice* 14, no. 2 (2008): 275–301.

19. Kimberly Kay Hong, "How the History of Spas and Sex Work Fits into the Conversation About the Atlanta Shootings," *Vox*, March 18, 2021, https://www.vox.com/first-person/22338462/atlanta-shooting-georgia-spa-asian-american.

20. William Shakespeare, *Hamlet*, ed. Barbara Mowat and Paul Werstine (Folger Shakespeare Library, n.d.), act 4, scene 7, https://www.folger.edu/explore/shakespeares-works/hamlet/read/4/7/.

21. Elaine Showalter, "Ophelia, Gender, and Madness," British Library, 2016, https://web.archive.org/web/20160322163935/https://www.bl.uk/shakespeare/articles/ophelia-gender-and-madness.

22. Elaine Showalter, "Representing Ophelia: Women, Madness, and the Responsibilities of Feminist Criticism," in *Shakespeare and the Question of Theory*, ed. Patricia Parker and Geoffrey Hartman (Routledge, 1985), 81–82.

23. Simonetta Falchi, "Re-Mediating Ophelia with Pre-Raphaelite Eyes," *Interlitteraria* 20, no. 2 (2015): 177.

24. Quoted in Falchi, "Re-Mediating Ophelia," 177.

25. Carolyn Day, *Consumptive Chic: A History of Beauty, Fashion, and Disease* (Bloomsbury Visual Arts, 2019), 88–89.

26. Day, *Consumptive Chic*, 125.

27. Day, *Consumptive Chic*, 57. See also Marjorie Levine-Clark, *Beyond the Reproductive Body: The Politics of Women's Health and Work in Early Victorian England* (Ohio State University Press, 2004).

28. For more on this shift, see Lynn Abrams, "Learning to Be a Woman," in *The Making of Modern Woman* (Routledge, 2016), 43–66.

29. Day, *Consumptive Chic*, 60.

30. Day, *Consumptive Chic*, 60.

31. Day, *Consumptive Chic*, 53.

32. Quoted in Emily J. Orlando, "'That I May Not Faint, or Die, or Swoon': Reviving Pre-Raphaelite Women," *Women's Studies* 38, no. 6 (2009): 613.

33. W. M. Rossetti and Harold Hartley, "Dante Rossetti and Elizabeth Siddal," *The Burlington Magazine for Connoisseurs* 1, no. 3 (1903): 273.

34. Rossetti and Hartley, "Dante Rossetti," 273.

35. See the full image in the collection of the Maas Gallery, https://www.maasgallery.co.uk/content/feature/66/artworks-9850-elizabeth-siddal-1829-1862-the-lady-of-shalott/.

36. Lord Alfred Tennyson, "The Lady of Shalott," 1832, https://www.poetryfoundation.org/poems/45359/the-lady-of-shalott-1832.

37. Orlando, "That I May Not Faint, or Die, or Swoon," 633.

38. For one summary and explanation of this data, see Richard V. Reeves, *Of Boys and Men: Why the Modern Male Is Struggling, Why It Matters, and What to Do About It* (Brookings Institution, 2024).

39. For examples, see Mark Driscoll (@markdriscoll), "Young men are in crisis," Instagram, February 26, 2025, https://www.instagram.com/reel/DGjfUgmPRy3; and Ruth Whippman, *Boymom: Reimagining Boyhood in the Age of Impossible Masculinity* (Harmony, 2024).

40. Andrew Tate is one of the most popular "manosphere" influencers, and his ideas are echoed by numerous other content creators. Shanti Das, "Inside the Violent, Misogynistic World of TikTok's New Star, Andrew Tate," *The Guardian*, August 6, 2022, https://amp.theguardian.com/technology/2022/aug/06/andrew-tate-violent-misogynistic-world-of-tiktok-new-star.

41. Adelina Modesti, *Elisabetta Sirani* (Getty Publications, 2023), 56–73.

42. Modesti, *Elisabetta Sirani*, 77.

43. Babette Bohn, "The Antique Heroines of Elisabetta Sirani," *Renaissance Studies* 16, no. 1 (2002): 56.

44. For a helpful, accessible overview of how Mary Magdalene's story has evolved over time, see Jennifer Powell McNutt, *The Mary We Forgot* (Brazos, 2024).

45. Michelle Moseley-Christian, "Mary Magdalene in Early Modern Material and Visual Culture," in *The Oxford Handbook of Mary Magdalene*, ed. Diane Apostolos-Cappadona (Oxford Academic, 2024), https://doi.org/10.1093/oxfordhb/9780197669907.013.12.

46. These Florentine examples include *Mary Magdalene with Eight Scenes from Her Life* by the Master of Magdalen, ca. 1280–85, in the Accademia, Florence; the Santa Reparata altarpiece in the Duomo; and frescoes in Santa Trinita and Santa Maria Maggiore.

47. Giorgio Vasari, *Lives of the Artists*, trans. George Bull (Penguin, 1965), 176.

48. The first description is from David Lindsay, *Donatello* (Duckworth & Co., 1903), 144; the second two are from Alfred Gotthold Meyer, *Donatello*, trans. P. G. Konody (Velhagen & Klasing, 1904), 127.

49. Fred S. Kleiner, Christin J. Mamiya, and Richard G. Tansey, *Gardner's Art Through the Ages*, 11th ed. (Harcourt College Publishers, 2001), 559.

50. See Deborah Strom, "A New Chronology for Donatello's Wooden Sculpture," *Pantheon* 33, no. 3 (1980): 239–48; this dating is also affirmed in Moseley-Christian, "Mary Magdalene in Early Modern Material and Visual Culture."

51. Martha Levine Dunkelman, "Donatello's Mary Magdalen: A Model of Courage and Survival," *Woman's Art Journal* 26, no. 2 (2005): 11.

52. Dunkelman, "Donatello's Mary Magdalen," 10–13.

53. Dunkelman, "Donatello's Mary Magdalen," 12.

54. Brian Pullan, *Tolerance, Regulation and Rescue: Dishonoured Women and Abandoned Children in Italy, 1300–1800* (Manchester University Press, 2016), 96.

55. Diane Apostolos-Cappadona, *Mary Magdalene: A Visual History* (T&T Clark, 2023), 103.

56. Dunkelman, "Donatello's Mary Magdalen," 12.

57. Examples include *Mary Magdalene with Eight Scenes from Her Life*, by the Master of the Magdalen, ca. 1280–85, in the Accademia, Florence; an anonymous fresco of Mary Magdalene, fourteenth century, in Santa Maria Maggiore, Florence; and Bernardo Daddi's tempera on panel painting of Mary Magdalene, part of a larger altarpiece, 1340–45, in the Accademia, Florence.

58. Dunkelman, "Donatello's Mary Magdalen," 11.

Chapter 4 Mother

1. For an introduction to different ways the Virgin Mary has been represented in Christian art, see Beth Williamson, "The Virgin Mary," in *Christian Art: A Very Short Introduction* (Oxford University Press, 2004), 15–33.

2. For an introduction to the growing veneration of Mary and how it developed in visual culture, see Department of Medieval Art and The Cloisters, "The Cult of the Virgin Mary in

the Middle Ages," The Metropolitan Museum of Art, October 2001, https://www.metmuseum.org/essays/the-cult-of-the-virgin-mary-in-the-middle-ages.

3. Plum Sykes, "Gwyneth's Guide to Life," *Vogue*, May 2008, 259–61, 314.

4. Susan J. Douglas and Meredith W. Michaels, *The Mommy Myth: The Idealization of Motherhood and How It Has Undermined All Women* (Free Press, 2004).

5. See also Linda Rose Ennis, *Intensive Mothering: The Cultural Contradictions of Modern Motherhood* (Demeter Press, 2014).

6. Elisabeth Elliot, *Let Me Be a Woman: Notes on Womanhood for Valerie* (Tyndale, 1976), 53.

7. Douglas and Michaels, *Mommy Myth*, 1. Later scholars have further developed this work, summarized in Ashley Noel Mack, "Critical Approaches to Motherhood," in *Oxford Research Encyclopedia of Communication* (August 28, 2018), https://doi.org/10.1093/acrefore/9780190228613.013.579.

8. I discuss this idea further in Elissa Yukiko Weichbrodt, "The Archive," in *Redeeming Vision: A Christian Guide to Looking at and Learning from Art* (Baker Academic, 2023), 45–64.

9. See more on this history in Jane Tibbetts Schulenburg, *Forgetful of Their Sex: Female Sanctity and Society, ca. 500–1100* (University of Chicago Press, 1998).

10. See Merry Wiesner-Hanks, "Martin Luther on Marriage and the Family," in *Oxford Research Encyclopedia of Religion* (Oxford University Press, 2016), https://doi.org/10.1093/acrefore/9780199340378.013.365.

11. For more on this history, see Lyndal Roper, *The Holy Household: Women and Morals in Reformation Augsburg* (Oxford University Press, 1991). I'm grateful for Beth Allison Barr first pointing this out to me in her chapter "The Cost of the Reformation for Evangelical Women," in *The Making of Biblical Womanhood: How the Subjugation of Women Became Gospel Truth* (Brazos, 2021), 101–28.

12. See Wayne E. Franits, *Paragons of Virtue: Women and Domesticity in Seventeenth-Century Dutch Art* (Cambridge University Press, 1993).

13. See Irene Cieraad, "Rocking the Cradle of Dutch Domesticity: A Radical Reinterpretation of Seventeenth-Century Homescapes," *Home Cultures* 15, no. 1 (2018): 73–102.

14. See Martha Peacock, "Housewives," in *Heroines, Harpies, and Housewives: Imaging Women of Consequence in the Dutch Golden Age* (Brill, 2020), 317–456.

15. Gregg Johnson, "The Biological Basis for Gender-Specific Behavior," in *Recovering Biblical Manhood and Womanhood: A Response to Evangelical Feminism*, ed. John Piper and Wayne Grudem (Crossway, 1991), 282.

16. Peter Raissis, "The Well-Beloved Mother," in *Prints and Drawings: Europe 1500–1900*, Art Gallery of New South Wales, 2014, https://www.artgallery.nsw.gov.au/collection/works/111.1999/#about.

17. Denis Diderot, "The Salon of 1765," in *Diderot on Art: The Salon of 1765 and Notes on Painting*, trans. John Goodman (Yale University Press, 1995), 96.

18. Carol Duncan, "Happy Mothers and Other New Ideas in French Art," *The Art Bulletin* 55, no. 4 (1973): 570–83.

19. See Jean-Jacques Rousseau, *Emile, or On Education*, trans. Barbara Foxley, originally published 1762 (Floating Press, 2009).

20. Rousseau, *Emile*, 26.

21. Jean-Jacques Rousseau, *Jean-Jacques Rousseau: His Educational Theories Selected from Émile, Julie and Other Writings*, ed. R. L. Archer (Barron's Educational Series, 1964), 46.

22. See Carol Blum, *Strength in Numbers: Population, Reproduction, and Power in Eighteenth-Century France* (John Hopkins University Press, 2002).

23. Rousseau, *Emile*, 709.

24. Rousseau, *Emile*, 28.

25. For more on these debates, see Lynda Lange, ed., *Feminist Interpretations of Jean-Jacques Rousseau* (Pennsylvania State University Press, 2002); and Matthew David Mendham, *Hypocrisy and the Philosophical Intentions of Rousseau: The Jean-Jacques Problem* (University of Pennsylvania Press, 2021).

26. Paula Rea Radisich, "Que peut définir les femmes? Vigée-Lebrun's Portraits of an Artist," *Eighteenth-Century Studies* 25, no. 4 (1992): 449.

27. Radisich, "Que peut définir les femmes?," 449.

28. Radisich, "Que peut définir les femmes?," 446.

29. Rousseau, *Emile*, 824.

30. Rousseau, *Emile*, 824.

31. Rousseau, *Emile*, 824.

32. Quoted in Radisich, "Que peut définir les femmes?," 452.

33. Elisabeth Vigée-Le Brun, *The Memoirs of Elisabeth Vigée-Le Brun*, trans. Sian Evans (University of Indiana Press, 1989), 28.

34. Vigée-Le Brun, *Memoirs*, 28.

35. Julia Kristeva, "Women's Time," trans. Alice Jardine and Harry Blake, *Signs* 7, no. 1 (1981): 31.

36. Kristeva, "Women's Time," 31.

37. Kristeva, "Women's Time," 31.

38. Kristeva, "Women's Time," 31.

39. Geoffrey Batchen, "Hiding in Plain Sight," in *Hidden Mother*, ed. Linda Fregni Nagler (MACK, 2013), 5.

40. See, for example, D. Lynn O'Brien Hallstein, "Introduction to Mothering Rhetorics," *Women's Studies in Communication* 40, no. 1 (2017): 1–10; and Sophie M. Mary, Robbie Duschinsky, Louise Davis, Susan Dunnett, and Barry Coghlan, "Representations of Motherhood in the Media: A Systematic Literature Review," *Information, Communication, and Society* 28, no. 1 (2025): 169–86.

41. See Elizabeth Johns, *American Genre Painting: The Politics of Everyday Life* (Yale University Press, 1991).

42. Wendy J. Katz, "Lilly Martin Spencer and the Art of Refinement," *American Studies* 42, no. 1 (2001): 22, 23.

43. Quoted in April F. Masten, "Shake Hands? Lilly Martin Spencer and the Politics of Art," *American Quarterly* 56, no. 2 (2004): 357.

44. Lynn Abrams, *The Making of Modern Woman* (Routledge, 2016), 36.

45. Masten, "Shake Hands?," 358.

46. Quoted in Masten, "Shake Hands?," 359.

47. For some different approaches, see Helen S. Langa, "Lilly Martin Spencer: Genre, Aesthetics, and Gender in the Work of a Mid-Nineteenth Century American Woman Artist," *Athanor* 9 (1990): 37–45; and David M. Lubin, "Lilly Martin Spencer's Domestic Genre Painting in Antebellum America," in *Picturing a Nation: Art and Social Change in Nineteenth Century America* (Yale University Press, 1994).

48. A few examples include photographers Carmen Winant (*My Birth*, 2018), Elinor Carruci (*My Belly After Giving Birth and C Section*, 2004), and Catherine Opie (*Self-Portrait/Nursing*, 2004). Carrie Mae Weems's quietly powerful *Kitchen Table Series* (1990) specifically explores the complexity of navigating Black womanhood as a mother. Wendy Red Star (*Amnía* [Echo], 2021) and Magdalena Campos-Pons (*Replenishing*, 2001) have also explored the relationships between mothers and daughters, particularly the transmission of memory and cultural responsibility between generations.

49. Rosemary Betterton, "Louise Bourgeois, Ageing, and Maternal Bodies," *Feminist Review* 93, no. 1 (2009): 40.

50. Whitney Chadwick, *Women, Art, and Society*, 6th ed. (Thames & Hudson, 2020), 61.

51. Fiona J. Griffiths, *The Garden of Delights: Reform and Renaissance for Women in the Twelfth Century* (University of Pennsylvania Press, 2007), 235–26.

52. Griffiths, *Garden of Delights*, 233.

53. See the facsimile at https://hdl.handle.net/2027/gri.ark:/13960/t7wm7sz16.

54. Griffiths, *Garden of Delights*, 118.

55. Griffiths, *Garden of Delights*, 32.

56. Griffiths, *Garden of Delights*, 230.

57. Griffiths, *Garden of Delights*, 153.

58. Griffiths, *Garden of Delights*, 214.

59. Griffiths, *Garden of Delights*, 98.

60. Hiu Ki Chan, "Sicut Apis Operosa: Honey, Bees, and Chastity in the Early Medieval World," *Ex-position* 45 (2021): 49.

61. Quoted in Griffiths, *Garden of Delights*, 93.

62. Griffiths, *Garden of Delights*, 238.

63. Griffiths, *Garden of Delights*, 217.

64. Elise Kammerer, "Activism Behind the Veil of Sentimentality: The Amy Matilda Casey Friendship Album," *Critical Studies: Interdisciplinary Journal of the Humanities* 2, no. 1 (2016): 112–21.

65. Britt Rusert, "Sarah's Cabinet: Fugitive Science In and Beyond the Parlor," in *Fugitive Science: Empiricism and Freedom in Early African American Culture* (New York University Press, 2017), 194.

66. Katherine Isabel Bondy, "Freedom Flora: Botanical Revision and Community in African American Friendship Albums," *The Journal of Nineteenth Century Americanists* 10, no. 1 (2022): 56–57.

67. Bondy, "Freedom Flora," 61.

68. Elizabeth Felicetti, *Unexpected Abundance: The Fruitful Lives of Women Without Children* (Eerdmans, 2023), 19, Kindle.

Chapter 5 Monster

1. Jeffery Jerome Cohen, "Monster Culture (Seven Theses)," in *Monster Theory: Reading Culture* (University of Minnesota Press, 1996), 13.

2. For more examples, see Scott G. Bruce, ed., *The Penguin Book of the Undead: Fifteen Hundred Years of Supernatural Encounters* (Penguin Books, 2016).

3. See James H. Charlesworth, *The Good and Evil Serpent: How a Universal Symbol Became Christianized* (Yale University Press, 2010).

4. Nancy Madeville Caciola, "Serpents and Lies," *Speculum* 93, no. 1 (2018): 106.

5. Caciola, "Serpents and Lies," 109.

6. For more on the origin and spread of the story of Lilith, see Janet Howe Gaines, "Lilith: Seductress, Heroine or Murderer?," *Bible Review* 17, no. 5 (2001): 12–20.

7. Emma Green, "How Mike Pence's Marriage Became Fodder for the Culture Wars," *The Atlantic*, March 30, 2017, https://www.theatlantic.com/politics/archive/2017/03/pence-wife-billy-graham-rule/521298/.

8. Katelyn Beaty, "A Christian Case Against the Pence Rule," *The New York Times*, November 15, 2017, https://www.nytimes.com/2017/11/15/opinion/pence-rule-christian-graham.html.

9. Claire Cain Miller, "It's Not Just Mike Pence. Americans Are Wary of Being Alone with the Opposite Sex," *The New York Times*, July 1, 2017, https://www.nytimes.com/2017/07/01/upshot/members-of-the-opposite-sex-at-work-gender-study.html.

10. For a biography of Baartman and an exploration of her legacy, see Clifton C. Crais and Pamela Scully, *Sara Baartman and the Hottentot Venus: A Ghost Story and a Biography* (Princeton University Press, 2009).

11. See the poster in the Wellcome Collection, "Just arrived from London, and, by permission, will be exhibited here for a few days at Mr. James's Sale Rooms, corner of Lord-street : that most wonderful phenomenon of nature, the Hottentot Venus: the only one ever exhibited in Europe," 1810, https://wellcomecollection.org/works/pg5nsuur.

12. Sander Gilman, "Black Bodies, White Bodies: Toward an Iconography of Female Sexuality in Late Nineteenth-Century Art, Medicine, and Literature," *Critical Inquiry* 12, no. 1 (1985): 204–42.

13. Robin Mitchell, *Vénus Noire: Black Women and Colonial Fantasies in Nineteenth-Century France* (University of Georgia Press, 2020), 35–36.

14. Mitchell, *Vénus Noire*, 33.

15. London Museum, "We Want the Vote," https://www.londonmuseum.org.uk/collections/v/object-289813/we-want-the-vote/.

16. See this cover for *The Suffragist* at https://archive.org/details/suffragist01cong_0.

17. Patricia Simons, "The Crone, the Witch, and the Library: The Intersection of Classical Fantasy with Christian Vice during the Italian Renaissance," in *Receptions of Antiquity, Constructions of Gender in European Art, 1300–1600*, ed. Alison C. Poe and Marice Rose (Brill, 2015), 264–304.

18. Simons, "Crone," 265.

19. Simons, "Crone," 288.

20. Simons, "Crone," 300.

21. Lotte Van de Pol, "The Whore, the Bawd, and the Artist: The Reality and Imagery of Seventeenth-Century Dutch Prostitution," *Journal of Historians of Netherlandish Art* 2, nos. 1–2 (2010): https://doi.org/10.5092/jhna.2010.2.1.3.

22. Pierre-Jules Hetzel, *L'esprit des femmes et les femmes d'esprit* (Michel Lévy Frères, 1856), 21.

23. Quoted in Lucy Gellman, "Absent Mothers, Anxious Fathers, Babies in the Bathwater: Honoré Daumier's 'Les bas-bleus,'" *Yale University Art Gallery Bulletin* (2014): 56. Gellman cites and translates Jules Barbey d'Aurevilly, *Les bas-bleus* (Victor Palmé, 1878), 10.

24. Gellman, "Absent Mothers," 55.

25. Janis Bergman-Carton, "Conduct Unbecoming: Daumier and *Les Bas-Bleus*," in *Reclaiming Female Agency: Feminist Art History After Postmodernism*, ed. Norma Broude and Mary D. Garrard (University of California Press, 2005), 204.

26. Bergman-Carton, "Conduct Unbecoming," 208.

27. John Piper, "Is It Okay for Mothers to Work Outside the Home?," Desiring God, June 22, 2010, https://www.desiringgod.org/interviews/is-it-okay-for-mothers-to-work-full-time-outside-of-the-home.

28. Bergman-Carton, "Conduct Unbecoming," 203–15.

29. Bergman-Carton, "Conduct Unbecoming," 205.

30. In the later, Roman version of the story, Medusa was initially a beautiful maiden but was turned into a monster after being raped by a god.

31. See Yael Even, "The Loggia dei Lanzi: A Showcase of Female Subjugation," *Woman's Art Journal* 12, no. 1 (1991): 11.

32. Margaret Carroll, "The Erotics of Absolutism: Rubens and the Mystification of Sexual Violence," *Representations* 25 (1989): 5. See also Christine Corretti, *Cellini's Perseus and Medusa and the Loggia Dei Lanzi: Configurations of the Body of State* (Brill, 2015).

33. Sarah Blake McHam, "Donatello's Bronze 'David' and 'Judith' as Metaphors of Medici Rule in Florence," *The Art Bulletin* 83, no. 1 (2001): 35.

34. Even, "Loggia dei Lanzi," 11.

35. Carroll, "Erotics of Absolutism," 6–7.

36. Two important examples are Hélène Cixous, "The Laugh of the Medusa," trans. Keith Cohen and Paula Cohen, *Signs* 1, no. 4 (1976): 875–93; and Judith Plaskow, *The Coming of Lilith: Essays on Feminism, Judaism, and Sexual Ethics, 1972–2003* (Beacon Press, 2005).

37. Rachel Corbett, "Kara Walker Secretly Filmed You Taking Selfies in Front of Her Sphinx," *Vulture*, November 19, 2014, https://www.vulture.com/2014/11/kara-walker-filmed-you-in-front-of-her-sphinx.html.

38. Michael G. Sundell, *Mosaics in the Eternal City* (Arizona Center for Medieval and Renaissance Studies, 2007), 8.

39. Peter Murray and Linda Murray, *The Oxford Companion to Christian Art and Architecture* (Oxford University Press, 1996), 224.

40. Mary M. Schaefer, *Women in Pastoral Office: The Story of Santa Prassede, Rome*, ed. Joyce Louise Rilett Wood (Oxford University Press, 2014), 9.

41. Inocent-Mária V. Szaniszlo, "Strong Sisters in Roman Antiquity: Saints Pudentiana and Praezede, Daughters of Senator Pudens," *ASTRA Salvensis* 10, no. 1 (2022): 786.

42. See, for example, the historiographic overviews offered in Miri Rubin, "A Decade of Studying Medieval Women, 1987–1997," *History Workshop Journal* 46 (1998): 213–39; and Paula M. Rieder, "The Uses and Misuses of Misogyny: A Critical Historiography of the Language of Medieval Women's Oppression," *Historical Reflections* 38, no. 1 (2012): 1–18. A delightfully accessible introduction to women's experiences in the medieval period through images can be found in Gemma Hollman, *Women in the Middle Ages: Illuminating the World of Peasants, Nuns, and Queens* (Abbeville Press, 2024).

43. Valerie Garver, *Women and Aristocratic Culture in the Carolingian* World (Cornell University Press, 2009).

44. I have a deep affection for the San Zeno Chapel too. You can read about it in Elissa Yukiko Weichbrodt, "Wondering at God's Transcendence: Abstract Art," in *Redeeming Vision: A Christian Guide to Looking at and Learning from Art* (Baker Academic, 2023), 105–26.

45. See Schaefer, *Women in Pastoral Office*, especially chaps. 4, 5, and 6.

46. See this review of Schaefer's book for an example: Robin M. Jensen, "*Women in Pastoral Office: The Story of Santa Prassede, Rome* by Mary M. Schaefer," *Journal of Early Christian Studies* 23, no. 2 (2015): 318–20.

47. Schaefer, *Women in Pastoral Office*, 318.

48. See Sundell, *Mosaics in the Eternal City*.

49. Claudia Bolgia, "New Light on the 'Bright Ages': Experiments with Mosaics and Light in Medieval Rome," in *New Light on Old Glass: Recent Research on Byzantine Glass and Mosaics*, ed. L. James and C. Entwistle (British Museum Series, 2013), 217.

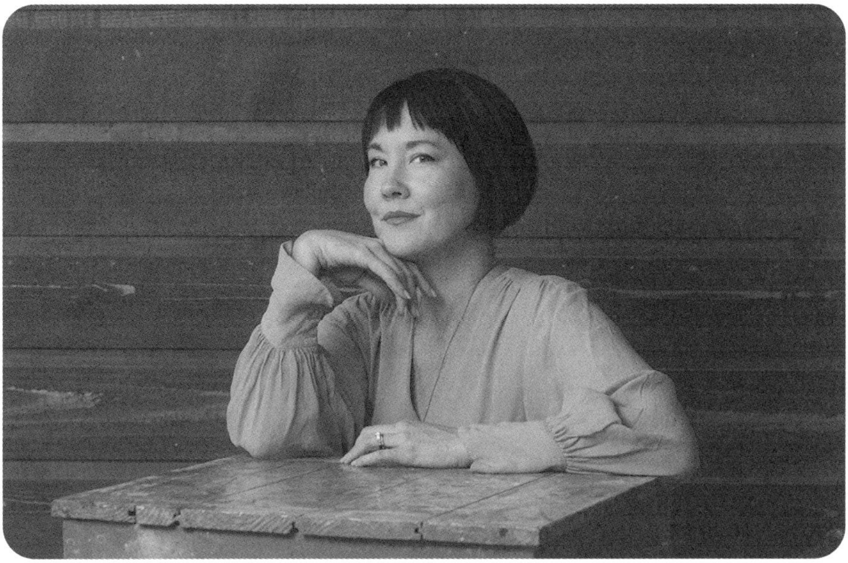

Elissa Yukiko Weichbrodt (PhD, Washington University in St. Louis) is professor of art and art history at Covenant College in Lookout Mountain, Georgia, and author of the award-winning book *Redeeming Vision: A Christian Guide to Looking at and Learning from Art* (Baker Academic, 2023). As a biracial, Japanese-white woman, she navigates the joys and tensions of a hybrid identity. Her research and teaching focus on representations of race and gender, material culture, and the role of art in spiritual formation. She has published scholarly articles and chapters on contemporary African American photographers, Hawaiian landscape painting, and material culture of the Japanese American internment. Her greatest joy, however, is introducing new audiences to the richness of engaging art. Her writing has appeared in *Christianity Today*, and she speaks regularly at conferences and church events.

CONNECT WITH ELISSA

www.elissa.weichbrodt.org

@elissabrodt

elissayukikoweichbrodt.substack.com

@elissabrodt